ECO-TYPES

Eco-Types
Five Ways of Caring about the Environment

Emily Huddart Kennedy

PRINCETON UNIVERSITY PRESS
PRINCETON AND OXFORD

Published by Princeton University Press
41 William Street, Princeton, New Jersey 08540
99 Banbury Road, Oxford OX2 6JX

press.princeton.edu

All Rights Reserved

ISBN: 978-0-691-23956-9
ISBN (e-book): 978-0-691-23957-6

British Library Cataloging-in-Publication Data is available

Editorial: Meagan Levinson and Jaqueline Delaney
Production Editorial: Jenny Wolkowicki
Production: Erin Suydam
Publicity: Kate Hensley and Kathryn Stevens
Copyeditor: Jane Simmonds

Jacket image: Andrew Zarivny / Alamy Stock Photo

This book has been composed Adobe Text Pro and Gotham.

Printed on acid-free paper. ∞

Printed in the United States of America

10 9 8 7 6 5 4 3 2 1

For Margaret and Morris Dunn, my grandparents, who taught me there are many ways to care about the environment

CONTENTS

ACKNOWLEDGMENTS

I wrote an early draft of this book during the first wave of the Covid-19 pandemic. I am fortunate to live near Pacific Spirit Regional Park, a protected area of temperate rainforest, and I composed much of this book while walking on its trails. I am so grateful for the serenity and inspiration that it offered me.

Although it is my name on the front cover, this book is the result of years of conversations and collaborations with a great many people—so many that I cannot begin to list them all here.

Thank you to the family, friends, and colleagues who read early drafts of this book and had long conversations with me about the ideas in it. I am so grateful for your support, ideas, and encouraging feedback: Camilla Speller, Elizabeth Dunn, Stephen Huddart, Catherine Rideout, Celina Tumbach, Mary Lucas, Riley Dunlap, Neil Guppy, Shyon Baumann, Gerry Veenstra, Christine Horne, Richard York, Harvey Krahn, Lindsay Cuff, and Jennifer Givens. A special note of thanks to Amin Ghaziani—my shepherd through the intimidating and opaque world of academic book publishing and to four anonymous reviewers whose comments were immensely helpful.

The data collection for this project would have been far less efficient and less fun without assistance from Jake Hammond, Darcy Hauslik, and Jesse Mendiola. Also, a big thanks to Mark Billings for his skills in participant recruitment. It also would have been impossible to collect the data without financial support. For that, I want to acknowledge the Washington State University New Faculty Seed Grant and the College of Arts and Sciences for the funds to start this project. Additional funding from the Social Sciences Research Council of Canada allowed me to collect the survey data and complete this book.

The real heart of the book you are reading is the voices of my participants. I'm frequently surprised and grateful at how many people are willing to take time out of their busy days to have a conversation with a stranger. I'm deeply thankful to everyone who shared their feelings, thoughts, and reflections with me. It is truly a privilege to be able to take the time to travel to new towns and cities and meet people from so many walks of life.

Many other people helped me to carry this book over the finish line. The team at Princeton offered invaluable guidance and support. In particular my editor, Meagan Levinson, was a generous and enthusiastic part of this project from day one. I am so grateful for her encouragement and support through the process of writing this book. I could not have been in better hands. Two of my graduate students at the University of British Columbia (UBC), Parker Muzzerall and Carly Hamdon, also supported this project with their careful editing skills.

Every single day, I am thankful to Mike, Maya, and Ollie Kennedy for their affection, effervescent energy, and love of adventure.

The best thing we can bring to any fight is a calm and compassionate mind.
—GEORGE SAUNDERS[1]

There is a beach near my home in Vancouver, British Columbia (BC). The beach lies at the base of a steep hill—so steep and so long that I need to commit to nearly 500 stairs to get from the top to the bottom (and, more dauntingly, from the bottom back up to the top). The stairs wind through a forest that is beautiful, in any season. In summer, the deciduous trees are fully leafed-out and giant, big leaf maples give a viridescent tint to the air. On a January day, the maples are hibernating, but cedars and Douglas fir still tower overhead, and prehistoric-looking sword ferns cover the hillside. There is often mist or light rain in the air as I walk to the beach.

In the midst of so much evidence of the devastating impact humanity has had on the planet, the beach offers me reprieve. Seals poke their heads above the water, seemingly curious about a new visitor. Waterfowl of all colors paddle lazily, occasionally calling out to one another; and often, a bald eagle soars overhead. This place is a respite, partly because here the earth feels healthy and strong.

On my way back up the stairs, I pass a sign that always makes me smile: *Clothing is required beyond this point*, it reads. I imagine taking a photo and sending it to a friend with a tagline like, "Party's over," or something funnier that I haven't thought of yet. I would never take my clothes off at this beach. But many people do. On a winter morning, I see no one in the nude. But on a midsummer day, the beach is packed with hundreds upon hundreds of naked people. Why am I talking about nude beaches? Because when this beach is crowded with naked bodies, I don't ever find myself thinking, "What terrible people!" but rather, "Huh. How interesting. Why is this something they like to do?" This is relevant because it is the sort of attitude we need to have toward one another when it comes to our relationships with the environment. When we intuit that someone we encounter doesn't care about the environment, when we find ourselves thinking another person is unethical because of their beliefs about climate change or the type of vehicle they own, we should pause and reconsider; reflect. We should stop ourselves from going down the path of making character judgments and instead cultivate a sense of curiosity about that person and the conditions of their life. We should do that because granting this basic gift of trust and dignity to those around us is an essential part of developing the sort of civil society that can protect the environment.

To be honest, this, "Huh. How interesting" attitude is not always my first reaction when I encounter other people's comments about and actions toward the environment. When I see people throw trash out of their car window, my first thought is typically something along the lines of, "What an asshole." While reading a book written by a wise and knowledgeable woman, who, at one point, instructed her readers not to buy food that wasn't produced using organic methods, my first impulse was to think, judgmentally, "how judgmental!" If, after many years of research culminating in a book that tries to convince people not to make character judgments based on others' relationships with the environment, I still do, is this pointless? No.

I am confident that our society and our planet would be better off if we could habitually respond to unfamiliar environmental beliefs and behaviors by thinking, "Huh. How interesting. Why is this something they think or do?" This kind of thinking does not just happen. Even if you read this whole book, and you have moments where you can put yourself in someone else's shoes and feel where they are coming from, if you're like me, you still have years of habitual thinking pushing you away from empathy. Cultivating curiosity is a practice. Just like trying to eat more healthily or exercise more or meditate, training ourselves to be curious instead of making character judgments based on scant information takes practice. But it's worth the effort. In fact, I am often asked, "What is the one thing I should do to help the environment?" And people expect me to answer along the lines of: "install solar panels" or "give up meat." These actions may feel like the right ones for some and will certainly offer material benefits in the way of emissions reductions. But these days, the suggestion I'm increasingly inclined to offer is centered on cultural change: if you find yourself making a character judgment of someone because of their environmental actions or opinions, try to cultivate a sense of curiosity instead. Because a civil society divided lacks the power and will to fight for a better world and is too vulnerable to resist powerful actors who profit from divisiveness.

Let me tell you why a Canadian sociologist spent three years interviewing and surveying American households about their relationships to the environment. I began my university education in forestry, studying natural resource conservation. This focus put me in classes with other students who shared my passion for the environment and my concern with industrial logging practices. But in the summers, to pay for my education, I worked in the forest industry. That experience, moving between an urban environment, where my peers held an antagonistic stance on loggers and the forest industry, and a rural setting, where my peers held an antagonistic stance on environmentalists and environmental nongovernmental organizations, showed me that neither group fully understood the other. Even more significant, I noticed that the antagonism these two groups held toward one another eclipsed important common ground: all of the people I studied and worked with cared about the environment, although they did so in ways that seemed at times to be incompatible.

I started my first academic job at Washington State University in Pullman, a small town located a few miles west of the border with Idaho. My experience in forestry and university in Canada struck me as a tension between so-called blue-collar workers, whose livelihoods depended on natural resource extraction, and comparatively "white-collar" students who were embedded in a knowledge economy. But when I moved to Washington, I sensed much of the same antagonism in conversations with neighbors, other parents, and fellow hockey team-members, none of whom worked in the forest sector or any other extractive industry. In this context, I sensed that the two sides were not blue-collar and white-collar, but conservative and liberal. As an outsider, it was perhaps easier to recognize common ground and shared interests, and I embarked on this project in order to understand the place of the environment in people's lives.

There is no shortage of evidence that there are deep rifts between individuals in the United States right now. Whether we experience these divisions based on race, geography, age, education, income, or religion, it certainly can feel that there is more that separates us than unites us. Many studies have demonstrated that these rifts act as a barrier, preventing decision makers at all levels from taking meaningful actions to uphold and advance the common good. This includes our ability to protect the environment. The tragic irony is that alongside the divisiveness of US civil society right now, we share an appreciation and respect for the environment. We don't agree on what the right relationship to the environment is, or who should take a leading role in protecting the environment, nor how they should do so. These points of difference are accentuated in Congress, on social media, over dinner table conversations among friends and family. This tendency to focus on our differences rather than our similarities skews our perceptions of how those unlike us relate to the environment. Too many people have lost sight of our common ground: that we all care about the environment.

My hope is that this book will challenge your assumptions about how people different from you feel about the environment. In my research I found that, for many people, their relationship to the environment is deeply emotional. While a significant number feel the planet is vulnerable, in a state of crisis, and feel a moral responsibility to reduce their own impact on ecological systems, this is not an exhaustive account of how people care about the environment. I also spent time with people who believe the planet is powerful and resilient and who exercise their relationship with the environment through reverence and witnessing wild places. My goal is that by demonstrating various modes of caring about the environment, I can dissuade readers from making judgments about a person's character based on their environmental beliefs or behaviors, instead encouraging a sense of curiosity about the social and biophysical factors that influence the place of the environment in someone's life.

ECO-TYPES

Introduction

Who cares about the environment? What images come to mind when you try to answer that question? Who do you think cares about the environment, and how can you tell?

For now, don't worry about the person's gender, age, or any other demographic characteristic, but think about the sorts of things you imagine them doing. Perhaps you imagine someone who rides a bike or drives a hybrid car, who doesn't eat meat and may buy their food at a farmers' market. You might picture them attending climate protests. But maybe you don't picture any of these things. Maybe you imagine an outdoors enthusiast—someone who demonstrates deep knowledge of their local environment, who lives in a rural area, and who may enjoy hunting, fishing, snowmobiling, or gardening. What I will argue in this book is that both of these examples can reflect caring about the environment. The term "eco-type" in evolutionary biology refers to variation within a species of plant or animal that is shaped by that species' environment. I invite you to look at your own and others' orientation toward the planet in the same way: different eco-types exist. We all care about the environment in ways that are shaped by our upbringing and the context in which we live our lives. And so, while this imagination exercise may feel like a simple and relatively unimportant matter of personal preference, these two imagined eco-types reflect the chasm that divides American civil society's orientation to the environment.

This seemingly benign exercise is deeply implicated in current patterns of political polarization over environmental protection. This is, in part, because it is not just that some people picture a bike-riding vegetarian while others picture a conservation enthusiast, but that the people who picture one eco-type are so often antagonistic toward those who feel more closely connected to the other eco-type. In other words, the sort of person who admires the bike-riding vegetarian may not extend the virtue of caring for the environment to some outdoors enthusiasts. Similarly, the person who hunts and fishes, or values those who do, may argue that the vegetarian who goes to climate protests does not really understand the environment. This is also because there is a pattern in who associates caring about the environment with sustainable consumption and who associates it with nature-based recreation. These examples have become cultural ideals that alternatively attract or repel us in ways that are tied particularly to our political beliefs. As a general rule, if you are politically liberal, you will be more likely to associate efforts to reduce individual environmental impacts with caring about the environment.[1] If you are politically conservative, you are more likely to feel that someone who cares about the environment is intimately familiar with the land, whether that's a family farm or a national park.[2]

In this introductory chapter, I invite you to join me in rethinking, and understanding more deeply, the story of who cares about the environment. Current trends measuring public opinion suggest a widening gulf between liberals' and conservatives' views on environmental protection, as well as a growing tendency to misjudge how (and how much) people different from us care about the environment.[3] Political liberals think other liberals care most deeply, and political conservatives challenge that assertion, claiming that other conservatives are most likely to care for the planet. A democratic state cannot meaningfully confront catastrophic ecological decline with a divided public. It is essential to cultivate curiosity about others' relationships with the environment in order to overcome political polarization.

Political Differences in Human-Environment Relationships

How do people experience ecological decline? Why is it that some people seem to care more about the environment than others? One of the earliest attempts to address these questions is by environmental sociologists Riley Dunlap and William Catton Jr. in their conceptualization of the Human Exceptionalist Paradigm and the New Environmental Paradigm.[4] Dunlap and Catton suggested that a Human Exceptionalist Paradigm (HEP) underpins humanity's destruction of the environment. Endorsing the HEP is expressed through beliefs such as the notion that humans have a right to exploit nature, the view that we will develop technological solutions to address environmental issues, and a sense that claims of an ecological crisis are exaggerated. Dunlap and various coauthors describe the HEP as a dominant and "anti-ecological" worldview.[5] This characterization is important to notice because, as I will discuss in greater detail further on, it captures a dynamic that has come to play a role in political polarization. In contrast to the HEP, early environmental sociologists characterized a New Environmental Paradigm (NEP) as a cultural foundation for restoring ecological health.[6] People endorsing a NEP believe there are natural limits to growth, that is, the earth cannot sustain human growth and development indefinitely, human and nonhuman species must live in harmony to survive, and nonhuman species do not exist in order to be used by humans.[7] Early environmental sociologists characterized the NEP as pro-ecological.[8]

There is a strong and enduring connection between political ideology and the paradigm a person endorses with respect to the environment and humanity's impacts on ecological systems. Over dozens of surveys conducted during and since the 1970s, environmental social scientists have found that political liberals are far more likely to hold a NEP and conservatives more likely to endorse a HEP.[9] This pattern is not unique to studies of the HEP and NEP: research into environmental values, environmental concerns, and multiple domains of environmental behaviors illustrate a similar pattern of liberals self-reporting more strongly pro-environmental orientations. For instance, recent work shows that liberals are more likely to endorse biospheric values than conservatives.[10] Biospheric values prioritize benefits to the environment, even if this means a cost to oneself.[11] Survey research also indicates that liberals tend to be more concerned about the environment than conservatives.[12] These contrasts have only become greater in the context of climate change—evidence shows not only political variation in what individuals in the private sphere believe about climate change, but also in how elected representatives from across the political spectrum act on climate change in their leadership roles.[13]

Political conservatives in the US—in particular, white, male conservatives—are most likely to question climate science and oppose efforts to mitigate climate change.[14] In the context of what many describe as a climate emergency, published research suggests that one is far more likely to encounter a conservative climate denier than a liberal one, and a liberal voter is far more likely to support environmental protection legislation than a conservative voter.[15] Analyses of concern over global warming, conducted by the academic group Climate Change in the American Mind, show that since at least 2008 when they began polling, political party and political ideology have been key factors explaining why some people are more concerned about climate change than others. The same poll also notes important age-related shifts, with younger Republicans more likely than older Republicans to accept that climate change is happening.[16]

Social scientists offer several explanations of why liberals and conservatives might feel so differently about addressing environmental issues. Sociologists Aaron McCright and Riley Dunlap argue that conservative individuals are more likely to challenge evidence of environmental decline and solutions to address it because they tend to have a positive view of capitalism and industrialization.[17] Their theory involves three related claims. First, that people who embrace industrial capitalism are less likely to support environmental protection policies. This gives rise to the second and third claims: that skepticism about environmental issues such as climate change results from a lack of critical reflexivity about industrial capitalism, and that this skepticism is reinforced by messages calling attention to the ways industrial capitalism supports human flourishing. In later research, McCright tested and confirmed these claims with survey evidence indicating that conservatives are less likely to engage in critical reflection on industrialization and more likely than liberals to doubt evidence that capitalism creates problems for people and the environment.[18]

If conservatives are not often critically reflecting on the impacts of industrialization, it must be partly due to a long-standing, corporate investment in disseminating pro-industry, climate-skeptic messages, particularly to those on the political right. Pro-industrialization, climate-skeptic messages are fed into public discourse by prominent, wealthy conservatives like the Koch brothers and fossil-fuel companies like ExxonMobil. For decades, these powerful actors have invested vast sums of money into think tanks and lobby groups whose purpose is to undermine climate science and promote the social value of industrialization in order to ensure future profits. The historian Naomi Oreskes has identified advertising campaigns that, for decades, deliberately tried to cultivate climate skepticism by misleading audiences about climate change. For example, in 1991, the Edison Electric Institute (an association representing investor-owned electric companies) ran an advertisement reading, "If the Earth is getting warmer, why is Kentucky getting colder?"[19] That claim was unsubstantiated and contradicted evidence from the American Meteorological Society showing a 1.0–1.5 degrees Fahrenheit warming in the Minneapolis area over the twentieth century.

In a more recent example of climate misinformation, ExxonMobil spent nearly $5 million on Facebook ads targeted to political conservatives. One example is a photograph of an oil worker behind text that reads, "Unnecessary regulations slow our economy down."[20] In a clear illustration of corporate investment in political polarization, Exxon simultaneously ran an ad targeted to liberal Facebook users highlighting the company's investments in clean energy. US senators have called this fossil-fuel financed network of funding for climate skepticism "the web of denial."[21] In short, prevailing wisdom holds that conservatives are less likely to value environmental protection and more likely to value industrialization, a pattern exacerbated by messages challenging (or questioning) climate science and lauding the gifts of industrial activity.

The web of denial also impacts the voting practices of elected representatives from the two major US political parties. Among elected representatives who set the course of the government's mandate, conservative, Republican representatives are less likely to propose environmental protection legislation and more likely to try to block efforts from their liberal, Democrat counterparts to enact environmental protection policies.[22] In one analysis of the political gap in support for clean energy laws at the state level, sociologists Jonathan Coley and David Hess show that Republicans are less likely to support bills seeking to generate more energy from renewable sources. But they also offer two important insights into the contextual factors that shape this political divide. First, Coley and Hess find that in states with a weak fossil-fuel industry, Republicans are more likely to support renewable energy laws. This pattern substantiates arguments that the web of denial thwarts efforts to diversify energy production.[23] Their second insight is not generally recognized by social scientists studying political polarization in civil society. They found that the political divide in support for environmental protection policies was also smaller where environmental advocacy groups were weaker, labor-environmental coalitions absent, and where there were fewer Democrats in the legislature. Coley and Hess suggest it is possible that conservative opposition to environmental protection is, in part, a "*reactive effect* against green energy policies in more progressive settings."[24] A key argument I make in this book is that reactive effects are an overlooked cultural driver of political polarization—and one that we each have the power to disrupt.

This summary of research on political differences in views on environmental protection is bookended by points that are important to note as you read this book: first, for decades, environmental sociologists have characterized views on the environment that tend to be held by conservatives as "anti-ecological"; and second that reactive effects are one of the factors shaping how elected representatives vote on pro-environmental legislation. These points are important because, as I will demonstrate, these reactive effects take place within civil society as well as in state legislatures. My explanation of the cultural dynamics that exacerbate political polarization is a key contribution of this book. Another contribution is the way in which I reconsider the importance of values for understanding human-environment relationships. Much of the research I just summarized focuses on individuals' views on the environment by scrutinizing values. Values, as a concept, represent a strong theme in literature on human-environment relationships and in research on political polarization over environmental protection. But the task of disrupting the reactive effects that drive political polarization will be easier if we have a language that decenters values and focuses instead on relationships.

Studying Eco-Social Relationships, Not Values

Environmental social scientists have a long-standing interest in understanding human-environment interactions.[25] This book builds on that tradition by seeking to understand the place of the environment in people's lives or, more succinctly, eco-social relationships. The idea of an eco-social relationship is central to this book. With this term, I refer to the intensity and direction of a person's orientation toward the planet. In the same way that a long-term relationship with another person can take on many forms, so too can our relationships to the planet. Some people relate to their backyard. Others relate to the image of the planet from space. Others relate to a web of human and nonhuman interactions. Some exercise their relationship to the environment by trying to protect it. Others by celebrating and enjoying the outdoors. Others by gazing at our world, and beyond, through cameras, or telescopes, or televisions. We don't all have the same relationship to the planet, and an eco-social relationship is not static—it will shift along with other changes in our social context and personal history. Regardless of what our eco-social relationship looks and feels like, one thing remains constant: the eco-social relationship we have is one that makes sense for us, given our biography and the parameters of our lives.

THE STANDARD FRAMEWORK OF
HUMAN-ENVIRONMENT RELATIONSHIPS

In order to explain why I chose to study eco-social relationships it is first important to clarify the framework of human-environment interactions that I am not using in this book. What I call the "standard framework" of human-environment relationships makes people's values a central focus. Let me be clear about what values are and how some scholars see them working. Values are defined as goals that feel desirable to the people who hold them—they generally act as guiding principles for us, shaping our decision making.[26] For example, if we value benevolence and helping people more vulnerable than us, then when faced with an invitation from friends to enjoy a night out on an evening that we dedicate to volunteer work, we would (theoretically) turn down the invitation. Environmental social scientists who study values share a belief that values influence behavior by directing our attention when we make decisions.[27]

The psychologist Shalom Schwartz proposed two broad axes of values: self-enhancement and self-transcendence.[28] Self-enhancement values represent a broad category encompassing two types of values orientations: hedonistic values that motivate people to do what feels good and requires minimal effort, and egoistic values (like achievement) that steer people toward opportunities to increase their wealth and status. Self-enhancement values are goals that drive people to better their individual outcomes. Environmental social scientists applying this framework in survey research have found that people who are strongly oriented toward self-enhancement values (hedonistic or egoistic) seem neither to care about the environment nor to do much to protect it.[29]

In contrast to self-enhancement values, self-transcendence values set the individual aside in order to focus on other-oriented goals. Specific orientations within this broad category include altruistic and biospheric values. Altruistic values motivate people to make choices that benefit others, while biospheric values direct our attention toward choices that benefit nonhuman species. There is no shortage of research from environmental social scientists demonstrating that people who endorse biospheric values adopt behaviors that are intended to be good for the environment—I have published this research myself. These studies find that people who espouse self-transcendence values (altruistic or biospheric) are concerned about the environment and frequently engage in pro-environmental behaviors.[30] One of the major contributions of this book is to update this way of thinking in order to more fully account for how the social and environmental context of our lives shapes our relationship with the environment.

Critiquing the Standard Values Framework

The framework I just described assumes our values drive our behaviors. Yet, anecdotally, many of us can likely recognize there is a difference between what causes us to act and what we may later justify as causing us to act. The sociologist C. Wright Mills long ago addressed this phenomenon with the phrase, "vocabulary of motives," pointing at the way in which people reframe actions in order to make them appear to act consistently with their values and with values that they perceive to be well-regarded by their audience.[31] For example, the fictitious volunteer from the previous section might choose to cancel their volunteering plans to spend time with their friends. They might stress to others, who they sense share a value for benevolence, that this is because their volunteer commitments are a long-term project and they need to sustain their energy. To the friends they join for an evening out, the same person may report that going out to socialize felt more appealing than volunteer work. In another example, imagine someone telling others about donating generously to a nonprofit organization, emphasizing a motivation to do good in the world, and downplaying the motivation to receive a tax credit. There are many ways that most of us use a vocabulary of motives to showcase our more public-spirited side and withhold interests we think others may deem selfish.

If we apply this notion of a vocabulary of motives to the relationship between holding biospheric values and adopting pro-environmental behaviors, we can generate new insights. It may be just as likely that the relationship between biospheric values and pro-environmental behaviors is bidirectional and strongly influenced by context. In other words, the people for whom being good to the environment and demonstrating that goodness through participating in a climate march, carrying a reusable mug, and buying food at a farmers' market are important, are likely the same people who will tell survey researchers they value the natural environment. It is entirely possible that contextual factors, such as where we live and whom we spend time with, shape our behaviors. In this line of thinking, we articulate values statements post hoc, as a way of justifying an alignment between our goals and our actions.[32]

A more political critique of the scholarship on values is that as scholars design tools to measure how much people care about the environment, they inadvertently make and reproduce moral judgments.[33] These tools include measures of environmental values, environmental attitudes, and environmental behaviors. When researchers develop survey questions to measure these concepts, they use examples that are familiar to them, and that resonate with their own eco-social relationship. With this in mind, perhaps it is not surprising that so many studies implicitly asking "Who cares about the environment?" ultimately find that those who care are educated, politically liberal, and professional in their fields of employment. To put this more directly, perhaps researchers find that the people who care about the environment share their beliefs, practices, and sociodemographic traits because they design and use measurement tools that assume their own orientation to the environment is the correct one.

A New Approach: Interests, Not Values

Critiques of the conventional, or standard, values framework have given rise to alternative approaches to understanding human-environment relationships. One project that aimed to address the political critique of how environmental social scientists study values is Willett Kempton, James Boster, and Jennifer Hartley's book, *Environmental Values in American Culture*, published in 1995. Impelled by their concern that most scholarship on environmentalism is based on "methods that assume that the investigator knows in advance which values and beliefs comprise environmentalism," the authors instead listened to Americans in order to describe their environmental values.[34] To do so, they interviewed people from organizations that are often opposed to one another on environmental issues, such as coal miners, environmental activists, and policy makers. Even though their research was published more than two decades before I started this study, in a different part of the country, I come to the same general conclusion: people from all walks of life value the environment, but they don't value it in the same way.[35]

My book refines, updates, and builds on this earlier work in a few ways. First, by focusing on relationships instead of values, I can more directly bring the biophysical and social worlds into my explanation of why people feel about the environment the way they do. Second, political polarization over environmentalism is a more prominent theme in the public realm now and I examine the connections between eco-social relationships and political divisiveness. And third, the survey sample I draw on more accurately reflects the US adult population—at least on political ideology, education, and income.[36]

In an effort to disrupt the standard framework of values and behaviors, some cultural sociologists argue for replacing values with the concept of "interests."[37] Interests don't assume directionality between, for instance, the acting subject and an acted-upon object, but simply a relationship. When we consider interests, we are focused on connections between subjects (people) and objects (which is a broad term encompassing other people, consumer goods, ideas, the natural environment, and so on). Qualities of the object and the subject determine the connection between them. In abstract terms, people perceive objects as having qualities that make them more or less appealing.[38] In terms of understanding eco-social relationships, this reframing has the advantage of giving the environment a more prominent and tangible role than exists when we look solely at values.

Consider an environmentally relevant example of how we can study topics related to human-environment reactions using a model emphasizing interests instead of values. In their book *Beyond Politics*, Michael Vandenbergh and Jonathan Gilligan demonstrate that many households have invested time and money in technologies like rooftop solar panels and electric vehicles. They do not explain these investments as an extension of individuals' altruistic or biospheric values, but argue that people who adopt these renewable energy technologies perceive objects like solar panels as offering cost-savings and as conveying a symbolic commitment to supporting climate mitigation. In this example, solar panels are the objects in relationship with people. Solar panels have qualities that make them appealing to some people and unappealing to others. People's perception of these qualities also depends on the context within which solar panels play a role: whether there are rebate policies, whether other people in one's neighborhood have solar panels, and a range of other factors. Vandenbergh and Gilligan draw readers' attention to the qualities of eco-friendly technologies that make people more or less interested in adopting them, not on the motivating values people identify as shaping their decisions. In my book, rather than study people's interests in objects like eco-friendly technologies, I focus on eco-social relationships in order to understand people's interests in the environment itself.

Focusing on eco-social relationships allows me to shed light on two things that are missing from the standard framework linking values and environmental behaviors. I illuminate the importance of the environment itself and the qualities of the environment that make it of interest to people. And I describe a cultural schema of what it looks like to care about the environment among the people I interviewed. I label this cultural schema "the ideal environmentalist" and demonstrate how this schema shapes the ways in which people evaluate their own and others' eco-social relationships. The way I conceptualize eco-social relationships focuses on qualities of people

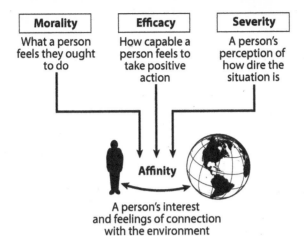

FIGURE I.1. Conceptual model of eco-social relationships

and the environment that influence the affinity people feel for the natural world (see figure I.1).

It is timely and important that we take a closer look at eco-social relationships, since the political polarization that is evident in the American landscape today is a significant barrier to enacting the sorts of environmental protection measures needed to confront ecological decline. Solutions to ecological crises must resonate with, or at least make sense to, a wide array of people if they are to be sustainable in the long term. Part of this strategy must be to recognize the diverse qualities of the environment that appeal to others and the many ways people put their affinity for the environment into action. In this way, it should be more inviting to build common ground on shared interests or at least to feel respect for or curiosity about relationships to the environment that look different from our own.

Conceptual Framework of Eco-Social Relationships

The conceptual framework of eco-social relationships moves away from a focus on individual values toward a focus on the *relationship* between people and whatever they conceive of as "the environment." The heart of an eco-social relationship is this sense of affinity for the environment (figure I.1). Although cultural sociologists use the term "interest" to capture this phenomenon, I prefer the word "affinity." To have an affinity for something is to feel an emotional connection, a pull toward it. When I interviewed people, I sensed variation in this affinity. While some people cried when I asked,

"What comes to mind when I say 'environment'?" and went on to describe specific details about places that they love, others were nonplussed and non-committal. They might answer, "I don't know, trees and stuff," or simply look at the buildings and landscape around them and say, "all of this," with little emotional valence. An affinity for the environment is a way of characterizing the intensity of the relationship between a person and whatever they define as the environment. In keeping with cultural sociological research arguing that our interests or affinities are shaped by perceived qualities of the object and by qualities of ourselves, I identified characteristics of people and the environment that affected affinity. Although affinity captures the intensity of the relationship between a person and the environment, people do not all envision the same things when they think about the environment.

Perception of the severity of ecological decline was the most prominent quality of the environment that my participants described.[39] "Severity" captures people's sense of the urgency and intensity of ecological deterioration. Although very few people argued that the environment is healthy, and most perceived the planet to be under threat, people varied in terms of how severe they felt that threat to be. At one extreme, you can imagine a person who sees the environment as extremely vulnerable, sees humans as a violent species, and worries a great deal about the fate of the earth. At the other extreme, picture someone who sees the planet as highly resilient and who believes that while humans can be destructive, our species is not powerful enough to disrupt and destroy ecological vitality. For example, someone who sees the planet as vulnerable might look at a clear-cut forest and see it as an assault on the natural world, while someone who sees the environment as resilient might focus on how quickly new plants begin to grow on the site.[40] There are many gradations between these poles that I will describe in later chapters, but for now, understand that this is a perceived quality of the environment that affects people's affinity for nature.[41]

In the relationship between a person and the environment, the person also has qualities that matter. The two qualities I focus on are morality and efficacy. Morality, or personal moral responsibility, describes what a person feels they ought to do (not whether or not they actually do so) vis-à-vis their relationship with the environment. You might be passionate about the environment and perceive ecological decline to be more akin to ecological catastrophe, but these reactions may not exist alongside a feeling that you are personally responsible for doing something to protect the environment.[42] A person's perception of their moral responsibilities to protect the environment is partly shaped by their sense of what causes environmental issues. Some of my participants believed that our actions as individual consumers create environmental problems. Many of the participants I interviewed who felt this way also communicated a strong personal moral responsibility to protect the environment. But other participants scoffed at the idea that individual consumers are responsible. They perceived ecological decline to be a result of corporations' capacious drive for power and profits and governments' acquiescence to corporate power. These participants felt very little personal moral responsibility.

The second quality of individuals and the final element of my framework of eco-social relationships is efficacy. Efficacy refers to the extent to which people feel capable of actualizing their ideal relationship with the environment. In trying to understand the place of the environment in people's lives, I noticed that some people I spoke with exuded a sense of control and confidence when discussing their environmental beliefs, actions, and impacts; others conveyed a deep sense of powerlessness.[43] I interviewed people who proudly told me that they oriented their entire lives around their passion for protecting the environment—where they worked, where they lived, how they got around, what they ate. But I also interviewed people who told me they felt guilty every day for not doing enough to protect the environment. Although this sense of how effectively we are protecting the environment might seem tangential to human-environment relationships, instead, I found this to be a surprisingly salient theme throughout my interviews.[44]

Our relationship with the environment is made and remade in a social, cultural, and physical context. Because of this, eco-social relationships are dynamic and relational: our upbringing matters, as does the culture of our current social context, including the friends we associate with and the neighborhoods in which we live, the physical parameters of the communities we inhabit, and the information we take in about ecological issues in our communities and beyond. The politics of our context matters as well—What sort of people are given the most authority and respect? Whose experiences are marginalized or overlooked? These themes shape our relationship with the environment and one another. The way each of us interprets, experiences, and responds to ecological decline is also shaped by our own life history: by our connections to the people with whom we spend our time and the places where we live and work. Since all of these components can change, so too can our eco-social relationships—people who hold one relationship for a period of time can shift into another. But a person's eco-social relationship always makes sense for them, in the context of their life.

In this book, I use the four elements of an eco-social relationship to delineate five eco-social relationship archetypes, or, put concisely, eco-types. In

Washington, where I conducted my interviews, the four elements—affinity, severity, morality, efficacy—gave rise to five eco-types, but the nature and key characteristics of these eco-types will likely vary across time and geography. If you are interested in identifying your own eco-type, see the questions listed in box I.1.

BOX I.1 Identify Your Own Eco-Type

Like any framework, this one does not pretend to describe everyone (or anyone) all the time. Eco-social relationships are dynamic, and you may be able to see yourself in more than one eco-type. To identify where you best fit, answer the questions below and see the instructions in the right-hand column (see figure I.2). Once you've identified your eco-type, you can read more about it in Overview of the Book, below.

Questions

Eco-type

Affinity

Do you think about the environment often?
Is the environment extremely important to you?
Do you value keeping up with news or information about the environment?

If you mostly answered yes, you would score high on the affinity measure.
If you mostly answered no, you would score low on the affinity measure and may reflect the **Indifferent** eco-type.

Severity

Would you characterize the state of the environment as worse than it used to be?
Do you think humans are using up the earth's resources?
Do you feel that protecting the environment should be the country's top priority?

If you mostly answered yes, you would score high on the severity measure.
If you mostly answered no, you would score low on the severity measure and may fit the **Optimist** eco-type.

Morality

Do you feel a moral responsibility to reduce your own impact on the environment?
Do you worry about your impact on the environment?
Do you try to consume less to protect the environment?

If you mostly answered yes, you would score high on the morality measure.
If you mostly answered no, you would score low on the morality measure and may reflect a **Fatalist** eco-type.

Efficacy

When you evaluate your own efforts to protect the environment, do you feel as though you're living up to your ideals?
Have you made choices in your life motivated by a desire to reduce your environmental impact?
Do you generally feel capable of reducing your environmental impact?

If you lean toward yes, you would score high on the efficacy measure and may fall under the **Eco-Engaged** eco-type.
If you lean toward no, you would score low on the efficacy measure and may fit the **Self-Effacing** eco-type.

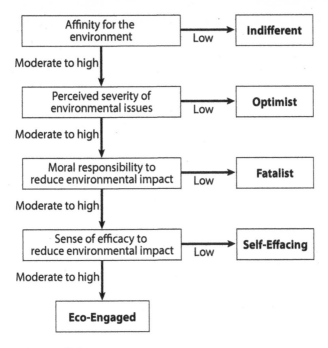

FIGURE I.2. Estimate your eco-type

Data and Methods: Learning More About People's Relationships with the Environment

Because I wanted to identify the place of the environment in people's everyday lives, rather than test a framework of environmental values, I needed to speak with a wide array of people, not just committed eco-enthusiasts. This is what led me to embark on a three-year research project interviewing and surveying American households about their relationships to the environment. Because past research showed that support for environmental protection and engagement in eco-friendly activities varies most by political ideology, education, and place of residence, the approach I took to recruiting a sample of interview participants was aimed at capturing heterogeneity on these sociodemographic characteristics.[45] That is, while others have studied those at the vanguard of environmentalism, my focus was on everyday routines and beliefs and I interviewed many people who would not identify as environmental activists or dedicated sustainable consumers.[46]

Starting in Washington State, where I lived and worked, I recruited 63 politically and socioeconomically diverse households across various types of communities to participate in an interview about the environment.[47]

I interviewed people in Pacifica, an amenity-rich rural area where nature-based tourism is the mainstay of a healthy economy; and people in Olympia, Washington State's uber-progressive capitol whose unofficial slogan is, "Stay weird, Oly."[48] I interviewed people in Pullman, the small college town where I lived, and in Whitman, a rural farming community.[49] The first two sites are predominantly liberal. Pullman has a relatively even mixture of Democrat and Republican voters, and Whitman is a Republican voting base.[50]

In the first section of the interviews, I asked people to tell me what they pictured when I said "environment," to tell me what emotions that image evoked, and then to tell me how concerned they were (on a scale from 1 to 10) about the environment and how important they thought it was that we protect the environment. I asked participants to qualify their answers, explaining how they came up with the numbers they did. Our conversations also touched on the phenomenon of voting with your dollars (or political consumerism), people's senses of their moral responsibilities to protect the planet, their ability to fulfill those responsibilities, and their judgments of who cares— and who doesn't care—about the fate of the planet. I analyzed the interviews with an eye to understanding the place of the environment in people's lives.

The data analysis began with a structured analytic memo that my research assistants and I would write immediately after the interview. The purpose of this memo was to create a bridge between the interview and the work of answering research questions through line-by-line qualitative data coding. I built the analytic memo template around a series of questions, such as "How would you describe this person's relationship with the environment, noting their emotions, opinions, etc.?" and "How does this participant understand their environmental impacts?" The memos allowed me to identify a number of themes in my data. In the second stage of analysis, I coded excerpts of text from interview transcripts with the labels of those themes as I read the transcripts line-by-line. In the third phase, I read through all of the transcripts to identify additional themes, coding text accordingly in an iterative process. In this way, I identified affinity as a theme capturing the intensity of a person's relationship with the environment, and identified severity, morality, and efficacy as qualities of the environment and people, respectively, that bear on affinity. Based on the direction of my participants' comments on these four themes, I created codes for five types of eco-social relationship, that I labeled the Eco-Engaged, the Self-Effacing, the Optimists, the Fatalists, and the Indifferent. I coded lines of text from the interview transcripts that epitomized these orientations to the environment.[51] I also used data on each participant's sociodemographic attributes to see whether there was any variation within and across those themes, and if so, along what attributes. I describe the five eco-types in more detail in the overview of the book.

After spending two years analyzing the qualitative data, I wanted to get a sense of whether these Washington State–based patterns also existed in the general population. I hired the survey research firm Qualtrics to administer a survey I designed to a sample of their panel of US residents. The 2,619 survey respondents reflect much of the diversity in the US adult population in terms of political ideology, income, and education. The survey data represent respondents from all 50 states. To analyze the survey data, I use a cluster analysis to delineate the five eco-types, basic descriptive statistics to characterize their eco-social relationships, and a series of regression analyses to identify who is most likely to embody each of those relationships and understand variation within the eco-types.[52]

Studying Eco-Social Relationships

I have spent years reflecting on the question of who cares about the environment. These reflections were prompted by reading books and articles and taking courses about human-environment relationships, but also by my years studying forestry and working as a forester in resource-dependent towns. As a forester, I worked with people who often conveyed an antagonistic orientation toward environmental activism, many of whom did not support environmental protection policies, and whose views seemed to reflect the HEP that Dunlap and his coauthors described. Yet, as my colleagues in forestry shared photos they had taken of plants they encountered in the forest and told me the names of birds in the area and mimicked their songs, it was clear to me that my coworkers clearly felt passionate about the environment. Would I be comfortable concluding they were anti-ecological? No. Conventional explanations of human-environment relationships do not adequately capture how those who might express a HEP feel about the environment.

There is also more work to be done to complicate how we understand people who endorse biospheric values and the New Ecological Paradigm. I have many colleagues, friends, and family who fit this description. They have oriented their lives to reducing their environmental impacts, but for some, these commitments often entail leaning into market-based solutions rather than taking a wholesale critical stance on capitalism and industrialization. When I hear friends and colleagues proudly describe some of the market-based solutions to environmental problems they invest in and learn about, from solar panels and the circular economy, to reusable mugs and farmers' markets, I question McCright and Dunlap's thesis that only conservatives embrace industrialization.[53] Liberals seem to support industrialization in a different way. While my peers and I may voice our critiques of capitalist systems, many of us are also proudly engaged in multiple forms of eco-conscious consumerism that appear to promise little to nothing in the way of challenging the distribution of power and privilege that global capitalism has given rise to.

Compounding these doubts about the bifurcation of pro- and anti-ecological orientations are my observations of the consumption patterns of the people I have known and interacted with in my life. Is the ideal environmentalist whom my friends and family admire any better for the environment than the stereotypical conservation enthusiast? Like me, many of my colleagues, friends, and family live in relatively large homes, fly frequently, and may even buy quite a bit of stuff. Several years ago, my colleagues and I analyzed data from a representative survey of households in Alberta, Canada, and we found that people who held pro-environmental values also had a large carbon footprint. We found that income, not values, mattered when it came to determining a household's carbon emissions.[54] I am not raising this point in order to lay blame on well-intentioned individuals. I do so to demonstrate why, instead of asking the more common question, *Why do some people care about the environment?* I chose to ask, *What is the place of the environment in people's lives?*

The Alberta study taught me that environmental social scientists focusing on values might not be measuring what matters, but is my approach any better? I think so; first, because my answer to the question of what role the environment plays in people's lives is derived from spending hundreds of hours listening to people in Washington State talk about the environment. Also, my results are based on an analytic approach aimed at understanding why a person's way of making sense of and responding to ecological decline is right for them. Through this process, I learned that many people care deeply about the environment. But people whose eco-type is not culturally associated with caring about the environment often experience frustration and resentment at being misunderstood or maligned. Recognizing this phenomenon is significant for understanding and overcoming political polarization and strengthening civil society, because it forces us to admit that we have misunderstood people who are not like ourselves, and invites us to identify areas of common ground where we might find unlikely allies in the fight to disrupt ecological decline.

Overview of the Book

Over the next eight chapters, I will lay out the groundwork for my argument that we all care about the environment and that an underrecognized driver of political polarization is the way in which liberals and conservatives misjudge one another's eco-social relationships. To do so, I begin chapter 1 by introducing the cultural ideal that my interview participants alluded to when evaluating their own and others' eco-social relationships. This cultural schema served as something of a specter in so many of my interviews—revered by liberals and derided by conservatives. The framework of eco-social relationships that I described in this chapter gives rise to five eco-types, and I unpack each of these in subsequent chapters, allocating a chapter to each eco-social relationship.

Chapter 2 introduces the Eco-Engaged. This eco-type is characterized by a deep affinity for the environment, bolstered by a strong belief that ecological decline is urgent and severe. The Eco-Engaged feel personally responsible for confronting that decline and generally feel capable of acting on that moral responsibility. This is the eco-type environmental social scientists often study when we want to know what motivates people to take personal and political actions to protect the environment.

Chapter 3 describes the Self-Effacing, who share the Eco-Engaged participants' perception of the environment as vulnerable and threatened by humanity and who feel a moral responsibility to help protect the environment. However, the Self-Effacing experience a profound lack of self-efficacy to act on their moral ideals. I believe much previous research has overlooked this eco-type.

In chapter 4 we meet the Optimists, who feel a strong affinity for nature and confront an environment they perceive as powerful and resilient. As a result, they accept neither diagnoses of an imminent ecological catastrophe nor appeals to reduce their personal levels of consumption. The Optimist eco-type reflects past research on the conventional climate denier as well as the embodiment of the HEP. But as I argue in the chapter, these characterizations misunderstand and overly simplify the Optimist eco-type.

Chapter 5 presents the Fatalists, an eco-type that has been overlooked or mischaracterized in existing research. Fatalists have a deeply pessimistic outlook for humanity and feel powerless to confront what they believe is driving ecological decline: corporations who are driven to endlessly maximize profits, aided by a state too powerless to stop them and uphold the common good. This eco-social relationship has received little attention from social scientists to date.

Chapter 6 introduces the final eco-type: the Indifferent. The Indifferent express a weak affinity for the environment. Other studies have characterized a "disengaged" group of Americans and I think that adequately reflects the Indifferent.[55] For the Indifferent, other issues feel more immediate and more relevant than their relationship with the environment.

My goal in writing the chapters on eco-social relationships is to demonstrate that we all care about the environment, but do so in ways that can be unrecognizable to others. The final chapters of the book build on this foundation to demonstrate how failing to appreciate the diversity of eco-social relationships that exists, and critiquing how others care about the environment, affects political polarization. Chapter 7 brings in evidence of the cultural dynamics driving political polarization over environmental protection from my interviews with Washington State residents. In chapter 8 and the conclusion, I identify key lessons from closely studying eco-social relationships. I summarize the current landscape as encompassing seemingly incompatible relationships to a natural environment that is universally valued.

As long as we critique *individuals'* relationships to the environment and make judgments of their moral worth on this basis, we exacerbate the divisiveness of civil society. This pattern of individualizing ecological decline also obfuscates the role of the state and market in perpetuating unsustainable and inequitable production and consumption practices. If we can instead cultivate curiosity about other people's eco-social relationships, and direct our critique toward decision makers in the market and state, we can strengthen the power of civil society to protect the environment. Next, I introduce the ideal environmentalist, a cultural schema that my participants referred to when explaining what it looks like to care about the environment.

1

The Ideal Environmentalist

The Good Place is a fantasy sitcom that follows four young, good-looking people into the afterlife. The four are told by a demon-in-Ted-Danson-clothing that they have ended up in heaven, when in fact, they are in an elaborate torture scenario because the "points" they accumulated in their lives landed them in the "bad place." Over the course of many episodes, the protagonists come to realize (spoiler alert:) no one has made it to the "good place" in over 500 years, and this is largely because each and every human's daily consumption choices trigger a cascade of social and ecological damage. For instance, a person shopping for a tomato, believing it to be a healthy dietary choice, is unwittingly accumulating negative points due to the carbon dioxide emissions from producing that tomato, the bleak working conditions for tomato-pickers, and the impacts of toxic pesticides on people and the environment. As Ted Danson's character explains, "Humans think that they're making one choice, but they're making dozens of choices they don't even know they're making."[1] This view of consumer goods as fraught with moral significance is now central to how many people in Western industrialized societies make sense of ecological decline. *The Good Place* showcases a prominent perception that I encountered in my interviews: a sense that in mainstream culture, demonstrating an ethical relationship to the environment demands being conscious of ecological decline, caring about one's own environmental impacts, and being committed to reducing those impacts. My interview participants also conveyed a belief that these three characteristics are made visible in the domain of consumption. The embodiment of these traits represents a cultural schema that I call the *ideal environmentalist*.

My conceptualization of an ideal environmentalist is similar to sociological scholarship on the ideal worker.[2] The concept of the ideal worker serves as a cipher to understand how gender affects who is granted authority in the workplace. As the sociologist Joan Acker argued, gendered perceptions of employees' innate abilities in the workplace shape who is hired, promoted, and paid well. Employers tend to privilege masculine ideal worker norms, for instance, strong leaders and logical thinkers who are unlikely to be distracted by family. The prominence of these ideal worker norms obscures, marginalizes, and disadvantages many women's participation in the labor force.[3] In a similar way, the ideal environmentalist is a schema that helps make sense of why conscious consumers are so widely presumed to care about the environment.[4] That is, people whose practices and attitudes convey a commitment to using consumption decisions to clean up their environmental impact are used as the benchmark or prototype by which people evaluate their own and others' relationships with the environment.[5] As I'll explain later in this chapter, the people I interviewed have a prototype of this ideal environmentalist that is relatively high-status, politically liberal, white, and female.

But how did it come to pass that this conscious, caring, committed consumer was so prominent in my Washington State participants' perception of who cares about the environment? First, we need to get to know the ideal environmentalist in more detail and we will do so by hearing how my participants imagined (and envisioned others imagining) what caring about the environment looks like.

Defining and Understanding the Ideal Environmentalist

What does it look like to care about the environment? The ideal environmentalist is widely viewed as someone who is worried about human impacts on the planet and who exercises their environmental concerns through conscientious choices in the marketplace.

As a sociologist who studies sustainable consumption, I often feel that my work is a bit tangential and less serious, in contrast to the work of my colleagues who focus on production. So, it came as a surprise to me to see how prominent consumption choices are in people's sense of which beliefs and behaviors reflect caring about the environment. Although I asked my interview participants about how they perceived their daily actions to affect the environment, which inevitably led our conversation to a focus on consumer practices, I did not mention consumption until after I asked people what they thought it looked like to care about the environment. Across virtually all of my interviews, participants' comments indicated that you can tell (or that most people think you can tell) if someone is aware of environmental issues and cares about those issues by looking at the choices they make as a consumer. My participants also told me that there is a general sense, in their social context, that being committed to environmental protection means being thoughtful about consumption and waste choices.[6] In fact, when my participants shared their theories of why humanity has caused such catastrophic ecological decline, most pointed at what they deemed to be excessive levels of household consumption, rather than implicating nations, corporations, militaries, or other entities that impact the planet.

THE IDEAL ENVIRONMENTALIST: CONSCIOUS, CARING, AND COMMITTED

I asked my Washington State–based interview participants who they pictured as a good environmentalist. First, they picture people who are *aware*. Awareness means worrying about environmental issues and being cognizant of what you're buying and how much you're using up. James, a Fatalist and conservative, says he believes that environmentalists are, "more environmentally conscious." The term "conscious" comes up a lot, and I take it to represent a synonym for aware. While James explains that he is referring to people who follow environmental issues, others link consciousness to consumer choices. Amber, a strong conservative who I labeled as having an Indifferent eco-social relationship, envisions environmentalists in this way: "in everyday life they are more conscious about their decisions, maybe as far as purchasing food, water, and then how they dispose of the trash. And those types of daily decisions are way more conscious I think, for environmentalists." Scott, an Optimist and political conservative, says being an environmentalist means, "Being aware. Being that global consumer, that global citizen." When I asked Myra, an Indifferent liberal, who she would describe as an environmentalist, she mentions the father of a child she looks after. When I ask why he comes to mind, Myra tells me, "He's just more informed and aware than other people, about the environment." Across all eco-types and across political ideologies and party preference, people associate environmentalists as people who are conscious of the environment. As Amber and Scott's comments indicate, for many participants, being aware is intimately tied to daily consumer choices.

The ideal environmentalist is also *caring*. Ideal environmentalists care how they impact the environment. This means they are seen as unselfish and ethical; they are quick to make personal sacrifices to their own comfort and convenience in order to ensure that their impact on the environment is as small as possible. Again, these sacrifices are primarily located in the realm of consumer choices. When I asked interview participants to tell me what an environmentalist is, they told me it is someone who cares about the environment, but also that it is someone who cares in a particular way. Environmentalists, people suggested, care by trying to reduce their carbon footprint—or at least, other participants told me, that's what a lot of people think. Annie, an Eco-Engaged participant who supports the Green Party, says an environmentalist is, "anyone who has care and concern and tries to live a minimal, simple lifestyle without so much consumerism." Care is intimately tied to using consumer choices to lessen their footprint on the earth. Sarah, a lifelong Republican voter in the Indifferent eco-type, says she believes environmentalists, "make better decisions," and elaborates that she means people who make consumer choices that prioritize sustainability over cost. Caitlyn, Self-Effacing and politically liberal, tells me she not only associates conscious consumption with environmentalism, but also that she admires people who buy eco-friendly products: "you can tell they care more about their bodies, and the environment too." The Eco-Engaged associate this caring ideal with themselves. Like Denny, a self-proclaimed "far, far left liberal," who says he pictures himself when asked to imagine an environmentalist: "I picture yours truly. People that bicycle, people that drive electric cars, people that turn off the front porch lights at night." Only the Eco-Engaged mentioned themselves when I asked who came to mind as someone who cares about the environment.

Finally, the ideal environmentalist is someone *committed* to protecting the environment, which is recognizable by what they buy, what they eat, and how much waste they produce. To return to *The Good Place*—the ideal environmentalist knows that a tomato comes with heavy socioecological baggage, is upset about that, and responds by purchasing their tomatoes at a local farmers' market or growing their own. Myra references this specifically, as she says, "environmentalists are just more committed. They will shop at the farmers' market. They're not lazy." More broadly, Angela, Eco-Engaged and politically moderate, describes an environmentalist as, "someone whose actions and choices are made to not hurt the environment." In our cultural imaginary, people who care about the environment try not to leave a big footprint. Ellen, Self-Effacing and politically liberal, describes what it looks like to be the ideal environmentalist: "Trying to have the smallest possible footprint." She specifies: "Zero to little fossil-fuel usage. Collecting water or being conscientious of water management. Opting for things that have the least amount of shipping to live on. Walkers, bikers. It is both good for them and not bad for anybody else. Those are the basic things."

Ellen introduced some of the specific practices that people associate with the ideal way to care about the planet. Here are some other examples: Addy, an Eco-Engaged participant who supports the Green Party, has a picture in her mind of, "somebody who rides their bike more than they drive, and is conscious about the products they purchase, not getting plastic bags at the store." Cheryl, a lifelong Democrat who I characterize as having a quint-essentially Self-Effacing eco-type, concentrates on transportation choices and civic engagement: "they buy a Prius, they join Sierra Club, ride bikes. All that." Cheryl's comments indicate the ways in which membership in environmental organizations can be part of the ethos of the ideal environ-mentalist, although few participants mentioned membership. Overall, this is what my participants told me: it is possible to be an environmentalist who buys eco-friendly products and goes to protests, but you are probably not an environmentalist if you go to protests but care little about how and what you consume. The social scientist Dave Horton describes a similar phenom-enon based on his time spent observing environmental activist groups in the United Kingdom. In these activist groups, status and belonging centered less on activism than on each member's engagement in ethical consumer choices, such as choosing to bike rather than drive.[7] In my interviews, I did not observe any eco-friendly consumers trying to differentiate themselves based on their political activism, nor did I hear my participants look down on someone for not being politically active in the same way as some did toward people they saw as being excessive in their consumption of resources.

I'll elaborate on what my participants described when they envisioned a commitment to reducing environmental impact through consumption choices. People have quite specific images of what eco-friendly consumption looks like. Charles, a Fatalist and Democrat, focuses on food: "they would be people who would be very conscious of what types of food they bought. They wouldn't buy a lot of packaged foods." Shauna, an Optimist and con-servative, emphasizes waste: "trying to take steps in your day-to-day life, like recycling or composting and things like that." Ina, an older Eco-Engaged woman who did not share her political ideology, also zeros in on waste, but focuses on efforts to reduce waste and calls attention to her own actions: "People like me, who compost and never throw away anything." And Judy, Self-Effacing and liberal, focused on home energy use when defining an environmentalist: "somebody that is being really careful with their energy use. Maybe somebody who has their house 100% solar. Somebody who's trying really hard not to leave a big footprint." Caring about the environment is tied to an array of ethical consumer choices—from picking which tomato to buy to choosing low-carbon transportation options. The themes of awareness, care, and commitment as characteristics of the ideal environmentalist are interconnected. For example, when I asked Travis (Self-Effacing, liberal) to tell me what comes to his mind when he thinks of someone who has a positive impact on the environment, he raises the themes of awareness and commitment. He pictures someone who is "really aware of the externalities of things, of what's being used up. I would say it's someone who sort of takes all that into account when calculating what to buy."

There are particular practices that are culturally coded as signifying concern for the environment. These sorts of practices are likely familiar to readers. Sustainable consumption scholars often categorize household environmental impacts in domains: eating, transportation, waste management, dwelling in the home, leisure, and so forth.[8] I notice that food, ground transportation, and waste are the areas of household environmental impact that my participants most commonly targeted and mentioned. Home energy use (either the source or the amount) is not emphasized so much, nor is leisure travel or spending on fashion and electronics. And within the targeted domains, certain practices have much more cultural weight than others. For instance, in the domain of food, my participants mentioned practices like buying organic and local foods far more often than reducing food waste. In the domain of transportation, my participants emphasized driving a hybrid or electric car and bicycling far more than cutting back on air travel.

The practices my participants placed so much weight on connote caring about the environment at this time and place.[9] They are also the practices the Eco-Engaged almost effortlessly integrate into their daily lives, as I describe in the next chapter. In the previous chapter, I began by asking what sorts of practices you associate with caring about the environment. As I showed here, many people I interviewed envisioned someone concerned about ecological decline, worried about their personal environmental impacts, and committed to reducing those impacts through actions like cycling, buying local food, and recycling.

Who Is the Ideal Environmentalist? High-Status, Liberal, Female, and White

Now that you have a better idea of which behaviors typify the ideal environmentalist, we can focus on the sociodemographic characteristics people associate with this stereotype. It is difficult to get people to talk about stereotypes in an interview, but when pressed to describe their image of a person who cares about the environment, participants described a high-status, politically progressive, white woman.[10]

Shelby, who fits in the Self-Effacing eco-type and is strongly liberal, said that when she imagines a person who is "really into the environment," she pictures, "a professor-type." Shelby's comments allude to a person whose position in the professional managerial class conveys high cultural capital and status.[11] Amber envisions someone who is really invested in reducing their environmental impact as, "a woman holding a wagon with a lot of fresh foods from the farmers' market. She is probably a stay-at-home wife or mother." Amber elaborates, "they would be thinking maybe they are more righteous for making that decision and 'I am so much more environmentally friendly than you are for buying this fresh stuff.'" In these excerpts, Amber is suggesting that her prototype of an ideal environmentalist is female, wealthy, and someone who looks down on others. Nadine, Eco-Engaged and strongly liberal, when I asked how she puts her environmental concerns into actions, described how much she enjoys shopping at her local farmers' market. When I asked who she pictures as an environmentalist she said, succinctly: "someone like me." Jim, Self-Effacing and undecided on his political orientation, says he pictures someone "a little pretentious, but that might be a defensive judgment on my part." Overall, most of the people I interviewed assumed that the ideal environmentalist is the sort of person who is relatively higher up in our social hierarchy.

The other place I noticed this association between social status and the ideal environmentalist is in how difficult it was for my participants to imagine a low-income household being committed to environmental protection, or having a relationship to the environment at all. My colleague Christine Horne and I have written about this more extensively, but here I will note simply that when people envision the environmental contributions of low-income households, they either characterize them as "accidental environmentalists," who have a small footprint due to their limited income and not, as Eileen (Eco-Engaged, liberal) says, "because they actually care about the environment."[12] Or they picture low-income households as having a negative impact on the environment because they are not aware of environmental problems. For instance, Greg, an Optimist and a strong conservative, conflates stereotypes of poverty and race when picturing a household that is bad for the environment: "Now if you get into a poor neighborhood where you have a huge Black community of third or fourth generation welfare, they don't care. There's probably not going to be an awareness there." Other participants alluded to the same phenomenon by invoking Maslow's hierarchy of needs: the idea that we cannot develop an interest in higher-order needs like environmental protection if we don't have our basic needs met.

Aside from Greg's blunt and racist remarks and other participants' allusions to Maslow's hierarchy, my participants made only a few direct judgments about the gender and race of the ideal environmentalist. But I noticed gendered and raced patterns in how people spoke of a prototypical "type" of environmentally concerned actor and in who people named as iconic figures in environmentalism. Like Amber, who pictures a stay-at-home mother shopping at the farmers' market, people were more likely to envision a woman as the ideal environmentalist. But when my participants offered a specific name as reflective of an environmentalist, they tended to name white men: John Muir, Aldo Leopold, Wendell Berry, Daniel Berrigan, Edward Abbey, Ralph Nader, Al Gore, Henry David Thoreau, Paul Ehrlich, Paul Watson, and Bernie Sanders. None of the men in my sample named a female environmental leader and the women I interviewed who referred to female environmentalists only named white women (Rachel Carson and Jane Goodall). That is, people imagined unnamed women to be more likely to make consumer choices to demonstrate care for nature, and spoke glowingly about (mostly) white, male environmental heroes who they knew by name.

Participants' comments about race were even more subtle than their remarks about gender and the ideal environmentalist. Sociologist Elijah Anderson uses the term, "white space" to describe arenas in society that are culturally coded as white.[13] These are spaces that can be highly uncomfortable and exclusionary toward people of color. Is environmentalism a "white space"? First of all, a couple of participants explicitly pictured the ideal environmentalist as white. For example, Travis says he pictures an environmentalist to be, "a white person from a middle-class or upper-middle-class background who's privileged enough to buy, like, organic cotton." Other scholars have commented on a tendency for academics and the public to assume that people of color are uninterested in environmental protection or feel powerless to effect any meaningful change.[14] And yet, surveys of Black and Latinx people's environmental concerns reveal a strong commitment to environmental issues.[15] My interview participants reproduced the notion of environmental protection as a white person's concern by only naming white environmental leaders and by drawing on racialized stereotypes of immigrants, Black people, and Latinx as poor and lacking the capacity to care about the environment.

My participants' perceptions of Indigenous peoples took a different tone. For instance, Jeff (Optimist, conservative) described Indigenous peoples as "living in harmony with the environment." Several interviewees associated Native Americans with environmentalism, but did so in general and nostalgic terms like Jeff's. This is an enduring and prominent pattern in mainstream US culture, culminating in what some scholars refer to as the myth of "the Ecological Indian," or the "Noble Savage."[16] Some Indigenous scholars argue that when settlers suggest that Native Americans have an inherent capacity to live in harmony with the environment, they are romanticizing a history of colonialism, genocide, and enclosure and portraying Indigenous peoples as simple and lacking agency.[17] For many Indigenous peoples, acknowledging the violence of settler colonialism is an essential first step to understanding and addressing environmental issues. My participants didn't envision contemporary Indigenous peoples as demonstrating an ideal eco-social relationship. Rather, they romantically imagined Indigenous communities pre-colonialism. In this way, Indigenous peoples don't serve as contemporary examples of valued eco-social relationships, but are instead relegated to a past whose violence and ongoing legacies are ignored.

Most of the people I interviewed agreed that the ideal environmentalist is upper-middle-class, drew associations to how men and women implemented the ideal differently, and romanticized Indigenous peoples' relationship to nature. These are the similarities. Political ideology is the sociodemographic factor that seems most salient in characterizing the differences in how my participants imagined the ideal environmentalist. Many participants stereotyped the ideal environmentalist as a liberal and many conservative participants made a point of noting that the ideal environmentalist reflects liberals' connections to the environment, not their own. Conservatives often challenged the notion that this ideal is the best—or the only—way to care about the environment. In turn, liberals tended to characterize conservatives as anti-environmental. Conservatives did not apply this label to liberals, but they did challenge liberals' knowledge of the environment and what they perceived as an unearned moral high-ground, by characterizing the ideal environmentalist as misguided or hypocritical.

None of my liberal participants characterized caring about the environment as reflecting politically conservative values. Brian, Self-Effacing and politically liberal himself, tells me that "someone who's politically liberal is more likely to be very passionate about saving the environment and caring for it." My liberal participants frequently denounced conservatives for caring more about profit than the planet (a failure to live up to the "caring" element of the ideal). For instance, I asked Lexi (Self-Effacing, liberal), a 21-year-old college student who also works as a nanny, what she pictured when she thought of someone with a negative impact on the environment: "A Republican!" Kim, Self-Effacing and liberal, elaborates: "Republicans! They're so worried about profit, they don't even care about the environment, they just care about getting less regulations about the environment." And when I asked Elena (Eco-Engaged, liberal) if most of her friends felt as passionately about environmental issues as she did, she said, "I don't think our conservative friends do. . . . Their views on things like the environment are so self-centered." This speaks to a perception that conservatives lack both awareness of ecological decline and a meaningful relationship with the environment.

Conservatives themselves recognized (and challenged) the view that a conservative political ideology is seen as diametrically opposed to the ideal environmentalist. Bill (Optimist, conservative) said that when he pictures the stereotypical environmentalist, he pictures his politically liberal sister, who lives in a condominium in Seattle, buys organic foods, and composts her kitchen waste. Bill says when his sister visits, she always critiques him and his family for buying plastic water bottles and not recycling enough. In other words, Bill feels that his sister evaluates him using the benchmark of the ideal environmentalist—an ideal he recognizes but does not seek to emulate. Hannah (Optimist, libertarian), who comes from a farming family and still works in the agriculture industry, contrasts liberals' and conservatives' perceptions of one another's relationships to people and the environment. She recounted a recent instance where well-educated liberals (as Hannah perceived them) from the Environmental Protection Agency (EPA) fined a local farmer for not fencing off a creek to stop cattle from walking in the waterway. In the discussion that followed, I asked Hannah if she felt that liberal outsiders were judgmental of the conservative townspeople. She says, "Yeah, for sure. But we do the same thing to them." She explains these misunderstandings: "I would say their judgment is that we are behind the times, that we're not doing everything that we can to protect the environment. We're being lazy." She is also aware of judgments that people in her town have of urban liberals: "our judgment is that liberals are just city people and they have no idea, which is, that's an awful characterization, but at the same time, some of these laws and rules come down from the liberals and we're just like, 'Are you kidding me?'"

As Hannah explains, she senses that because in her state, liberals have the cultural and legislative power to define how people should care about the environment and, more specifically, to shape farmers' livelihoods, they end up making decisions that harm farmers and help well-educated liberals.[18] Returning to Hannah's story of the EPA fining a farmer in her town, I'll offer more detail on why she feels that well-educated liberals in her state have the authority to craft policies that are in line with their own values, and deploy that authority in ways that ultimately make farming financially unviable. Hannah tells me that over time, policies like the one that requires fencing to protect waterways have made life in her town more difficult. As costs to adhere to environmental protection requirements balloon, local farmers such as the one fined in Hannah's anecdote end up laying off low-income employees who are often their neighbors and friends. These employees typically have few other local job prospects and are forced to move to seek employment elsewhere. On top of this, Hannah's sense is that the same set of policies ultimately create job opportunities for newly minted graduates of Masters and PhD programs—well-educated and more privileged people she assumes are politically liberal, who then set out crafting more policies, in the manner of a feedback loop. As this feedback loop cycles over time, there are increasing numbers of people with graduate degrees working in well-paid, environmental protection jobs, and declining numbers of farmers and farm laborers making less and less money for their work.[19]

Before moving on to a historical account of the rise of the ideal environmentalist, I want to connect with my data to check the accuracy of my participants' stereotype of the ideal environmentalist as liberal, high-status, female, and white. Of the five eco-types I identified, the Eco-Engaged bear the strongest resemblance to the ideal environmentalist, in terms of their beliefs and practices. But is the typical Eco-Engaged more likely to be a high-status, liberal, white woman? By analyzing the survey data, I found that the only trait here that is strictly accurate is political ideology—liberals are over twice as likely to embody this eco-social relationship.[20] But I need to make a note about status. Researchers and people in the general public often measure status by looking at a person's wealth and education. These variables are not related to membership in the Eco-Engaged eco-type. However, I included in the survey a measure of upbringing, in which I asked people how often their families growing up spent time in nature, talked about the environment, and adopted eco-friendly practices. Think of this as a measure of an inherited, high cultural capital eco-social relationship. I found that the Eco-Engaged are twice as likely as other eco-types to have been raised in this kind of household. And while this is not a measure of social status, it can be interpreted as reflecting an eco-habitus. Eco-habitus refers to people's orientations to the environment, perceiving this orientation to be something we inherit through the process of socialization, and something that is ingrained in us, shaping our beliefs and our actions in a semi-conscious way.[21] For example, I grew up with parents who ate vegetarian food for environmental reasons and although I now eat meat, I still find myself associating meat with environmental damage without really critically interrogating this association. The manifestation of the ideal environmentalist in daily life (the Eco-Engaged) is not any more likely to be female or male, or white or not. Not only do these traits fail to predict who has an Eco-Engaged eco-social relationship, but descriptive statistics also show that the Eco-Engaged is the most racially diverse and gender-balanced of the five eco-types.

Historicizing the Ideal Environmentalist

Next, let's consider how the cultural schema I described above came to occupy a position of such prominence in my study area. A rich historical analysis is beyond the scope of this book, but it is important to make note of some social structures and historical patterns that are relevant for creating a context where the decision of what tomato to eat is a moral one.[22]

It would be an oversight not to mention the interrelated roles of colonialism and capitalism in bringing us to a point in history when the episode of *The Good Place* that I described at the start of this chapter resonates with so many people. There is an extensive and compelling literature on how our contemporary relationship with the environment can be traced to the beginning of colonialism and the violent marginalization of Indigenous societies and their cultural practices.[23] One point made consistently across this multidisciplinary literature is that colonialism marks the beginning of a cognitive separation of people and the environment. Rather than being seen as part of a web of species, settlers came to the Americas with the notion that humans were separate from, and meant to rule over and benefit from, the nonhuman world.[24] To connect that to the case at hand: that a tomato could incur such high social and environmental costs is an extension of the relationship to the land that settler colonialists brought to the Americas and beyond. Early settler cultures prized activities that created economic value and expanded the presence of Europeans on the landscape.[25] Modern, globalized, monoculture agriculture is a manifestation of settler values. It is impossible to purchase an ethical tomato from a model of food production that does not seek just treatment for all actors in an ecosystem.

A second key point from the literature on colonialism is that when settlers came to the Americas, they imposed a social stratification that placed Europeans above Indigenous peoples in their social worth. As sociologists Allison Ford and Kari Norgaard explain, mainstream environmentalism in North America is likely to reflect the views and practices of settlers, given their power and dominance.[26] The two themes intersect: the social importance ascribed to European settlers imbues this group with more power to define what counts as an environmental problem and what solutions are appropriate for addressing those problems. The framing of both problems and solutions tends to perpetuate human dominance over and separation from nature, as well as settlers' domination over Indigenous peoples.

The rapid rise of capitalist political economic orders is widely (though not universally) seen as exacerbating and accelerating ecological decline and shaping the fabric of civic life. Two key points from this literature draw our attention to the harmful ecological impacts of capitalism and the way in which the market mediates everyday life. Turning to the first point, scholars such as John Bellamy Foster and Richard York continue the Marxist tradition of critically interrogating the impacts of capitalist systems on social equity and ecological integrity.[27] Their analysis points at the problem of wealth creation in capitalist societies. They demonstrate ways that individual profits are made at the expense of ecological integrity and publicly held wealth, benefiting a tiny fraction of individuals and creating a rift between people and nature. In the case of the moralized tomato, we can appreciate the ways that within capitalism, a primary aim of production is profit and that entails reducing input costs. In a drive to reduce the costs of production, markets have globalized, seeking cheap labor and land, and costs are artificially low because many natural resources are not accounted for in the price of a good.[28]

The second way in which capitalism should be considered as influencing the rise of the ethical tomato and the ideal environmentalist lies in the centrality of the market as a medium for participation in social change. Even when we focus on something that seems to have little to do with "getting and spending," like people's relationship with the environment, the marketplace still occupies a place of prominence. As the rich literature on conscious consumerism has made clear, many people seek to actualize their moral commitments, which include environmental protection, by "voting with their dollars."[29] This neo-liberalization of environmental protection did not simply happen; key interests worked deliberately to propagate the notion that saving the planet is up to us, as individuals.

The case of recycling is a powerful, environmentally relevant example of how industry groups cultivated a norm for individualizing the responsibility to protect the environment. As the sociologist Andrew Jaeger demonstrates, the beverage and packaging industries in the US have lobbied against extended producer responsibility policies since the early 1950s.[30] Meanwhile, actors in these industries carefully crafted a narrative that waste is everyone's problem, for instance, in the Keep America Beautiful campaign. By calling for people to stop being "litterbugs" and promoting household and community recycling, the beverage and packaging industry has continued manufacturing and selling plastic and glass containers, leaving the responsibility to deal with the resulting waste to households and municipal governments. In short, companies have invested in campaigns aiming to inculcate the idea that as individuals, we are responsible for the environmental pollution and waste our society produces.[31] In this context, we can see a connection between industrial lobbying aimed at individualizing environmental responsibility and the ideal environmentalist, who feels personally responsible for her environmental impacts.

This interest in and acceptance of household-level environmentalism is also a theme in the history of the US environmental movement. In the 1970s, after Americans participated in the first Earth Day, more environmental protection legislation was passed in the US than any time before or since.[32] And while there were some subcultural pockets of Americans engaging in lifestyle solutions to environmental issues, like voluntary simplicity or living in intentional communities, these were not mainstream practices.[33] In contrast, today the US federal government passes fewer pieces of environmental protection legislation and there are increased efforts to roll back or weaken existing legislation. In our contemporary context, lifestyle movements have become so ubiquitous that we now see ads at the Superbowl promoting "eco-friendly" vehicles, Netflix specials documenting homesteading, minimalism, and other household and community-level responses to consumerism, and environmental organizations promoting simple things *you* can do to save the environment.[34] Lifestyle movements have expanded from a counter-culture niche into mainstream communities of vegans, urban homesteaders, and zero-waste enthusiasts.[35] To ground these patterns in the context of the problematic tomato, people picture someone who is conscious of their personal moral responsibilities to reduce environmental impact as a prominent expression of caring about the environment because this is such a ubiquitous caricature in contemporary culture.

It is important to note that over the same time period, political polarization over the environment has also widened. In 1970, the country was deeply politically polarized—but not over environmental protection. The main rift between conservatives and liberals was over reactions to the Vietnam War.[36] Against this backdrop, bipartisan support for environmental protection was all the more striking. Today, federal Democrats and Republicans are often pitted against one another, fighting for or against, respectively, environmental protection legislation. Further, there are political differences in people's level of engagement in these more consumer-focused, everyday expressions of environmental commitments: liberals are more likely than conservatives to report a high level of engagement in these types of activities.[37] To return once more to our moralized tomato, political differences in who is more likely to engage in household efforts to reduce consumption map onto cultural schemas associating caring about the environment with liberal political ideologies.

As lifestyle movements become more popular, the American public is simultaneously growing increasingly skeptical of traditional politics. In a study of participants in voluntary associations, Elizabeth Bennett and her coauthors were surprised to find that no one wanted to describe their work as "political," even though they were engaged in what scholars would define as political action. The people in the study worked to distance their efforts from what they saw as a "tainted" sphere of society—they sensed that politics is coopted by people representing and advancing powerful interest groups.[38] These dynamics show up in political divisions on the topic of activism. Many conservatives I interviewed spoke derisively about climate activists but spoke far less combatively about eco-conscious consumers. Even the liberals I interviewed who were supportive of environmental activism and saw it as important, told me that it is a person's daily commitment to reducing their environmental impact that is most central to determining how much they care about the planet.

The way different actors and institutions respond to ecological decline is shaped by colonialism, capitalism, the environmental movement, and the nature of public engagement in contemporary civic life. This is a history that has left us in a place where many consumer goods carry a great cost to people and the planet. It is difficult for governments to achieve bipartisan consensus to offer sustained support for environmental protection; markets continue to produce an ever-expanding panoply of eco-friendly goods; and civil society generally conveys low levels of trust in traditional politics. In contrast to the tainted realm of politics, as individuals, we are often encouraged to make conscientious shopping choices in a marketplace that offers a growing number of "green" choices for everything from toys to tomatoes, cleaning products to cars. And now, not only is the array of "eco-friendly" consumer choices proliferating, but through advertising and marketing we are also frequently reminded that choosing these goods is an important way of caring about the planet.[39] The idea that conscious consumerism is a necessary element of environmental protection is commonly voiced in our cultural spaces, from the classroom, to books and magazines, to films and television shows like *The Good Place*. It is increasingly normal to encounter judgments of indulgent consumers as selfish and stupid and of green consumers as conscientious and caring.[40] So, here we are, in the era of the problematic tomato—individual consumer choices are front and center in human-environment relationships.

BOX 1.1. Explaining How the Ideal Environmentalist Influences
Eco-Social Relationships

This box connects to cultural sociological material that is helpful for understanding how it is that my diverse participants, living all over the state of Washington, could develop a shared understanding of what it looks like to care about the environment. This content is not essential to understand in order to follow the main argument in the book.

The theoretical model I describe here is taken from sociologist Omar Lizardo, who is trying to explain how culture shapes actions. He explains that people have a personal culture that we internalize and that we act on that cultural knowledge through "declarative" and "nondeclarative" processes.[41] At the same time, there is also a public culture of which we are all aware. I'll define these terms as I make use of them to explain how the ideal environmentalist influences eco-social relationships.

The ideal environmentalist is how we perceive caring about the environment to look and sound like in our *public culture*. We each also have a personal culture that comes about through declarative and nondeclarative processes. People identify and learn declarative culture through spoken or written language, and it is instilled in us when we are asked to evaluate, judge, reason, and categorize the world. Lizardo describes declarative culture in the language of photography: it can be stored after only "a small number of exposures" and retrieved as "flashbulb" memories. People can speak confidently about the declarative culture they "know." Taking this idea into the realm of how to care about the environment, we can see declarative culture at work when we hear people evaluate someone's profligate consumption as unethical and another person's eco-friendly choices as admirable.

If declarative culture is explicit, nondeclarative culture is implicit; as declarative culture is similar to a photograph, nondeclarative culture is more like an impression or a feeling. We attain nondeclarative culture slowly and over a long period of what Lizardo calls, "repeated encodings." For example, think of learning a new skill, like driving or typing. In research on sustainable consumption, some scholars use an approach like Lizardo's to argue that a great deal of our daily actions are relatively unconscious, and rely on repeated habits and routines that we ultimately take for granted. Alan Warde describes driving in this way—at the outset we change gears and indicate turns consciously, while proficient drivers seemingly do all of this without thinking.[42] Many of our consumption choices, from showering to grocery shopping, rely on nondeclarative culture. So too do status judgments, for instance when we make judgments of someone based on their race or gender or the way they care about the environment. As Lizardo argues, nondeclarative culture is put into use effortlessly, compared with declarative culture, which requires knowing that one is accessing stored knowledge.

Importantly, declarative and nondeclarative processes may be at work in the same domain of knowledge (e.g., how to care about the environment). That is, someone may be aware of cultural scripts associating cloth bags and organic produce with caring about the planet (public culture) and be familiar with evaluations of that public culture (e.g., the ideal environmentalist is admirable, or hypocritical). This is their declarative culture. Meanwhile, a person's nondeclarative culture affects the extent to which their habitual thoughts and practices align with public culture or not. Everyone I interviewed shares a "public culture" that sketches out the ideal environmentalist in their minds as someone who embraces eco-friendly consumer choices. Not everyone has a "personal culture" that aligns with the public ideal. The Eco-Engaged do—their upbringing in environmentally active households endows them with an eco-habitus, with nondeclarative cultural skills that align with the ideal environmentalist. They semi-consciously enjoy the benefits of having their personal culture (both declarative and nondeclarative) align with public culture. In contrast, others are aware of the public ideal but their own relationship to the environment is incongruent with this ideal. That is, their personal culture is out of step with public culture, and they may react to this incongruency in several ways: guilt (the Self-Effacing), withdrawal (Fatalists, Indifferent), or antagonism (the Optimists).

To briefly illustrate how this gap between a public ideal and personal culture can exist, I will return to the example of driving. For instance, most drivers presumably know there is a public rule about indicating to make a turn, or about driving under a speed limit. We learn this formally, through rulebooks and tests, and also informally, by watching or listening to others as they drive (e.g., getting a fine for speeding, yelling at other drivers for failing to use their turning indicator). Yet even if most people share this public culture—are knowledgeable about it—we don't all agree with or follow the rules. That is, shared public culture does not mean that we all act homogenously or harmoniously. Variation in driving practices is high. In the same way, most people may be aware of a cultural schema of an ideal environmentalist, but that doesn't mean that people agree with, or follow, the rules associated with that ideal.

The Moral Politics of a Tomato

Does the tomato in *The Good Place* feel problematic for all of us? Does everyone watching that episode catch the premise of the joke—that choosing a consumer good is a moral decision? If so, do they agree with the premise? Does everyone accept the cultural hegemony of the ideal environmentalist? In my interviews, I found that everyone is familiar with the idea that caring about the planet demands conscientious consumer choices. In fact, this is central to how people defined the "ideal environmentalist"—someone who cares about a planet in peril and responds by consuming conscientiously in order to reduce how much they impact the environment. My participants were aware of the suggestion that "good" people care what tomato they eat and try to procure the most ethical tomato they can. But I also observed a lot of variation in how people responded to this premise. Some of my participants agreed—yes, good people buy good tomatoes. Others disagreed, arguing that it is ridiculous to moralize a tomato in this way. What can explain this discrepancy? I found that political ideology seems to be the most important quality in terms of orienting a person toward or away from making moral judgments of the environmental weight of consumer choices.

When environmental social scientists study household-level environmentalism, we tend to study, or at least have in mind, the sort of people who care what tomato they buy. Most research (including much of my own) focuses on household environmentalism by examining subcultures of environmentally concerned people—subcultures we identify by finding people who do the sorts of things we think are important for protecting the environment. We know a lot about what motivates people living these ecologically oriented, alternative lifestyles.[43] This leaves social scientists in a position where someone watching *The Good Place* who worries about the socioecological impacts of a tomato is familiar to us. But we don't know if everyone feels that way, or if everyone is even familiar with the association between caring about the environment and choosing a tomato. What I found in my interviews with people in Washington, is that this cultural schema shapes how people value their own and others' relationships with the environment.

In the dominant cultural imagination (that is, the ideas that are shared by members of the same culture), caring about the environment involves caring which tomato you buy. As a cultural schema, we each interpret and evaluate the ideal environmentalist differently, and those differences are likely linked to our social and biophysical context and personal history. Each of the eco-social relationships I identified has a different orientation toward the ideal environmentalist. I depict the way that the ideal environmentalist shapes how people evaluate their own eco-social relationship in figure 1.1. The Eco-Engaged convey the sense that they *are* that ideal and the Self-Effacing tell me they want to be that ideal. The Eco-Engaged and the Self-Effacing tend to be politically liberal, while the Optimists, Fatalists, and Indifferent are more likely to be politically conservative. The Optimists are antagonistic toward the ideal, the Fatalists suggest the ideal environmentalist is well-meaning but misguided, and the Indifferent look on from the sidelines, curious about the ideal environmentalist, but doubtful that buying a tomato is a moral decision.

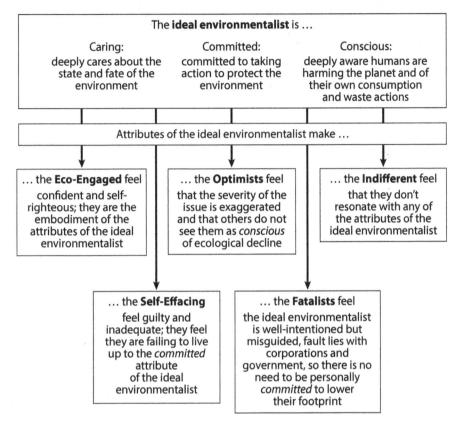

FIGURE 1.1. The ideal environmentalist and its influence on eco-social relationships

There is a great deal of power and privilege that comes with having the general public agree that your beliefs about how to interpret and respond to ecological decline are the preeminent example of what it looks like to care about the environment. A large part of the privilege the Eco-Engaged have as a result of reflecting the cultural ideal is the ease of feeling that they are doing the right thing in the face of ecological decline, and are generally respected for doing so. Their sense of morality and efficacy are, I argue, partly related to their alignment with the cultural ideal (see figure 1.1). Meanwhile, the Self-Effacing feel guilty and inadequate alongside the ideal environmentalist. The Optimists resent that their doubt about the severity of ecological decline undermines the moral worth of their eco-social relationship. The Fatalists and the Indifferent fail to connect with the ideal environmentalist, leaving them with a lack of avenues to connect their personal lives to environmental protection. Next, we meet the first of the five eco-types: the Eco-Engaged, who most closely reflect the cultural schema of an ideal environmentalist.

2

The Eco-Engaged

*Who do I picture as an environmentalist? I picture myself. That is
a big part of what I do in my life. That is who I picture.*
—EILEEN, UPPER CLASS, LIBERAL, 59 YEARS OLD[1]

Eileen is passionate about the environment. She works as a climate change
educator and, in our three-hour-long interview, I was struck by how thor-
oughly her commitment to environmental protection is woven into the fabric of her life. At the grocery store, Eileen only buys products made from
recycled materials, and foods that are organically grown. For years, she and
her husband, a medical doctor, have led many successful campaigns to protect natural areas. They eat a vegetarian diet and are currently trying to
transition to being vegan. But, as Eileen explains, there is still work to do.
They have two cars, though she is quick to point out that they rarely have
both on the road at once, and that one of their cars is a hybrid.

Eileen acts on her commitment to environmental protection through
education, political engagement, and conscious consumerism. Her desire
to protect the environment influences her whole way of being in the world,
including how she judges herself and those around her. She tells me that she
regularly experiences profound sadness about human impacts on the planet,
describing herself in these moments as, "Sobbing, depressed, down." But,
she explains, the best antidote is action. Eileen doesn't believe any of us
have a right to feel hope about the planet, "if we are not putting the energy,
the time, the money into it." Eileen absolutely does put in time, energy,

and money. She also expects that other people should do the same, and feels entitled to tell them so. This quality of confidence in correcting other people's environmental beliefs and actions is a unique characteristic of the Eco-Engaged eco-type.

At one point in our conversation, Eileen told me about an interaction in the grocery store she had with "a mom" she knows. This woman had attended one of the climate change education workshops that Eileen hosts in her community. Noticing the organic foods in Eileen's shopping cart, the woman described wishing she could afford to buy organic food for her children. Eileen recounts her response. She looked in her acquaintance's cart and told her, "Well, if you put the four-dollar package of Doritos back on the shelf, you have just subsidized the purchase of organic foods for your kids."

Why is Eileen so eager to share this story with me? Part of the answer surely lies in a cultural license to judge parents, especially mothers, based on the meals they give their children. Many sociologists have commented on the troubling ways that public scrutiny is particularly intense when it comes to low-income mothers' food choices. The ideal of the home-cooked meal, made from fresh, organic, whole foods is at once heralded in popular media, as many scholars have observed, and punitive for the women who do the work of feeding their families.[2] Certainly, Eileen is ignoring her own privilege—for example, the privilege of not having a financial barrier to purchasing high-priced, organic foods. Yet instead of trying to ascertain who is at fault in this situation, I want to use this interaction to understand where the Eco-Engaged are coming from.

Eileen experiences climate change as the most urgent of emergencies and is pained that everyone else does not share this feeling. Central to Eileen's relationship to the environment is her belief that environmental protection requires personal sacrifices from all of us. I hope you can see the alignment with the ideal environmentalist here, and the way that Eileen perceives the environment as vulnerable and in crisis (severity). She sees herself as morally responsible for doing something to help (morality), and she is confident in her capacity to do so (efficacy). Eileen feels justified in scolding her friend because that friend had expressed frustration that she could not afford organic foods. Seeing nacho chips in this woman's cart suggested to Eileen that her friend was simply not willing to compromise her desire for a treat (chips) to support an organic food production system that won't deteriorate soil health and accelerate climate change.

We can better understand the nature of Eileen's comments about the grocery store incident, insofar as they reflect her relationship to the environment, by looking at what she told me immediately after this story. Eileen described a show she watches, *Grace and Frankie*, which Eileen explains, is "about two menopausal women, and their husbands, who work together and have been in love with each other for 20 years. So, they finally divorce their wives, and their wives end up having to share one of the homes." The main characters, these two women, "are very, very different . . . and they start to grow together as friends." Eileen tells me this story because after she watched the last episode, she had, in her words, "a very blue day. I felt very blue. Very despondent." After reflecting on why she felt so upset, she concludes, "I realized that in the show, they're not worried about climate change." One of the characters even identifies as an environmentalist. But, as Eileen tells me, this character is also an artist, and in the show, she focuses on her art. This is the key to Eileen's sadness—that the character makes no sacrifices to care about the environment and only focuses on her art. Eileen realized, "these people are doing what they want to do. And I feel so bound to do what I feel I *need* to do, so I was envying these fictional characters." Eileen's sadness was a response to envying Grace and Frankie, specifically, "their freedom to do what they want to do."

For Eileen and her husband, there is no "right" way to live other than to strive in every moment to reduce their impact on the planet. Judging a friend for buying chips rather than organic food feels like an expression of her commitment to protect the planet. Seeing someone do what they *want to do*, rather than what they *know they must do*, is a painful reminder for Eileen of the sacrifices she has made to protect the planet, and the futility of doing so when she is surrounded by people who act as though they have the "freedom to do what they want to do." I did not interview the woman in Eileen's anecdote, but I did interview many people who had experienced feeling judged by the Eco-Engaged. Although Eileen had no ill intentions, her practice of acting on her ethical commitments in this instance likely created a sense of frustration, guilt, inadequacy, and perhaps even resentment, in her friend.

Getting to Know the Eco-Engaged

This chapter introduces the Eco-Engaged. This is the most prevalent eco-type among the people in my studies: nearly one-third of the participants in the interview study (32%) and the national survey (33%) embody this relationship to the environment. These figures illustrate the cultural dominance that this particular eco-type holds in our contemporary milieu. Not all Eco-Engaged are as passionate and as invested in environmental protection as Eileen, and I will document some of the variation that exists within this eco-type. First, though, I will provide a sociodemographic snapshot of the Eco-Engaged and then describe some of the common qualities of this eco-type.

Do you know anyone who fits the Eco-Engaged eco-type? In terms of their demographic traits, there are only a few clues. I examined how gender, age, political ideology, race, education, income, parents' education, and cultural capital are related to membership in this eco-social relationship. Of these sociodemographic variables, only political ideology and cultural capital remain significant when I control for the correlations between all of these measures.[3] Liberals are 70% more likely than conservatives to be Eco-Engaged. I used two measures of cultural capital: the first, engagement in environmental activities in childhood, is clearly relevant to the arena of environmentalism. I found that respondents who grew up in households where pro-environmental behaviors were common are almost 90% more likely than others to fit the Eco-Engaged eco-type. The second measure of cultural capital asks people how often they attend artistic performances.[4] I found that people who frequently participate in high culture are nearly 40% more likely to have an Eco-Engaged eco-social relationship than those who do not.

WHAT DOES AN ECO-ENGAGED ECO-TYPE FEEL LIKE?

The Eco-Engaged have a strong affinity for the environment, perceive ecological decline to be urgent and severe, believe they have a personal moral responsibility to protect the environment, and generally feel capable of doing so (figure 2.1). On a scale from 0 to 12, where 12 is the strongest possible affinity with the environment, the Eco-Engaged score 11.06. The environment has an extremely important place in their lives. This intense affinity is related to their perception that the planet is in crisis, that they are morally responsible for protecting the planet, and that they have the capacity to do so.

"I Feel No Separation Between Myself and the Environment": Strong Affinity for the Environment

In terms of their views on eco-social relationships, the Eco-Engaged share a strong interest in the natural world. When I asked the people who I

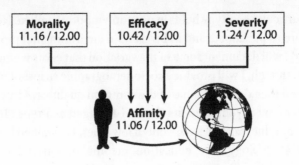

FIGURE 2.1. Eco-social relationship model for the Eco-Engaged
Note: 1–4 = disagree, 5–8 = neutral, 9–12 = agree.

interviewed to tell me what came to mind when they pictured "the environment," many described specific ecosystems and native plants and shared a feeling of inseparability from these other species. A good example of this is Annie, a realtor who lives in Olympia.[5] Annie, who is a lifelong Democrat tells me, "I feel no separation between myself and the environment." She tells me she thinks about environmental problems every time she takes out the garbage or fills up her car at the gas station. Annie expresses a deep appreciation for the natural world, which she attributes to her parents, who "were real outdoors folks."

Eco-Engaged survey respondents also show a very strong affinity for the environment. I asked respondents to indicate their agreement (0 = strongly disagree, 4 = strongly agree) with several statements measuring affinity. The Eco-Engaged score highest of all the eco-types on questions about their interest in environmental issues, the importance of the environment, and about how often they think about environmental topics (see "Affinity" score in figure 2.1). An analysis of the survey data demonstrates that the Eco-Engaged who report the strongest affinity for the environment are white survey respondents with university-educated fathers (parents' education is a measure that cultural sociologist Pierre Bourdieu used to estimate inherited cultural capital).[6] These results support the argument that feeling a strong affinity for the environment and having cultural capital go hand in hand.[7]

Among the Eco-Engaged that I interviewed, those who demonstrated an intense affinity for the environment often made a connection to important environmental lessons learned in childhood. The Eco-Engaged who conveyed more moderate levels of affinity did not describe these sorts of transformative childhood experiences. Betty, a realtor in Pullman, has a graduate degree, is in her 70s with no financial concerns, and conveys a strong affinity for the environment (Betty did not share her political orientation). For Betty, like Eileen, a commitment to protecting the planet is infused through all dimensions of her life. In her home, she is careful about reusing and repairing household items and she volunteers for an organization that provides support to victims of natural disasters. She explains that this is the ethos she was raised with, growing up on a working farm: "We were taught responsibility for the earth and how, even as a kid, you were responsible for it. You didn't muck around with it. It wasn't to be taken lightly 'cause that was your livelihood. I think that had a big influence on me." Yet not all Eco-Engaged described this sense of inheriting a commitment to environmental protection. Those who communicated a more moderate affinity for the environment tended to view the natural world pragmatically and did not refer to childhood experiences that brought them closer to the environment. Angela, a political moderate who works part-time as an accountant and grew up in a conservative, working-class family, has a more measured affinity for the environment than Betty. For Angela, the environment is a place for recreation—her expressions of appreciation and interest in the environment are tied to its role as a space for leisure, not as a sacred space needing her protection. Throughout our interview, Angela reiterated that while she frequently thinks about how to minimize her family's environmental impact, she does not feel emotionally invested in this goal.

"Protecting the Environment Should Be Our Top Priority": Perceiving Environmental Issues as Severe

From the impacts of industrial agriculture on soil health, to the effects of microplastics on marine life, and the disproportionate burden of environmental harms on people of color, the Eco-Engaged are passionate about discussing humanity's detrimental impacts on vulnerable people and the planet. They evaluate environmental problems as severe and worsening, and see resolving these issues as the highest priority for the country. I'll demonstrate this perception of severity by quoting an excerpt of my interview with Rachel. Rachel lives in Pacifica, the amenity-rich, rural, island community. She is politically liberal and comes from a farming background. She and her husband earn their living running a small construction business but Rachel spends time each day picking up trash on the beach and talking about environmental issues with friends and neighbors. Her commitment to recycling is only overshadowed by her efforts to reduce her level of consumption overall. At one point in our interview, Rachel tells me, "As you can see, I'm pretty passionate about this (meaning the environment)." When I ask

Rachel about her thoughts on the severity of environmental issues she states clearly, "It should be our top priority. Our top priority here in the United States needs to be protecting our environment." She elaborates, "You look at topographical maps from 20 years ago to now and you see how much of the mid-section is a desert, completely desolate." She believes these patterns will only worsen: "That's gonna spread. That problem's gonna get worse." Rachel feels like this about water, food, energy, and waste. She sees her fellow citizens as undermining ecological health in devastating ways, largely through our rapacious consumer habits.

For the Eco-Engaged, widespread evidence of ecological decline evokes intense and painful emotions. I witnessed these themes in my interview with Addy, on the front porch of the small home she shares with her husband and two young children. Addy and her family live in the same community as Rachel and moved here specifically for the natural beauty of the area. When I asked Addy to tell me about environmental problems that had affected her, I expected to hear her describe smoke from wildfires, or water quality scares; other people I interviewed in her community complained about air traffic. But Addy answered, "I worry about access to clean water a lot, on a lot of different levels . . . I worry about the state of our soil health." Overall, she feels like the planet is, "up against a lot of pollution and potential future pollution." Addy's concerns are not so much for herself or her family, but for the planet in general. Addy is typical of the Eco-Engaged in the breadth of her knowledge about ecosystems and environmental problems, and her evaluation of those problems as urgent and severe.

Eco-Engaged survey respondents also conveyed deep concerns about ecological decline. Of all respondents, the Eco-Engaged had the highest levels of agreement with statements about the seriousness of environmental problems. On a scale from 0 (strongly disagree) to 4 (strongly agree), the Eco-Engaged strongly agree that environmental problems are more serious now than they used to be, that humans are using up the earth's resources, and that protecting the environment should be one of the country's top priorities (see "Severity" score in figure 2.1). Drilling down into specific environmental concerns, I found that the Eco-Engaged survey respondents reported the highest level of concern among all eco-types for the environment generally, and for specific environmental issues from climate change to water pollution.

What sort of variation exists in the intensity with which the Eco-Engaged worry about the fate of the environment? Looking to the survey data, I find that variation among the Eco-Engaged is associated with political ideology and eco-upbringing. First, let's look at eco-upbringing, which has some interesting associations with perception of ecological decline. Perhaps counterintuitively, the Eco-Engaged who were raised in more eco-friendly families are less likely to see environmental issues as serious. It's possible that the Eco-Engaged who actively participate in the same eco-friendly activities they were exposed to as children feel that their engagement in these practices protects them from ecological decline. The suggestion that green consumption choices can make people feel safer from environmental harms aligns with environmental sociologist Norah MacKendrick's research on "precautionary consumption." MacKendrick found that people who purchase organic foods and other eco-friendly products described these choices as offering feelings of safety in a world of toxic chemical pollution.[8] In other words, consistently choosing products that are touted as being good for the environment might soften an intense fear of ecological decline. The other variable that was significantly associated with perception of severity among the Eco-Engaged is political ideology. Liberal Eco-Engaged tend to be more concerned about the state of the environment than others. This is certainly consistent with past literature, as liberals in general tend to be more worried than others about ecological issues.[9] Still, it is interesting to note that pattern holds within the Eco-Engaged relationship to the environment because it shows us that there is a liberal subset of the most environmentally concerned survey respondents who hold the most intense worries about ecological decline.

In the interviews, I noticed that participants with close ties to friends and family whose economic livelihoods depended directly on the environment were less likely to state unequivocally that the environment should be protected above all else. For example, one of the most powerful moments in my interview with Addy was when she spoke to the tensions in her community between relatively economically privileged preservationists who want to constrain further development on the island and the working-class community whose livelihoods depend on development. These tensions were close to the surface for Addy, as she told me, "I knew a guy that committed suicide last week," and explained that this was, "partly due to him being on the wrong end of litigation over an environmental issue. He had been a contractor and cut down trees on a property. The [local environmental organization], their mission is to preserve the environment mostly through litigation against land owners and business owners who do things that are deemed detrimental to the environment. They found out about this and fined him." She qualified, "I am not saying that . . ." and tapers off. So, I jumped in: ". . . that x caused y?" And she picks up again, "Right. But it was very related and present in his life and part of what put him in that circumstance." Addy is careful not to blame anyone: "That certainly is not [the environmental organization's] intent, and they would hate to be part of that. But it's hard on a small island to protect all the aspects of life that need to be protected."

Addy was one of the only Eco-Engaged I interviewed who was close to someone whose job depended on directly using natural resources. For those few Eco-Engaged whose social circles include family and friends whose livelihoods depended on the environment, the trade-offs between environmental protection and human well-being are emotionally charged and challenging to navigate. But for Eco-Engaged whose close social circles do not include people earning a living from natural resources, the economics of natural resource extraction pale in importance to the goal of protecting the environment. In contrast to Addy, Annie, the realtor quoted earlier, refers to deforestation in a way that suggests she has no social ties to industrial activity. For instance, she talks about the sort of environmental destruction that saddens her, noting "the logging and the fact that trees are coming out of these pristine places. And then you can look right across the water at the port and it's just stacked full of logs, and it's like, 'oh my god!'" For Eco-Engaged like Annie, preserving natural resources is uncomplicated. This reminds me of the way Eileen recounted the story of reprimanding a friend for buying Doritos, in that an environmental protection impulse that feels natural and uncomplicated to Eileen and Annie is more difficult and multifaceted for people who are familiar with economic uncertainty.

"It's Our Responsibility to Protect the Environment":
Strong Moral Responsibility

The Eco-Engaged share a firm belief that when it comes to addressing environmental issues, individuals have an important role to play and a moral responsibility to play it. Although they express a lot of admiration for environmental activists, the Eco-Engaged who I interviewed don't see activism as a moral responsibility—but they do argue that individuals ought to reduce their footprint on the planet. That is, although the Eco-Engaged are impressed by activists, they would not look down on someone who was not fighting for environmental protection in the public-sphere—but they do look down on those they perceive as making irresponsible consumption choices. While some interviewees with other eco-social relationships pictured corporations as having the most egregious ecological impacts, the Eco-Engaged tended to point the finger at greedy individuals who they perceived as consuming to excess.

More than any other eco-type, it is the Eco-Engaged who are most likely to endorse the belief that reducing environmental impact is a personal, moral responsibility that is best achieved through making a commitment to consuming sustainably. When I asked Annie whether she felt a moral responsibility to do right by the environment, she answered, emphatically, in the affirmative and immediately began describing her efforts to consume sustainably. Annie characterizes sustainable consumption as both important, and as requiring a small sacrifice of cost and convenience. When I shop, she says, "I'm choosing sustainability. The welfare of future generations over just the convenience of right now or saving a few extra pennies or dollars." It deeply saddens Annie that not everyone feels this way. In describing her sadness, Annie also helps bring into focus the way the Eco-Engaged give a moral valence to individual consumption choices. She explains, "once you get used to even just knowing what is a more sustainable product, it feels like a broadening of awareness and for maybe those who don't have that, I feel just a little bit of sadness." Annie elaborates, as she speaks to a hypothetical person who does not consume eco-friendly products: "Like, 'I wish that you felt differently or knew this or that better,' or something. It's kind of like if you're seeing someone who just eats a lot of packaged foods," Annie offers, "and that's their sense of how food can taste, as opposed to knowing how to put together this amazing delicious meal from whole foods and stuff and understanding how food can taste." She concludes, "You wouldn't be able to help but feel a little bit of sadness for someone who's never understood how to taste something truly delicious," and connects this example to her feelings about people who don't engage in eco-friendly consumption: "I kind of feel that same way for folks who maybe haven't gained the awareness. Like, feeling a little bit sad for them because they haven't found this new sort of deliciousness."

The "taste" that Annie describes is a foundational element of the Eco-Engaged eco-type. The Eco-Engaged are driven by a sense that a virtuous life is one centered on efforts to reduce their footprint. When I asked Nadine, a 47-year-old liberal who recently started a PhD in counseling, if she felt like protecting the environment was her moral duty, she answered: "Yes! It's my civic duty, my spiritual duty, my ethical duty. Absolutely. There's no separation." She elaborated that this is what motivates her to garden, to shop for local and organic products, and to pursue her dream of designing a home based on permaculture principles. The Eco-Engaged don't see collective actions like protests or participating in public debates as an individual's moral responsibility. Neither do they see spending time in nature as a moral imperative. But they do see engagement in individual, daily, consumer-based actions as integral to leading a moral life. In particular, the Eco-Engaged moralize the domains of food and household product consumption, household waste management, and ground transportation.

Eco-Engaged interview participants not only felt that people have a moral responsibility to protect the environment, they also saw this moral responsibility as shaping the health and vitality of ecosystems. The moral weight of an individual's impact was a strong theme throughout my interview with Denny, a 44-year-old, politically liberal firefighter. When I asked Denny what it looks like to care about the environment, he described someone who thought about their environmental impact and tried to reduce it by being conscientious about their diet, home energy use, and waste management practices. When I asked him if he believes people are morally responsible for taking these sorts of actions, Denny was perfectly clear: "Of course! If nobody felt that it was their civic duty to be concerned about the environment then we would be walking on candy wrappers, glass, paper towels, and garbage right now on this very spot." Denny spoke of his responsibility to future generations: "We are borrowing all of this. The universe gave us life, thought, love, passion. Why can't we have that care and concern for everything else around us rather than being selfish?" When it comes to imagining what will dictate whether he lives in a clean, healthy ecosystem or a filthy, polluted one, for Denny, the primary factor is whether or not he and others take responsibility for their environmental impacts.

The Eco-Engaged regularly practice a range of individual efforts to protect the environment and are distinct from other groups in both the frequency with which they engage in eco-friendly practices and the range of practices in their repertoire. At the household level, the Eco-Engaged I interviewed describe purchasing local, organic foods and products; avoiding packaging, plastic bags, and disposable drink cups; eating vegetarian or vegan meals; reducing, reusing and recycling; walking or cycling to avoid driving; choosing a hybrid or electric vehicle; saving rainwater and reducing water consumption more generally; using solar power and reducing energy consumption; and composting and gardening. In the civic sphere, they report talking to people about environmental issues, attending protests and marches, participating in or donating to environmental protection campaigns, and investing their money ethically.

In our interviews, the Eco-Engaged were unique in that they seemed to excitedly anticipate me asking about their involvement in environmental practices. To illustrate, I'll turn to my interview with Kyle, a conservative military recruiter in his early 40s. Kyle is the only Republican voter among my Eco-Engaged interviewees. He grew up in a conservative family in the Midwest and the tastes of the Eco-Engaged still felt new to him at the time of our interview. As he explained it, he grew up in a household where people valued the natural world but were not conscientious about their impacts on the environment. Based on his description, the household he grew up in would probably fit with the Indifferent eco-type I introduce later in the book. But Kyle's job in the military took him far from home. After living in Germany for many years and, more recently, in a college town, Kyle told me that he was really impressed when he saw people make efforts to reduce their impact on the environment. In Pullman, Kyle and his wife sent their daughter to an independent school where they met more politically liberal families. He noticed that these families made a number of different choices, from cycling instead of driving, to making conscious efforts to have less stuff, and he told me that he has been influenced by this. He says, "they don't strike me as materialistic, they live a very simple lifestyle, they're more about relationships and experiences." He and his wife, he tells me, "have tried to incorporate the best [parts] of that into our lives." Importantly, Kyle frames his adoption of some of his liberal acquaintances' practices as a shift that was made appealing because these practices struck him as offsetting materialism and dependence. In this way, even while practicing stereotypically liberal actions, Kyle maintains ties to his conservative upbringing.

Kyle and I had been speaking for nearly half an hour before I asked him what sorts of things he and his family did that he considered relevant to the environment. "Yay!" he said, "I was waiting for you to ask." And then he elaborated, "I like to think we have done some things to improve the environment. To help bring awareness about the environment and loss of species and things like that." He explains that he tries to do so by, "doing a little bit of conservation on a very rudimentary small scale, planting trees and such. And we recycle religiously." He also describes attending a public event celebrating biodiversity with his family. Kyle's answer is typical of the Eco-Engaged in both the enthusiasm with which he describes his own actions, the breadth of consumer-based and more public-sphere actions he engages in, and the confidence he conveys about the impact he's having on the world. There is still more Kyle wants to do—he is interested in eating less meat and living a more minimalist life—but he doesn't see any major barriers to taking on these new practices.

Eco-Engaged survey respondents also conveyed a strong feeling of responsibility to protect the environment and reported frequent engagement in efforts to reduce environmental impacts. I asked respondents three questions to gauge how strongly they felt a moral responsibility to reduce their impact on the environment, the extent to which they saw that responsibility as tied to reducing consumption, and whether they worried about their impact on the environment. The Eco-Engaged have the strongest levels of agreement with all three items, compared with other eco-social relationships (see "Morality" score in figure 2.1). I asked survey respondents to tell me how often they engaged in some of the household practices that my interview participants mentioned.[10] Compared to the average scores of the other eco-types, Eco-Engaged respondents have the highest level of engagement in every single behavior I included on the survey. These range from carrying a reusable mug to growing food in a garden. I used a statistical test that determines whether various survey items can be grouped together to create three groups of practices: eco-friendly consumption, like buying organic foods and shopping with cloth bags; reducing consumption, which includes efforts to reduce water, waste, and energy; and sufficiency and nature-based practices, like hunting, gardening, and spending time in nature. The last category of environmental practices includes items that are often left off of surveys of pro-environmental behaviors. But since these practices were noted by my interview participants as manifestations of their relationship to nonhuman nature, I included them on the survey. Across each of these types of practices, the Eco-Engaged reported the highest levels of engagement of all survey respondents, significantly higher than the average for the survey sample (figure 2.2).

Although the Eco-Engaged report the highest levels of participation in eco-friendly practices, there is some variation in frequency within this group. Eco-Engaged survey respondents who grew up in environmentally active households and who earn a high income practice eco-friendly consumption more often than others. These patterns shift when we look at reducing consumption practices: older Eco-Engaged with less education, but who were raised in households committed to environmental protection, self-report the highest levels of engagement in reducing their consumption. Finally, if we look at sufficiency practices, it is younger, more conservative Eco-Engaged respondents, who grew up in environmentally active households and had fathers with a university degree who engage in these practices most frequently. The patterns related to self-sufficiency indicate there is an Eco-Engaged impulse—one that appeals more to political conservatives than to liberals—that has received less attention in academic research and broader public discourse. These results also suggest that cultural capital is strongly associated with this more conservative expression of environmental commitments as well as with participation in eco-friendly consumption.

"It Feels Natural. It's Just What I Do": Strong Self-Efficacy

Personally, being committed to reducing my carbon footprint and translating that commitment into my daily practices is far from straightforward. I bike or walk to work every day largely to reduce

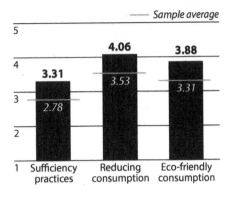

FIGURE 2.2. Eco-Engaged participation in eco-friendly practices
Note: 1 = never; 5 = always.

the carbon footprint of my lifestyle, but then I also travel to distant cities to present my research. I love the idea of eating only local, organic food, but that gets expensive, and sometimes I miss the weekly farmers' market in my neighborhood, or they don't have an ingredient I want. As my colleagues and I demonstrated in an earlier study, virtually everyone is, to varying degrees, limited from implementing eco-friendly practices by a lack of time, finances, availability of eco-friendly options, and other structural constraints.[11] Although the Eco-Engaged recognize those constraints, they nonetheless express a strong sense of self-efficacy about their ability to reduce their environmental impact.

The Eco-Engaged feel a sense of confidence and assuredness about their capacity to prioritize efforts to protect the environment. On the survey, I asked three questions to capture this element of eco-social relationships, assessing the extent to which respondents feel they do what they can to reduce their environmental impact, their perception of their own ability to do what it takes to lower their impact, and the extent to which they say they have oriented their life to reduce environmental impact. On each of these measures, the Eco-Engaged score the highest of all eco-social relationships (see "Efficacy" score in figure 2.1). There is extremely little variation in self-efficacy among the Eco-Engaged survey respondents. Nonetheless, I found that those Eco-Engaged who were raised in environmentally active households had stronger self-efficacy scores than those who did not. Otherwise, this shared characteristic spans education, income, gender, race, and political ideology. So, while having an Eco-Engaged relationship with the environment is strongly related to political ideology and cultural capital, within this eco-social relationship, self-efficacy is a predominantly shared experience across all of my respondents.

Many of my interview participants offered comments that illustrate this strong sense of self-efficacy. For example, Nadine said that when she pictures a sustainable consumer, she pictures herself. Since Nadine left her high-paying job to return to graduate school, her income has fallen dramatically. But she notes that she has continued to buy eco-friendly products, even though they cost more. As Nadine says, when describing what it means to be a sustainable consumer: "That's what I do . . . well, that's what I've been able to do, and I continue to do it, interestingly enough, in absence of money. It's weird. It just feels congruent; it just makes sense to me." In sociologist Pierre Bourdieu's language, Nadine demonstrates embodied cultural capital—her shopping choices are effortlessly oriented toward the sorts of practices that reflect the cultural ideal of an environmentalist that I described in the previous chapter.[12]

Nadine's comments illustrate the way that the Eco-Engaged see themselves as the sorts of people who care for the environment, which is one element of Self-Efficacy. Another element is the sense of confidence that their efforts are effective in reducing personal impacts on the environment—and that this focus on individual impacts is a meaningful response to ecological decline. Jerry is a 63-year-old, retired man and a Democrat, who showed up to our interview wearing Patagonia pants and carrying a bike helmet. He asked us to meet him at a local, independent café. During our interview, he told us that one way he protects the environment is through making conscientious shopping choices, though he quickly adds, "I don't do too much of my shopping." He explains that he "buys a lot of stuff online" and that he likes the company Patagonia, "because they contribute back to the environment." As a result, Jerry explains, "I try to support them quite a bit because I like what they do. They're going in the right direction." When he buys from Patagonia, he says, "that feels good." This feeling of purpose and virtue that comes from making consumption choices that feel like the right ones is an important part of the self-efficacy of the Eco-Engaged. Even when Eco-Engaged participants acknowledged that some pro-environmental behaviors can be difficult, they emphasized the rewards from feeling that they made the right choice. Annie offers up the example of choosing to use a push-mower for her lawn, in order "to go totally gasless." At times, she said, "it feels like, 'oh my god! It's gonna be a pack of work', but there's kind of a noble feel to it as well." At the end of the day, Annie says, "it feels good to know that maybe I went the hard way but made a little bit of difference." The

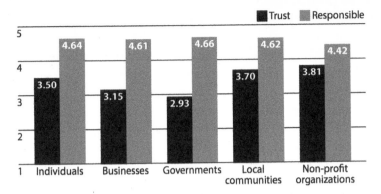

FIGURE 2.3. Eco-Engaged respondents' opinions of various actors' responsibility for environmental protection and trustworthiness
Note: 1 = not at all; 5 = very much.

Eco-Engaged feel proud of making choices that put environmental protection ahead of comfort and convenience, and these experiences generate a strong sense of self-efficacy.

The Eco-Engaged also have a relatively positive view of society's capacity to protect the environment. I asked those who took the survey to tell me how responsible they thought various actors and institutions are for protecting the environment. Because trust in social actors and institutions is part of how people construct a sense of social efficacy, I also asked respondents the extent to which they believed these institutions could be trusted to do so. The Eco-Engaged have the highest scores of any eco-social relationship on every single item measuring both perceived responsibilities to protect the environment and their trust that the institution or actor will do so (see figure 2.3). However, even though the Eco-Engaged have the highest scores on these items, it is important to look at the large gaps between trust and responsibility, most notably for the role of government in protecting the environment. This gap suggests that the Eco-Engaged doubt they can rely on elected representatives to protect the environment. Nonetheless, these scores indicate that the Eco-Engaged are unique in perceiving so many institutions as having the responsibility to protect the environment and trusting them to do so.

"Birds of a Feather": Strong Relationality

The Eco-Engaged consciously surround themselves with people who share their eco-type. I use the term "relationality" to capture variation in how important environmental beliefs and practices are for people when they evaluate the world around them. This concept encompasses the extent to which someone's social context is comprised of people who align with the ideal environmentalist and the extent to which they judge others based on alignment with that ideal. For example, I would characterize someone as having strong relationality who is from a family that instilled a sense that contributing to environmental protection is part of a moral life, whose social circles are largely composed of people who feel this impulse, and for whom that impulse is an important factor in determining whether or not to grant respect to another person. This concept might remind some readers of the cultural sociological term "boundary work," in that it captures the ways in which people identify in-groups and out-groups in their social worlds.[13] Although I don't use relationality in my framework of eco-social relationships, it is an important element to examine since it reflects the social and moral importance of household-level environmental protection. In her powerful analysis of social distinctions among American and French men, the sociologist Michèle Lamont proposes that a person's commitment to environmental protection may be part of class-based boundary work. Through the theme of relationality, I can take up that suggestion and demonstrate its accuracy.[14]

Of all eco-types, the Eco-Engaged are the most likely to have grown up in environmentally concerned and active households and to feel that how, and how much, a person "cares" about the environment is a meaningful parameter for evaluating their moral worth. It might be easiest to see these patterns through survey items first. Again, I included on the survey three items measuring relationality to assess the extent to which the people in the respondent's social network were worried about the environment and sought to reduce their environmental impact, and whether respondents preferred to spend time with people who cared about the environment. The Eco-Engaged had the highest levels of agreement with these items. Eco-Engaged respondents who grew up in environmentally active households were more likely than others to engage in this environmentally based boundary work. You may recall that people who grew up in environmentally active families are most likely to fit in the Eco-Engaged eco-type. By focusing on relationality, we can identify a way in which homogeneous social groups come to form: people from eco-conscious families express an Eco-Engaged orientation to the environment and prefer to spend time with others who feel the same way about the earth that they do. People who the Eco-Engaged feel are worthy of respect and friendship tend to be those who share the same eco-type.

The Eco-Engaged I interviewed who grew up in families that actively sought to lower their environmental impacts were proud of this, modeled their own families after this standard, and judged others' families accordingly. I interviewed a number of people with adult children and noted that the Eco-Engaged often commented on the extent to which their children's lives reflected their own orientation toward environmental protection. For some, it seemed to be a point of pride that their children were putting into practice learned environmental concerns. For example, Betty says she raised her children with strong environmental values. She makes a point of telling me that her daughter, "started out in environmental law but . . . now she's in a totally different thing, but she's still involved with the environment." Her son-in-law also works in an environmental field, and Betty says proudly, "as you can tell, we always talk about things like that. The environment is a major issue of concern in our family."

Not all of my participants had children who married environmentally concerned people. Annie tells me how she is trying to get her daughter-in-law to be more conscientious, because she's worried her grandsons are not learning how to care about the environment. She describes her daughter-in-law as, "not holding as much awareness as our family, probably very little actually, as far as the environment [is concerned]." Annie tries to compensate for her daughter-in-law because, as Annie explains, she has created, "a much more throw-away household." She does so by making subtle suggestions: "I'll say 'Where's your guys' recycle?' or, 'I think this can go in the recycle.'" As she explains, she is trying "to try to fill in a little bit of learning" for her grandsons. The Eco-Engaged were the most likely to describe growing up in families with a strong commitment to protecting the environment and were keen to tell me how they were instilling these same impulses in their own families.

The Eco-Engaged also tend to be friends with people who share their concerns about the environment and to distance themselves from people who don't. After I asked participants how concerned they were about the environment, I asked if most of the people they knew felt the same way. Elena, a politically liberal artist from Pullman, described how she and her social group tend not to invite their conservative friends out as often, because these friends do not seem to be concerned about the environment. As Elena explained to me, "Birds of a feather do flock together." Eileen compares people who aren't engaged in reducing consumption to people who smoke: "I don't spend time with them. I don't go out of my way to choose them as friends. It is a little bit like smoking. . . . It kind of grosses me out. . . . Most of our friends are people who think and feel the way we do." That is, finding out someone is not worried about the environment and committed to reducing their impact repels Eileen. I interviewed Eco-Engaged who were not as firm as Eileen in the boundaries they drew, but it was only when interviewing the Eco-Engaged that I encountered this tendency to deliberately create social distance from people perceived as not caring enough about the environment.

The Environmental Impacts of the Eco-Engaged

Environmental impacts could be measured any number of ways. In the interviews, I asked participants if they thought about their environmental impacts and, if so, what sorts of things they noticed. On the survey, I asked a series of questions to approximate each respondent's carbon footprint— the emissions associated with an individual and their household, based on estimates of their home energy use, ground and air transportation, dietary choices, and household recycling.[15] I had mixed feelings about using a carbon footprint calculator: this tool was initially funded by the fossil-fuel company, BP.[16] It seems unethical that a company profiting from its continued extraction of nonrenewable fuels would invest in an effort to encourage individuals to calculate their own, individual environmental impacts. But in this book, I report estimates of carbon footprints alongside a survey question asking respondents to describe their household's environmental impact as less than, the same as, or greater than the average American household. Overall, there was very little variation in carbon footprint across the five eco-types, yet there was much more variation in people's estimates of their impact, relative to the average. That is what I want to focus on, not on the amount of carbon emitted, though I will report emissions data as well.

The average carbon footprint of an Eco-Engaged household is 19.1 tons CO_2e, which is above the sample average of 18.1 tons and is the largest average footprint of all eco-types.[17] This average score obscures a considerable range: from less than one ton to 91 tons. This measure may falsely inflate the footprints of large households, so I also estimated a per person footprint: the average per person carbon footprint for the Eco-Engaged is 7.1 tons, which is equivalent to the sample average. Per person footprints among the Eco-Engaged range from less than one ton to 52 tons. The Eco-Engaged were most likely to believe their footprint is lower than the average American household: 71% believe they impact the environment far less than the average American.

BOX 2.1. Examining the Composition and Sociodemographic Antecedents of Eco-Engaged Carbon Footprints

Some readers may be interested in seeing the breakdown of the Eco-Engaged carbon footprint and in understanding what antecedent variables shape the size of the Eco-Engaged footprint, although this content is peripheral to the overall argument. Looking within the total footprint at the five domains that comprise the estimate (home energy use, ground transportation, air travel, waste, diet) offers some insight into which factors matter for variation in these different domains. First, I find that ground transportation comprises nearly half of the average Eco-Engaged carbon footprint (figure 2.4), while waste only makes up 2%. Roughly one-third of the Eco-Engaged footprint is a result of home energy use, which is a slightly smaller share compared to other eco-types (figure 2.4). Based on an Ordinary Least Squares regression analysis, the only sociodemographic predictor that is significant is home ownership—Eco-Engaged who own their home have a smaller footprint than those who rent. This is likely because they have both the desire to make investments in insulation and other energy efficiency measures and the ability and incentive to do so.

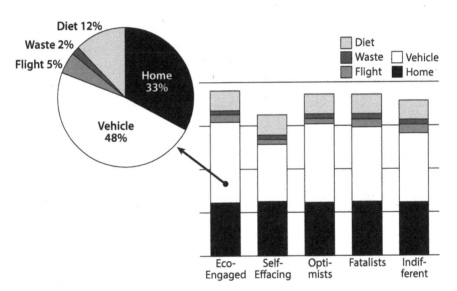

FIGURE 2.4. Composition of the average Eco-Engaged survey respondent's household carbon footprint against size and general composition of the footprint of other eco-types

The Eco-Engaged are the most likely of all eco-types to take the sorts of measures that are associated with the ideal environmentalist. They are the least likely to drive a gas-powered car, they are among the most likely to eat a meat-reduced diet, and they are avid recyclers. Nonetheless, these efforts do not significantly reduce their carbon footprint below the average.

Why do the Eco-Engaged so inaccurately estimate their impact relative to other Americans? It's not because they are hypocrites. Instead, I suggest it is related to the way that the Eco-Engaged adopt the practices people identify as indicative of caring about the environment (see figure 2.2). In the interviews, regardless of their eco-social relationship, my participants envisioned someone who cares about the environment as making efforts to reduce their impacts through food, waste, and transportation practices. For instance, Carissa, a liberal who I'll describe in more detail in the Self-Effacing chapter, says that when she pictures someone who wants to protect the environment, she imagines "a vegan who walks or bikes everywhere." Even when participants expressed antagonism toward this sort of person, this was still their association. These are the sorts of practices that the Eco-Engaged integrate into their daily lives.

A "flagship species" is a term used in conservation biology to refer to a species that is used to galvanize support for environmental protection, like the polar bear or the giant panda. I have come to think of certain green consumer practices as **flagship behaviors**. These are practices like carrying a cloth bag and reusable water bottle, shopping at a farmers' market, and cycling in order to avoid driving. The large cultural weight that these flagship behaviors carry is disproportionate to the more modest material benefits they offer to the environment. The Eco-Engaged have a strong affinity for these practices—as Nadine noted, even with a reduced income, she still shops for local, organic, sustainable foods and household cleaning products. They are drawn to these practices, incorporate them relatively effortlessly into their lives, and view them as evidence of a commitment to protecting the planet. The Eco-Engaged misjudge the size of their footprint relative to others because they are extrapolating from their truly higher level of engagement in flagship behaviors. The inaccuracy of their estimates of their environmental impacts is a result of the limited material effectiveness of flagship behaviors.

Relating to the Eco-Engaged

The Eco-Engaged elicit considerable anger and resentment, from the Optimists in particular, although early readers of this book also said they felt the Eco-Engaged seemed hypocritical and smug.[18] To dispel these sorts of reactions, I explain why the Eco-Engaged relate to the environment as they do, noting their biography and cultural context. If you grew up the same way the Eco-Engaged did and lived the lives they lead, you would probably feel and act as they do. They are doing what feels right for them—and particularly, what feels right in the face of ecological decline. The way each of us relates to the environment reflects our upbringing and our social networks and is shaped by the parameters of our lives and the society in which we live.

THE PERSONAL AND CULTURAL CONTEXT OF THE ECO-ENGAGED ECO-TYPE

The Eco-Engaged generally described growing up in households that cared about the environment and manifested that care through spending time in nature, talking about the environment, recycling, and buying products that are good for the environment. In other words, the impulse to talk about environmental issues, problematize those issues, and worry about those issues has been with the Eco-Engaged for a long time. Their upbringing inculcated in the Eco-Engaged a feeling that it was good to have a deep sense of curiosity and appreciation for nature, a perception that the natural world is vulnerable, an instinct that environmental destruction is driven by individuals, and a strong sense of moral responsibility to have as small an environmental impact as possible. These facets of their upbringing are a mark of pride for the Eco-Engaged, who described their environmentally concerned parents almost reverentially, and saw their family's environmentalism as a virtue that makes them proud of their heritage. As a result of their socialization, the Eco-Engaged have the cultural capital—the tastes, sensibilities, and know-how—to practice the sort of household-level environmentalism that typifies the ideal environmentalist.

With these instincts, it is understandable that the Eco-Engaged would be oriented toward people and practices that signal the aim of caring for the planet. Indeed, the Eco-Engaged are the most likely of all eco-types to have social networks populated by people who share their approach to environmental responsibility, particularly those who grew up in environmentally active households and who currently live in urban communities. A widely supported argument from psychologists is that we are strongly affected by the people around us—their opinions, their actions, and their habits.[19] The social circles of the Eco-Engaged are most likely to be drawn and redrawn based on evidence of someone's eco-social relationship. This means that the Eco-Engaged are very likely to be surrounded by people like them. Think back to Kyle's story. For Kyle, an Eco-Engaged eco-social relationship was relatively new and he pointed to his family's move to a college town and to emerging friendships with families engaged in efforts to reduce their environmental impacts as enabling a shift in his eco-type. Kyle sounded as though he had previously aligned with the Indifferent eco-type, and once he moved to Pullman and his social circle changed, he developed an admiration for and interest in eco-friendly practices.

There are also more mundane and logistical factors that shape this eco-type. The Eco-Engaged have enough money and relatively straightforward access to the infrastructure needed to manifest their eco-social relationship in everyday practices: they tend to own their homes and they live in places where you can buy green products and where it is "normal" to do so. For instance, no one in Whitman, the farming community, was in the Eco-Engaged eco-type and Whitman had virtually no eco-friendly consumption infrastructure—the town offered limited recycling facilities and there were no green products sold in local stores.

Dominant cultural narratives of environmental issues and solutions to those issues are an additional explanatory layer for making sense of Eco-Engaged environmentalists' commitment to their eco-social relationship. Being able to point to engagement in practices like shopping at a farmers' market and driving a hybrid car as proof of caring about the environment demands a cultural context that substantiates this association. What social scientist Michael Maniates termed the "individualization of environmental responsibility" captures the way that a growing share of governments, non-profit organizations, corporate actors, and members of civil society have accepted that protecting the environment begins with the individual.[20] This is infused throughout the marketplace and our cultural institutions, rendering this argument both hegemonic and ubiquitous. In conventional grocery stores, it is common to read banners like, "Buy Organic: Good for the Earth, Good for You," and vehicles from the Tesla line to the electric Hummer target consumers' desires to lower the environmental impact of their daily practices. A brand called, "If You Care" sells recycled and unbleached, chlorine-free bags and parchment paper, suggesting that people who don't care would buy the conventional versions of these products. As many scholars have already documented, the market for food and vehicles is replete with calls for consumers to vote with their dollars for a more sustainable world.[21] The prevalence of eco-conscious products and marketing shapes the way in which the Eco-Engaged act on their perceived responsibility to protect the planet. There are so few narratives in our public discourse that are both critical of consumer-driven approaches to change *and* offer an alternative vision of caring about the environment. As a result, it is not surprising that I did not encounter any Eco-Engaged who were critical of the cultural or material implications of their lifestyles and that so many felt entitled to tell others how to better care for the environment.

Finally, the way the Eco-Engaged perceive ecological decline reflects scientific assessments of planetary health from respected entities like the Intergovernmental Panel on Climate Change (IPCC), the United Nations' Millennium Ecosystem Assessment (MEA), and reports from prominent environmental nongovernmental organizations. The Eco-Engaged seek out information about environmental issues and they trust the science behind assessments that we are in the midst of an ecological emergency, whether that is presented in the popular media, in eco-documentaries and educational programming, or shared among friends. The Eco-Engaged I interviewed were the most likely of all interview participants to describe detailed knowledge of environmental issues and well-documented fears about water, plastics, and the climate when asked to picture the environment. Their trust in experts and their agreement with expert assessments of ecological decline leave the Eco-Engaged feeling extremely concerned about the fate of the planet.

A lot of people love to hate the Eco-Engaged. When I tell students and colleagues (many of whom would fit in the Eco-Engaged eco-type) that this group inaccurately thinks they have the smallest footprint, people do not seem disappointed, but delighted. The Eco-Engaged are one of the only eco-types (along with the Optimists) who are not self-deprecating about their own relationship to the environment. But while the Optimists defend their eco-social relationship against widespread criticism, the Eco-Engaged express a sense of confidence that theirs is the ideal relationship to the planet. Not only that, but they are also frequently instructing other people how to care more, and better, about the planet. Because they align with and reproduce the ideal environmentalist, the Eco-Engaged experience the advantage of having their eco-social relationship mirrored in public discourse, market spaces, and prominent cultural institutions. Although the Eco-Engaged certainly doubt whether humanity can continue to flourish within planetary limits, they have no doubts that their eco-social relationship is a virtuous one.

3

The Self-Effacing

It's just another way that I'm not measuring up. My reach is exceeding my grasp . . . So it's a feeling of, "Oh, yeah, that again." It's pretty familiar. The theme of this lifetime.

—CHERYL, MIDDLE CLASS, LIBERAL, 61 YEARS OLD

In my interview with Cheryl, I was struck by a tension: on the one hand, Cheryl thought about her environmental impact all the time. As a result, she tried to drive as little as possible, was conscientious about her household energy and water use, and described in detail her efforts to choose eco-friendly products. But on the other hand, Cheryl was extremely critical of her efforts. She berated herself for not buying green products more regularly and for driving a gas-powered car because she felt that her efforts are "not enough to really solve the issue [of climate change]." When I asked her how she felt about this, she said: "It's just another way that I'm not measuring up. My reach is exceeding my grasp . . . So it's a feeling of, 'Oh, yeah, that again.' It's pretty familiar. The theme of this lifetime." Unlike the Eco-Engaged, who feel a sense of frustration and hopelessness when they contemplate others' lack of commitment, Cheryl's distress stems from a feeling of personal failure.

One of the most distinctive things about the Self-Effacing eco-type is how they answered my question about their concern for the environment. In each interview, I asked people to rank their concern, verbally, on a scale from 1 (low) to 10 (high), and then explain their answer.[1] Cheryl's response is typical of the Self-Effacing eco-type: she says she'd place her concern at a "seven or eight," identifying two rationales. What is pushing her concern higher up the scale is, in Cheryl's words, "Climate change." She explains that "Since I've lived here [Olympia], the summers have been really hot. I've only been here three years but people have said this is so unusual, this isn't normal." Cheryl interprets these patterns as evidence of ecological decline that is caused by people like her. To put this in the context of the framework of eco-social relationships, Cheryl's perceptions of the severity of ecological decline shape her affinity for the environment, making that affinity more intense. For instance, Cheryl tells me, "The natural world is the place where I go to recharge. It's like a treasure and I hate to see what humanity has done to it, like the huge changes that have occurred because of the way we live our lives." But this answer sounds like a ten out of ten on the environmental concern scale. There is something pulling Cheryl's score down (or weakening her affinity)—it is not her perception of the severity of environmental issues, but her opinion of her own contribution to effecting pro-environmental change. As she describes, "I still have a gas-powered car. I haven't replaced all my light bulbs yet. I give some money to environmental causes but not a great deal. I don't have a lot of confidence that whatever I do is gonna make a difference."

The Self-Effacing frequently evaluate themselves against the prototypical ideal environmentalist (see chapter 1). This ideal is widely recognized as the consummate expression of caring for the environment. Emulating the ideal entails making sustainable consumption choices, whether that is a major decision, such as whether or not to buy an electric car, or a more perfunctory choice such as buying recycled paper towels—or whether to buy a car or paper towels at all. The Self-Effacing show us how fraught the eco-friendly marketplace can be, replete with uncertainty and conflicting ideals. For the Self-Effacing, a trip to the grocery store is a reminder that they are "not measuring up." This theme comes up again and again in my interview with Cheryl, who is retired from her career as a social worker and moved to Olympia in part because of the natural beauty of the area. Cheryl thinks about her carbon footprint all the time. She has used online calculators to estimate "how many cubic feet of carbon I put into the air," and considers this whenever she is deciding whether to walk or drive, or whether to turn the heat on in her house or not. But she tells me she thinks of herself as being "at the low end" in terms of being an environmentalist. She says that's because too often she, "buys stuff that's not particularly renewable or sustainable." She says this is because she's too "impulsive" and she admires people she sees at the store buying these more sustainable products. But Cheryl finds a trip to the store to be "overwhelming" because "there's too much choice. What's the difference between this one and that one? I'm 61—I'm a little behind the curve on a lot of this stuff." When I ask her what that contrast feels like, between how she wants to consume and how she consumes, she explains, "part of me just, like, feels overwhelmed with all the things I should be doing to improve the planet."

The Self-Effacing look up to the ideal environmentalist—they admire people who seem to effortlessly buy organic foods and electric cars. They do what they can to reduce their consumption of energy and water, but they struggle to consistently choose sustainable products and they berate themselves as a result. This is a way of experiencing ecological decline that is overlooked in research on eco-social relationships.

Getting to Know the Self-Effacing

In this chapter, we meet the Self-Effacing eco-type. This is a common orientation to the environment—27% of the survey sample and 29% of the interview sample fall into the Self-Effacing eco-type. The Self-Effacing acknowledge and respect the ideal environmentalist. They see this ideal as the highest form of eco-social relationship and aspire to emulate it. Although many Self-Effacing participants expressed a deep sense of curiosity and appreciation for nature, this is not as ubiquitous as it is among the Eco-Engaged. You are unlikely to see the Self-Effacing driving hybrid cars and shopping at Whole Foods Market, but they would like to. As they admire (and sometimes resent) others' ease with green consumerism, the Self-Effacing characterize themselves as inadequate ecological citizens. Yet the Self-Effacing overlook the ways in which their lifestyle already aligns with their goals of living lightly on the planet because they do not have an effortless preference for the flagship behaviors I described in the previous chapter.

Do you know anyone with a Self-Effacing eco-type? Does this fit your own orientation to the environment? In terms of the sociodemographic profile of the Self-Effacing, a person is most likely to reflect this eco-type if they are politically liberal, white, and live in a suburban community or large city. The Self-Effacing are unlikely to have grown up in an eco-engaged household.[2] Let's explore more fully what it feels like to have this eco-social relationship.

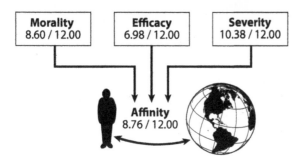

FIGURE 3.1. Eco-social relationship model for the Self-Effacing
Note: 1–4 = disagree, 5–8 = neutral, 9–12 = agree.

WHAT DOES A SELF-EFFACING ECO-TYPE FEEL LIKE?

The Self-Effacing have fairly high scores on all elements of eco-social relationships, but their sense of self-efficacy is low relative to their affinity for the environment, perception of severity, and sense of moral responsibility to protect the planet (figure 3.1). Those whom I categorize as Self-Effacing share an affinity for environmental protection, a perception that current patterns of human behavior are ecologically unsustainable, a belief that individuals are morally responsible for protecting the environment, and a critical view of their own efforts to do so. While the Eco-Engaged are most likely to express sadness about the state of the planet, the Self-Effacing communicate both sadness about ecological decline and guilt over their role in it.

"It's a Very Welcoming Place. It's a Home of Sorts":
Strong Affinity for the Environment

In my interviews with the Self-Effacing, I heard two themes that reflect an affinity for the environment. First, participants spoke about their connection to natural areas in the places they live. This connection did not have the sort of emotional intensity and intimacy that the Eco-Engaged conveyed, but there is certainly a strong sense of appreciation. When my students and I were recruiting participants for this project, we would go door-to-door, asking residents if they would be willing to participate in an interview about their community and the environment. In Pacifica, one of our target neighborhoods was located at the top of a hill. The homes here had beautiful views of the Pacific Ocean and were surrounded by Douglas fir trees. At one point, walking between houses, a Jeep pulled up behind me and William, a heavy-set, bearded man in an American flag tank-top leaned out the window and barked, "What are you selling?" "Research," I answered, "I'm looking for people to interview about the environment." I was nervous and intimidated, and surprised when he introduced himself and said he would be happy to be participate. One of the first things I asked William was to tell me what he liked about his community. He told me, "The trees. The rain. The rainforest." And he continued, "I love it. It's just a very welcoming place. It's a home of sorts." Throughout our two-hour long interview, William described his affinity for the natural environment, but this was commonly succeeded by his concerns about threats to this ecosystem. William (who says he has not voted for a long time) told me about how much Styrofoam he sees on the beaches where he lives, and described his sadness that new developments on the island are displacing wildlife habitat.

Like William, other Self-Effacing interview participants often paired their appreciation for nature with their concerns for human impacts on the planet. This is the second theme that characterizes Self-Effacing environmentalists' affinity for the environment. My interview with Judy, a 52-year-old Democrat who lives in Olympia, was deeply emotional. Right from the beginning of our interview, Judy's affinity for the environment was transparent. When I asked her what emotions came up when she thought about the environment, Judy began to cry as she told me, "Makes me want to cry actually, that's weird." After taking a breath, she said, apologetically, "It's funny, I wasn't expecting that," and then tried once again to answer the question: "The environment gives me kind of a sense of comfort and home and really deep concern and kind of a feeling of sadness."

The sadness that Self-Effacing participants described as evoked by thinking about the environment was more specifically borne from reflecting on what humanity has done to the planet. When I asked Caitlyn, who is a politically liberal, 38-year-old bartender in Pacifica, to tell me what she pictured as "the environment," she says, "climate change." She explains that she also envisions "water, air, trees, and the built environment," but that as a "word association exercise, forefront in my mind is climate change, hands down." Tom, a political liberal who works in an outdoors store in Olympia and is completing a graduate degree in environmental studies, tells me about books he read in his classes that argue humans and the environment are not separate entities.[3] As he explains, "We have an impact on the environment but we're also part of the environment. I feel like we're not separate from the environment. We affect it but we are part of it too." For Tom, this means that "We are a creature on the planet too, like a deer." But unlike deer, Tom articulates, humans have had far-reaching and negative impacts on ecosystems everywhere. I spoke with Eco-Engaged participants who also communicated this same sense of interconnectedness with nonhuman species, but the Self-Effacing were distinct in how quickly they added details about how much damage humans have done to the planet.

Overall, the Self-Effacing have a strong affinity for the environment, second only to the Eco-Engaged. The average Self-Effacing survey respondent agrees with the statements, "I am very interested in issues relating to the natural environment," "The natural environment is very important to me," and "I often think about environmental topics" (see the "Affinity" score in figure 3.1). The strength of agreement is not as strong as among the Eco-Engaged, but, as underscored by the qualitative analyses above, these two eco-social relationships share similar impulses: they both appreciate having access to places that are relatively undeveloped and they worry about the impact humans have on the planet. There was little variation in affinity for the environment, but younger Self-Effacing respondents in my survey report higher scores than those who are older.

"My Thoughts on the Environment Aren't Positive. It Makes Me Really Sad": Confronting the Severity of Ecological Decline

When I asked interview participants to picture the environment, the Self-Effacing emerged from this exercise with an air of sadness, regardless of whether they listed a litany of environmental issues, or whether they focused more acutely on the effects of climate change. Shelby is a politically liberal woman who moved to Pullman because she believes it to be a safe place to be in a climate emergency. She offers an assessment of the state of the environment that is typical among the Self-Effacing: "My thoughts on the environment aren't positive. It makes me really sad." Climate change is the issue that is most immediate to the Self-Effacing that I interviewed. Travis (liberal) explains that his biggest fear about the environment is, "the cumulative changes of the greenhouse gasses." He connects this to fears for his son's health in the future, but notes that "it's not just about my kid being sick, it's also other kids being sick, and the environment as a whole being sick." These fears for future generations are common. Self-Effacing participants described witnessing changes in the climate over the course of their lifetimes—changes like seeing spring come earlier than ever before, and experiencing hotter, drier summers now compared to the past. The Self-Effacing worry that the next generation won't, as Caitlyn comments, "inherit a world as carefree as what I grew up in." Caitlyn worries that the coming years will bring, "a lot more variability and a lot more fear associated with what the weather can do to you." Caitlyn concludes by saying, "We need to do something. What? I don't know. Something." Caitlyn's comment opens up space to discuss the second theme of severity, which is the view that ecological crises can only be addressed if enough caring, committed individuals take action.

The Self-Effacing often raised the view that there have been important improvements in human-environment interactions over the past few decades. Brian, who works as an instructor at the university in Pullman and has three children at home, agrees that "humanity has damaged the environment." But he feels hopeful that, in his words, "Now, more than ever, we're conscious about it, trying not to harm, trying to help it get back." Brian, and the Self-Effacing who share this view, believe that individuals becoming more attentive to ecological damage is a hopeful sign. In particular, they believe that having more people caring about the ways they affect the environment is a crucial element of eco-social change. William says, "it pisses me off to see people trashing the environment," but notes that there is less litter around these days, which indicates to him that more people are taking responsibility for reducing ecological harm. Tom's overall assessment of the environment reiterates this point—he thinks, "there's still hope," because individuals are starting to recognize the deleterious impacts humans have had on the environment, and to respond in turn by adopting responsible consumption and waste practices.

The Self-Effacing are similar to the Eco-Engaged in terms of evaluating the planet to be in a crisis. Their scores on the survey for the items, "Humans are using up the earth's resources," "Environmental problems are much more serious now than they used to be," and "Protecting the earth should be among our country's top priorities" (see "Severity" score in figure 3.1) are second only to the Eco-Engaged. The Self-Effacing are also second in intensity to the Eco-Engaged in their concern for environmental issues. On a scale from 1 (not at all concerned) to 5 (extremely concerned), the average score for concern among the Self-Effacing is above "4" for each item: environmental issues generally, climate change, plastic pollution, plant and animal extinction, air pollution, water pollution, and health risks from toxic chemicals.[4] But why is their perception of the severity of ecological issues not equivalent to the Eco-Engaged? The interview data offers some clues.

The first reason why the Self-Effacing may not perceive ecological issues to be as severe, compared with scores for the Eco-Engaged, is biographical. The Self-Effacing are less likely to have grown up in environmentally active households. As a result, the difference—which Self-Effacing participants characterized as an improvement—in their eco-social relationship compared to their parents, might indicate to them that society is becoming more aware over time. Indeed, the Self-Effacing stressed their perception that more people are aware of environmental issues and care about these issues than ever before. The Eco-Engaged did not make comments along these lines. Perhaps because the Eco-Engaged grew up in households that were conscious of ecological issues, they don't see this awareness as something new. But for the Self-Effacing, who differ from the families they grew up in because they recycle, try to drive less, and talk to friends about climate change, their awareness is a hopeful sign of social change.

A second reason why the Self-Effacing are less likely to perceive environmental issues as severe is that they sense that a large proportion of the population is committed to environmental protection. While the Eco-Engaged align with the ideal environmentalist, they feel that they are in the minority; that people like the Self-Effacing are not wealthy or educated enough to care in the same way. Thus, the Eco-Engaged may doubt the extent of concern for the environment that exists in the population because they see themselves as the only sort of people who care in the right way. Among the Self-Effacing, a sense that positive changes are happening—that improvements are taking place despite their own sense of not doing enough—dampens their perception of the severity of ecological challenges.

The third reason I offer to explain why the Self-Effacing do not evaluate ecological decline to be as severe as the Eco-Engaged do, is connected to my observation that the Self-Effacing were more likely to emphasize a concern that efforts to protect the natural environment affect the working classes disproportionately and negatively. In the previous chapter, I shared Addy's account of having a friend die by suicide after being sued for cutting down trees on a construction site. This sort of tension was far more prevalent among the Self-Effacing. For instance, even though William, who I described earlier, talked about how sad he felt when he saw habitat destroyed to build new homes, he followed up these remarks by explaining that, as a carpenter himself, he understood firsthand that people need to make a living. Similarly, Cheryl told me that seeing areas of forest being clear-cut is devastating for her. As she says, "It's kind of like having the rug pulled out from under me." But she explains that although she feels, "a combination of anger and despair," she also knows that "the people who are doing it, they're doing it probably for good reasons, like they're supporting their families with their salaries." This sort of awareness that environmental protection often comes with a human cost seems to lessen the degree to which the Self-Effacing diagnose environmental issues as severe.

Among the Self-Effacing survey respondents, perception of the severity of ecological decline varies. This variation is driven by respondents' political ideology and by the extent to which their families growing up were involved in environmental practices. Conservative Self-Effacing environmentalists who grew up in eco-engaged households report lower scores on the measures of severity. The political patterns are consistent with existing research that reports lower levels of concern for the environment among political conservatives, and the influence of upbringing suggests that early socialization can buffer some people from acute fears of ecological decline.[5]

"I Care About It . . . But Not to the Point Where I'm Getting Involved": Moderate Sense of Moral Responsibility

The Self-Effacing feel a moderate degree of personal moral responsibility to protect the environment. They picture that responsibility manifesting in ways that are consistent with the sorts of practices that characterize the ideal environmentalist—in particular, choosing eco-friendly products and reducing household consumption. For the Self-Effacing, it is consumption that most directly ties us to the planet, which comes across clearly when they describe their role in environmental protection. For example, Brian tells me he "knows" that the "right thing to do" is always the greener option, although he doesn't feel he does a good job when it comes to making "better choices." Brian's sense of what choices are "better" includes, "buying recycled plastic, choosing to not drive, using less water, less power, less resources in general." He explains that these choices are obvious, because, in his words, "If we ruin our environment, we're doomed. That is a no-brainer. You don't let your house fall down around you." Consuming profligately is akin to letting your house fall down around you. Carissa, who works in public health, envisions people and the environment as connected largely through the ways that people harm the planet. She says that whenever she hears or reads the word "environment," she immediately thinks of large-scale human impacts ("Are we polluting it? Are we being good for it?") and individual responsibilities to ameliorate those impacts ("Are you recycling? What are you doing for the environment? What's your carbon footprint?"). For Carissa, and other Self-Effacing participants I interviewed, exercising a moral responsibility to protect the planet means reducing how much you are consuming and choosing eco-friendly products. Facing barriers to integrating these sorts of practices and purchases into daily life, Carissa, like other Self-Effacing participants, struggles to put her ideals into action. As Carissa says, "I care about it . . . but not to the point where I'm getting involved."

Self-Effacing survey respondents report fairly strong levels of agreement with the items about moral responsibilities. On each item, "I have a moral responsibility to reduce my impact on the environment," "I worry about my impact on the natural environment," and, "I try to reduce the amount I consume in order to protect the environment," the average score among the Self-Effacing indicates agreement with these statements (see "Morality"

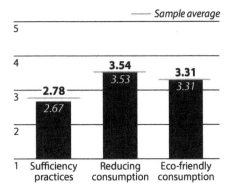

FIGURE 3.2. Self-Effacing engagement in eco-friendly practices
Note: 1 = never; 5 = always.

score in figure 3.1). The variation in how strongly respondents agreed with these statements is shaped by two sociodemographic measures: gender and income. Female Self-Effacing survey respondents with higher incomes report a stronger sense of moral responsibility than others. This suggests that feeling personally responsible for one's environmental impact is shaped externally by gender norms and internally by one's sense of efficacy.

Despite maligning themselves for not reflecting the ideal environmentalist, the Self-Effacing are second only to the Eco-Engaged in eco-consumption and reducing consumption, and their engagement in sufficiency consumption practices is typical among the survey sample (figure 3.2). The variation within the Self-Effacing for eco-consumption can be partially explained by respondents' age, political ideology, level of education, residence, and cultural capital. Specifically, older, well-educated liberals living in suburban communities are more likely to engage in eco-consumption, and this group is likely to have grown up in environmentally active and well-educated households. These patterns echo the argument I made in chapter 1 that participating in eco-friendly consumption both reflects and communicates power and privilege. With regard to sufficiency practices, such as hunting and gardening, within the Eco-Engaged, politically conservative respondents reported more engagement than liberals. But there is no political variation in engagement in sufficiency practices within the Self-Effacing eco-type. Instead, those who live in urban areas practice self-sufficiency less than those in rural areas, and people from eco-engaged households engage more frequently in self-sufficiency practices. The rural advantage here is logical, given that such practices require access to large tracts of land.

The inherited skills also make sense, since feeling competent in things like gardening and hunting requires knowledge, practice, and familiarity.

"I Could Definitely Do Much, Much More": Low Self-Efficacy

If there is one salient, defining characteristic of the Self-Effacing, it is the extent to which they criticize themselves for not doing enough. As I elaborate in the section on environmental impacts, below, the Self-Effacing have relatively small carbon footprints, but they believe their own contributions to environmental protection are inadequate. I suggest this is because they believe the ideal environmentalist defines what it looks like to be "good" to the environment, and they struggle to align with this ideal. In my interview with Jim, a 29-year-old prep cook, I asked what he felt his moral responsibilities were, vis-à-vis environmental protection. He immediately focused on his role in the market, explaining that his choices are largely motivated by cost, but that he wished he could buy more sustainable products. He recounts a recent purchase to illustrate the tensions he feels between being a "good" consumer, in line with the ideal environmentalist, and being a "good" consumer, in line with dominant expectations of lower-income shoppers. He tells me about, "this organic coffee, 'Harvest'-something," that is sold at the local grocery store. He says, "last time I was there, I was like 'Oh yeah, it's organic coffee, that'll help the environment.' I did buy it; I tried it. But I couldn't really tell the difference so I went back to the cheap-o stuff." I asked him how it felt the next time he bought "the cheap-o stuff," and he said, "Like I had two more dollars! But it felt like, uh, like a compromise. Like I'm settling for the cheaper product. Like it would be nice to know where the product came from. To know it's sustainable and organic and all that." Jim identifies eco-friendly shopping as the preeminent expression of caring for the environment and is critical of his own resistance to regularly choosing these products.

In the previous chapter, I shared Eileen's anecdote of judging a woman at the grocery store for buying chips while expressing an aspiration to buy organic foods. Eileen could probably find something in Jim's cart to put back on the shelf to offset the $2 he needed to buy "Harvest-something" coffee. What Eileen never acknowledges, and Jim alludes to, are the conflicting consumer ideals that lower-income shoppers are held to. Jim feels pressure to be frugal with his money, stretching a dollar as far as possible, but the ideal environmentalist demands a different standard—selflessly voting with our dollars to support ecologically beneficial production practices. The Self-Effacing frequently struggled with these conflicting normative standards.

The ethical consumption landscape that is relatively straightforward and nonproblematic for most of the Eco-Engaged is confusing and frustrating for the Self-Effacing. Here is the risk: by purchasing something that comes with a promise of sustainability, the lower-income shopper is making a gamble. In the face of ubiquitous greenwashing campaigns, they risk spending money wastefully if it turns out that the product is simply a marketing gimmick—more expensive but no more sustainable than its "cheap-o" counterpart. This precarious landscape leaves the Self-Effacing in a position of feeling very low self-efficacy to effect positive ecological reforms.

It is impossible to overstate how prominent a theme low efficacy is among my Self-Effacing interview participants. When the Self-Effacing justify their level of environmental concern, they integrate a critical view of their own contributions to environmental protection—and these criticisms are woven in and out of their comments on morality and self-efficacy. Carissa said that on a scale from one to ten, her level of concern is, "About a six. Like I care about it, because I enjoy it, but I don't care enough to where I am getting involved and doing things about it all of the time." Carissa wishes this were not the case: "I would like to pretend that I'm a better person that's doing a lot more for it, but I'm not." And as Carissa makes sense of this gap between her intentions and her actions, she blames herself: "I don't know, I guess I'm just lazy." Brian gives the same score and comes to a similar conclusion. He told me, "I could definitely do much, much more." And when I ask him what that would look like, he explains: "I could ride my bicycle and use my car a little bit less. I could somehow encourage my friends to do a little bit more in the good way and a little bit less in the bad way."

Part of the uncertainty I heard among my Self-Effacing participants, as Jim conveyed, is a feeling of lacking the skills and knowledge needed to make eco-friendly consumption choices. As Tom says, when explaining how he chooses which products to buy at the grocery store, "Do I know a lot about the company? Probably not." Tom seemed so frustrated as he said this, so I asked him how it felt, not knowing if the things he bought were better or worse for the environment. And he tells me, "I guess it's saddening. It makes me feel a little helpless. There's a lot of moving parts, a lot of people on the planet. It's a helpless feeling, like what can you possibly do as one person?" In my interview with John, a retired mail carrier and Democrat, a large part of our conversation was occupied by pickles. Yes, pickles. John explained that he wants to support local, sustainable businesses when he shops, and described a brand of pickles he has bought for years. Recently, he was bored and reading the label more closely, and noticed that it read, "Made in India."

John was flabbergasted. As he explained, "the label says, 'Great Northwest Taste since 1948, blah, blah, blah,' but the pickles are coming all the way from India!" Now, John visits websites to try to factcheck products and he is reading a book about truth in media and advertising, in order to equip himself to be a savvier shopper. Balancing his aims for buying products that are better for the planet with his wariness at being duped leaves John and others feeling adrift and uncertain in the eco-friendly marketplace. Similarly, Judy spoke at length about her uncertainty about what to do about her car. She told me, "honestly if I had my druthers I wouldn't even have a car." But she is overwhelmed by indecision and confusion about what it means to dispose of an old vehicle: "It would be great not to have a car, but that means my car is going to go either to somebody else or go to the dump. Maybe to get recycled, I hope, some of it." Judy explains that weighing these options is, "very uncomfortable because there is this desire to do the right thing and then there's these questions, 'what is the right thing? What is the best way to go about this? How can I afford it?'"

One of the arguments that environmental sociologist Kari Norgaard made in her book, *Living in Denial,* is that people try to avoid the feeling that their lifestyles are driving ecological deterioration. In order to avoid that feeling, people will construct rationales to suggest that things aren't so bad, they will compare their communities to places that are worse for the planet, and they might participate in daily efforts to feel like they are making a difference.[6] The Eco-Engaged point the finger at people whom they perceive as not taking responsibility for their impacts, and they focus on the many daily efforts they make to reduce their own impacts. The Self-Effacing also lay blame on "selfish" and "uncaring" individuals, but they convey a lot of guilt that they don't make more frequent efforts to reduce their own footprint on the planet. This latter point seems to be very frustrating for the Self-Effacing. For instance, Carissa described her fears about water shortages in the Pacific Northwest. But immediately after, she tells me, "I don't know that there's anything I can really do about it, you know what I mean? You try to stay positive, do the right thing and do what you can, I guess." When I ask what that looks like for her, she points to practices that seem only tangentially connected to water use: "I recycle and, and, uh, try to be good about stuff, but that's all I can really do." This feeling of helplessness in the face of ecological decline was common among Norgaard's Norwegian interview participants and the Self-Effacing Washingtonians I spoke with.

The Self-Effacing focus more on what they see as their transgressions than on the ways that their lifestyles likely generate a small carbon footprint.

Caitlyn is a good example of this. She lives in a small house, which she shares with roommates, has a large vegetable garden, and keeps bees. But she is extremely critical of the ways in which she fails to be an ideal environmentalist. Caitlyn tells me, guiltily, "I drive more than I should. I try to take the train whenever I can, but sometimes due to convenience, I drive." Because Caitlyn wants to have a vegetable garden and keep bees, she needs a backyard, which is expensive in the city where she works and explains why she lives far from downtown. Caitlyn recognizes that she can't balance all her ideals: her garden and apiary force her to drive. But she blames herself, rather than larger economic and political systems that structure her choices for housing and transportation, and rather than recognizing all that she is doing.

Compared with the other elements of an eco-social relationship—affinity, severity, morality—efficacy is notably weak among the Self-Effacing. In the survey, I asked respondents three questions to measure their self-efficacy. I asked how strongly they agreed with the statements, "I always do what I can to reduce my impact on the environment," "I have oriented my life around my desire to reduce my impact on the environment," and "I am able to do what it takes to reduce my impact on the environment" (see "Efficacy" score in figure 3.1). The Self-Effacing report similar scores on these items as the Optimists (chapter 4), even though they express stronger feelings of moral responsibility to protect the environment. The variation in these measures can be partially explained by age, race, political orientation, and eco-upbringing. Self-Effacing who are white and politically liberal report lower levels of self-efficacy, while older Self-Effacing and those from eco-engaged households report higher levels of self-efficacy. These patterns indicate that white liberal Self-Effacing may feel more pressure to conform to the ideal environmentalist and feel less successful at doing so, particularly compared to those who are older and who grew up in environmentally active households. Age is an interesting theme here: it may be that pressure to reflect the ideal environmentalist is more acute for younger people in the face of messages that climate change is threatening quality of life for the next generation.[7]

It is not only self-efficacy but also social efficacy that seems to feed the sense of powerlessness I heard from Self-Effacing participants. I asked survey respondents to indicate the extent to which they see various actors and institutions as responsible for protecting the environment, and the degree to which they can be trusted to do so, as a measure of broader social efficacy. The Self-Effacing attribute the greatest responsibility for environmental protection to the government, the least to nonprofit organizations, and see individuals, local communities, and businesses as moderately responsible

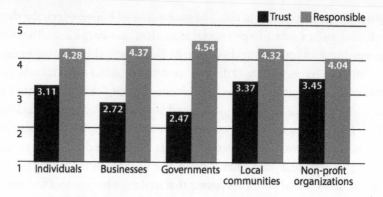

FIGURE 3.3. Self-Effacing respondents' opinions of various actors' responsibility for environmental protection and trustworthiness
Note: 1 = not at all; 5 = very much.

(see figure 3.3). Looking at the extent to which they trust these entities, I note the lowest levels of trust in the government and businesses, and the highest levels of trust in nonprofit organizations and local communities. Trust in individuals is moderate. The gap between trust and responsibility is smallest for nonprofit organizations and local communities and largest for governments and businesses. Seeing the government as most responsible for protecting the environment and not trusting them to do so might reinforce the view that environmental protection is best left to individuals.

"Some Care More, Some Care Less": Moderate Relationality

The Self-Effacing did not, as a general rule, grow up in households committed to sustainable consumption, and while they may have friends who are passionate about cycling and reusable straws, they also have friends who never talk about the environment and have little interest in reducing their carbon footprint. Cheryl captures this when describing her social network, "Some care more [about the environment], some care less." The Self-Effacing admire people who align with the ideal environmentalist, but they are unlikely to distance themselves socially from people who seem unaware of the virtues of conscientious consumption. This is distinct from the Eco-Engaged, who tend to differentiate themselves and their friends from people who appear uncommitted to environmental protection.

The Self-Effacing have learned how to orient themselves toward the environment in a way that is distinct from how they were raised. Recall that the Eco-Engaged tended to proudly describe how passionate their parents were about environmental protection and how committed they were to spending time in nature. This is not the case for the Self-Effacing. For instance, Carissa tells me she only learned about the importance of recycling as an adult after she was berated by a roommate for throwing newspaper in the garbage. She explains to me, "I didn't grow up recycling. Recycling was very much not a thing that was done." Now, when Carissa goes home, she finds herself feeling viscerally upset at her family's waste practices: "every time I go home it brings me, like, physical pain because I just have to throw things in the trash that should really be recycled or composted." Caitlyn, who grew up in a rural community, tells me her family is, "way more about hard work than they are about having fun in the environment." She didn't grow up doing any outdoor recreation, but she's learned to "love to hike and be outside." Although she didn't learn that from her family, she remarked that they do have "a respect for nature and an enjoyment of just sitting and watching things." As she describes, "my dad loves to just sit outside and just watch the backyard." She's noticed that "it doesn't matter whether it's a storm or whether it's watching deer or bunnies or whatever." Although this is different from her own way of relating to nature, Caitlyn sees a shared appreciation of the environment. As she explains, "He's not necessarily very pro-environment in what he does but that sort of reflection [on nature] is also very important to me and we have that in common." She summarizes the difference in how their appreciation for the environment manifests: "I recycle like a madwoman and try to drive less even though I loathe biking. He just sits still and smokes and watches his yard. But we both have that sort of 'enjoy nature' feeling." Caitlyn's ability to recognize a capacity to care about the environment even when it manifests in a way that looks distinct from her own eco-social relationship illustrates the orientation to others' eco-social relationships that I hope to foster through this book.

The Self-Effacing live, work, and socialize with people who have eco-social relationships both similar to and very distinct from their own. They describe their friends as representing a wide range of commitments to environmental protection. Tom tells me that his social circle ranges from "people who haven't even thought about the environment to people who are the same as me or who care even more." Travis notes that while his wife and siblings care deeply about the environment, his coworkers on the construction site seem much less interested in environmental issues. He elaborates: "the builders and laborers don't see what the big deal is, so much. They definitely see environmental protection as more of a burden."

Although the Self-Effacing seem content to socialize with people who care more and less about the environment, they nonetheless characterize their acquaintances with these sorts of labels. In our interview, Carissa told me about a "super-green friend," describing their home gardens, their efforts to reduce waste, and the way they never use a car. Travis tells me about friends he knows who have a small acreage and reuse water and only eat organic foods. Although he questions the self-righteousness that these friends convey, noting that not many people can afford to live that way, these are nonetheless the people he mentions when describing who in his social circle cares about the environment. Likewise, when I asked who she knows who cares a lot about the environment, Cheryl mentions a friend who has solar panels on their house and drives an electric car. The Self-Effacing often feel a bit insecure around these friends. As Carissa tells me, when she's with her "super-green friend," she "always feel[s] like a jackass" because she's "not doing nearly as much as she is."

Generally speaking, the Self-Effacing tend not to use evidence of caring for the environment to construct their social circles. The survey included three items measuring relationality: "Most of the people I'm close to are very worried about the environment," "Most of the people I'm close to try to reduce their impact on the environment," and "I prefer to spend time with people who care about the environment." The Self-Effacing have moderate scores on these items—much lower than the Eco-Engaged, but higher than other eco-types. Agreement with these items is related to age, political ideology, income, and eco-upbringing. Older, liberal Self-Effacing who earn a high income and grew up in environmentally active homes are more likely to describe their social circle as concerned about the environment and to say that a person's relationship to the environment influences their view of them. In short, the Self-Effacing who are going to use evidence of a person's concern for and commitment to the environment to determine their value as a friend are those most likely to be older, politically liberal, and wealthier.

The Environmental Impacts of the Self-Effacing

Despite the fact that, of all eco-social relationships, the Self-Effacing are the most critical of their own impact on the environment, their average carbon footprints are below the average for the survey sample. For household carbon footprints, the average for the Self-Effacing is 16.3 tons CO_2e, which is lower than the average across the survey sample as a whole (18.1 tons). Estimates of carbon footprint among the Self-Effacing range from less than one ton at the low end, to 69 tons at the upper limit. When we look at the average footprint per person, again, the Self-Effacing have the lowest

BOX 3.1. Examining the Composition and Sociodemographic Antecedents of Self-Effacing Carbon Footprints

---

Self-Effacing who live in towns and suburban areas have a smaller footprint than those in rural areas. Otherwise, there are no sociodemographic measures affecting variation in footprints. The Self-Effacing carbon footprint is largely made up of home energy use (39%) and ground transportation (40%). Their diet makes up a larger share compared to other eco-social relationships (see figure 3.4). Variation in home energy use is largely attributed to home ownership and age, as younger Self-Effacing who own their homes have a larger footprint than others. For ground transportation, wealthier Self-Effacing are more likely to have higher emissions. Variation in emissions from air travel is influenced by residence and income: high-income, urban Self-Effacing fly more frequently than others. Emissions from waste, predictably, vary by place of residence (with rural Self-Effacing having the largest waste footprint), but income and eco-upbringing also matter here: Self-Effacing who earn more and grew up in eco-engaged households are more likely to recycle, and therefore have a smaller footprint from their household waste.

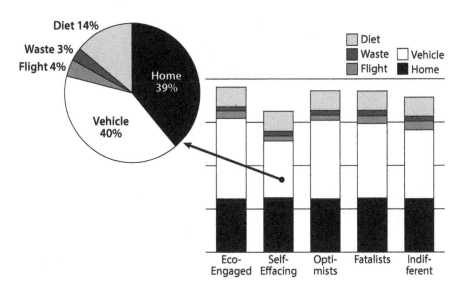

FIGURE 3.4. Composition of the average Self-Effacing survey respondent's household carbon footprint against size and general composition of the footprint of other ecotypes

level of emissions: the average per person carbon footprint is 6.2 tons (the survey average is 7.1 tons), ranging from less than one ton to 45 tons. Interested readers can review a brief discussion of the factors that contribute to variation in the Self-Effacing household carbon footprint (see box 3.1). Self-Effacing survey respondents were quite critical of their impacts on the environment. In contrast to the Eco-Engaged, 71% of whom believed their impact to be lower than the US average, only 53% of Self-Effacing thought they had below-average impacts.

The Self-Effacing don't adopt the flagship behaviors that the Eco-Engaged do. Of all the eco-social relationships, the Self-Effacing are the least likely to have solar panels and the most likely to own and drive a gas- or diesel-powered vehicle. They are unlikely to be vegetarian or vegan, and only about 70% recycle consistently. But at the same time, nearly 80% of the Self-Effacing do not use air travel at all (or at least not in 2019) and they are the most likely of all eco-types to not own a vehicle.

Relating to the Self-Effacing

Now I want to ask you to change gears, from the analytical reader I've demanded of you in this chapter up until now, to an empathetic reader. As I present a broad depiction of the eco-social world that the Self-Effacing confront as they navigate and articulate their relationship to the earth, you might get more out of this section if you make efforts to picture yourself in the shoes of the Self-Effacing. As in the previous chapter, I will refer to personal historical characteristics and cultural schemas in order to render the Self-Effacing eco-social relationship relatable and understandable.

THE PERSONAL AND CULTURAL CONTEXT
OF THE SELF-EFFACING ECO-TYPE

When I put myself in the shoes of the Self-Effacing, I picture growing up in a household where the environment was "out there"—a place you may have visited to go camping every now and then, or a place outside your window, but not a topic of conversation in daily life. When they grew up, household consumption practices may have been rooted in frugality (turning off the lights to save energy), but these actions were not tied to a moral commitment to leave a lighter footprint. Yet when the Self-Effacing started to make their own way in the world, they encountered a high cultural capital archetype they admired: the sustainable consumer who cycles or drives a hybrid car, buys organic foods and household products, shops at the local farmers' market, and maybe even has solar panels on their home. The Self-Effacing took steps to emulate that ideal—choosing a fuel-efficient vehicle, trying out eco-friendly cleaners and products that promised to be more environmentally sustainable. Once purchased, however, these products didn't have the patina of virtue that the Self-Effacing assumed they would. They felt duped—and then guilty for doubting the efficacy of eco-friendly shopping practices. Focused on the steps they weren't taking—driving an old, gas-powered car, living in a poorly insulated home, never getting that backyard composter set up—the Self-Effacing don't notice that their lifestyle effortlessly integrates many hallmarks of sustainable consumption.[8] They live in modestly sized homes and they use air travel rarely, once every couple of years. Although the Self-Effacing don't practice eco-consumption with the frequency that the Eco-Engaged do, they reduce their consumption of material goods and resources as part of their everyday practice.

The Self-Effacing and the Eco-Engaged relate to distinct images of the environment. The Eco-Engaged approach the environment as a sacred space. They feel awe and wonder and reverence when they reflect on the planet. In contrast, the Self-Effacing confront a much more profane space. For them, the natural world is more immediate. Depending on where they live, it may be the forests around them, the fields where wheat is cultivated, or the Pacific Ocean. They love to recreate in these spaces and appreciate the opportunity to do so. But their most emotional tie is not to the environment directly, but to their sense of failure to do more to protect it. This pattern showed up in the deep sense of guilt that the Self-Effacing expressed when they described their efforts to reduce their environmental impacts. For the Self-Effacing, "the environment" is synonymous with flagship behaviors—recycling, bicycling—anything that promises to reduce a household's carbon footprint. This is the sacred space to which the Self-Effacing are drawn; a space that can feel alienating as it serves as a painful reminder of their inability to align with ideals that they value. As Cheryl said, when describing how it feels to fail to live up to the ideal environmentalist standard: "Oh yeah, this again. The theme of this lifetime."

To understand the Self-Effacing eco-type, it's important to fully confront the experience of looking up to and failing to align with a cultural schema of caring for the environment. The Self-Effacing perceive the flagship behaviors of the ideal environmentalist to be virtuous practices, and they experience difficulties and barriers when trying to integrate these practices into daily life. But perhaps this experience of struggling to adopt green practices is less a reflection of the Self-Effacing not caring enough about the environment and is instead tied to their class position and cultural capital. As sociologists have noted, those who embrace low-waste and low-carbon lifestyles tend to be well-educated, relatively free from financial concerns, and to work in fairly prestigious jobs; they have high cultural capital.[9] Of all eco-social relationships, the Eco-Engaged have the highest levels of cultural capital, far higher than the Self-Effacing. Not surprisingly then, eco-friendly consumption, as a cultural practice, can be off-putting and intimidating and difficult for the Self-Effacing to integrate into daily life. From Jim experiencing frustration and envy when he encounters a shopper with green products, to Shelby and Kim who assume this shopper makes a lot more money than they do, the Self-Effacing feel distressed by their inability to be effortlessly green. They are keen to enter the arena of conscious consumerism, but agonize over the tension between frugality and sustainability, sensing competing cultural narratives of moral worth that do not affect the Eco-Engaged.

The Self-Effacing eco-social relationship strikes me as a particularly uncomfortable one. They worry about the fate of the environment but unlike the Eco-Engaged, lack the relatively effortless ability to emulate the ideal environmentalist. They did not grow up in eco-engaged households and they don't have the same level of cultural capital as the Eco-Engaged. Nonetheless, they share the Eco-Engaged environmentalists' fears about the instability and challenges that a changing climate will yield. They worry about the children in their own family, and about future generations more broadly. They look around and see visible reminders that the climate has already changed. In their cultural context, the most prominent model of engagement in environmental protection for civil society is the ideal environmentalist. They intuit that those who align with this ideal are more ethical than they are. In response, they experience a cavalcade of emotions: guilt for not being able to pull off the ideal of the sustainable consumer and resentment and envy toward those who can. Yet the Self-Effacing also have a relatively low carbon footprint, at least on average. While they are less likely to adopt flagship behaviors such as having a hybrid or electric car, eating a meat-reduced diet, and recycling as much of their waste as possible, as a result of their minimal air travel and small homes, their lifestyle generates fewer emissions than other participants in these chapters.

4

The Optimists

People sit and think "the environment" and they think "cars" and they think "pollution" and that is a concern, don't get me wrong. But I think that if they only knew where we were at then, compared to where we're at now . . . It's been a huge change! Things really are improving.
—JENNY, MIDDLE CLASS, LIBERTARIAN, 44 YEARS OLD

The Optimists I interviewed shared a pragmatic orientation to environmental protection, a commitment to community engagement, and a desire to have their relationship with the environment validated in the public realm. Jenny is an ideal example of these themes and characteristics. Jenny is a 44-year-old municipal employee in Whitman, the small farming town in eastern Washington. I interviewed her at work, and throughout our interview we are interrupted by her phone at least a dozen times. Despite being on her lunchbreak, Jenny agrees to the interview and fields calls from community members needing services, filing complaints, or just wanting to talk. Jenny treats each caller with her characteristic friendly nature and determination to help. This job is not Jenny's passion—she has a degree in outdoor recreation and dreams of working in this field when her kids are older and she doesn't need the steady income that her current job provides. Jenny has always had a passion for the outdoors. She grew up camping every summer, until her parents divorced and Jenny and her siblings moved with their mother from their rural community to Seattle. Once Jenny started college, she was able to get back into camping. She describes her hiking and mountain biking trips as giving her a "profound sense of peacefulness" and "euphoria." Jenny loves the environment. But she doesn't worry about environmental issues and bristles at the thought of some people thinking this means she doesn't care about nature.

When I ask Jenny to rate her concern on a 1-to-10 scale, she says her concern is at a "5." In explaining how she arrived at this number, she raises several themes. The first is centered on the environment and people's awareness of it. Like other Optimists, Jenny sees the earth as an immensely resilient system, and she is in awe of the power and robustness of the planet. Jenny tells me she knows there are people who are extremely concerned about the environment, but that she is skeptical of their claims. Her sense is that because she lives closer to the land than someone in a condo in the city, she can see firsthand that the environment is healthy, and she trusts that knowledge more than abstract claims of severe ecological decline. Jenny also shares her perception that things are improving as people's awareness of ecological decline increases. Jenny sees both patterns in her community: the farms around her are productive, which indicates to Jenny that they must be healthy and strong, and local farmers and other people in the town are increasingly aware of environmental issues. By way of example, Jenny tells me the mayor is an advocate of recycling and that many of her friends and neighbors were quick to start using Whitman's new recycling facility. The sources of Jenny's optimism are ecological (the planet is resilient) and social (people are becoming more conscientious).

An additional theme that seems to attenuate Jenny's environmental concern is her frustration that, in her view, many liberal elites reprimand people like her for their beliefs and lifestyles. By placing her concern at a five out of ten, Jenny is taking a stance against what she identifies as a hypocritical and self-righteous group of urban progressives who proclaim environmental doomsday scenarios are imminent. Her logic is that individuals like Hollywood actors and Silicon Valley elites are exaggerating the environmental crisis in part because they just don't know the environment like she does, and in part because they look down on people like Jenny and her neighbors. It annoys Jenny when cultural elites call for more engagement with some eco-friendly choices such as using a reusable water bottle, but fail to acknowledge their own problematic practices. As Jenny tells me, "Hollywood people love to stand up and champion, 'We need to do something for the environment!'" But when she hears them berate people like her for "drinking bottled water," or not "riding a bike," she can't take them seriously. In her opinion, "people like that don't think about how they're burning through clothes, or laptops.

They just tell us not to drive a car." To Jenny, and other Optimists, this is the iconic ideal environmentalist: someone who tells other people what to do and what not to do, but who lacks the knowledge and moral authority to make those judgments. Jenny resents both their cultural hegemony and their antagonistic orientation to her own lifestyle.

Although Jenny is skeptical that we are facing an ecological crisis and doubts the claims of the Eco-Engaged, she still feels it is extremely important to protect the environment. She ranks the importance of protecting the environment at a ten out of ten. That is, like other Optimists, Jenny is not anti-ecological. In fact, a connection to the environment is something she values and takes pride in. As Jenny says, "I'm definitely an outdoors person. I'm a water person. I definitely love the outdoors and my kids do too. We're an outdoor family." Some readers might prefer a label such as "Deniers" for the Optimists, but this would be problematic because it would not capture the ways that Optimists care about the environment. Optimists have a well-rooted affinity for the environment. But they question what they perceive to be overblown claims of an imminent ecological catastrophe.

Getting to Know the Optimists

Nearly 20% of survey respondents and 14% of interview respondents fall into the Optimist eco-type. The defining characteristic of the Optimists is their sense that claims of an ecological crisis are exaggerated. I suggest that this affects their affinity for the environment, but it does not imply that this group doesn't care. Optimists have an affinity for and connection to the natural environment. They pride themselves on knowing the land they live on—they are familiar with the forests and streams in their communities and they see humans as stewards of the environment.[1] The Optimists admire those who rely on natural resources for their livelihood, like farmers and hunters, because they feel these actors know their immediate environment intimately and have a vested interest in finding a balance between economic and environmental goals that also allows local communities to flourish.[2]

If you sift through your networks of friends, family, and acquaintances, can you identify anyone who may be an Optimist? I found that a conservative political ideology is the strongest sociodemographic predictor of the Optimist eco-type. Liberals are about half as likely as conservatives to fit into this eco-type. What I call "eco-upbringing"—the extent to which environmental practices were part of one's socialization—is also significant, indicating that the Optimists have more of an inherited familiarity with environmental

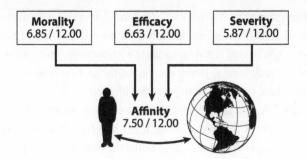

FIGURE 4.1. Eco-social relationship model for the Optimists
Note: 1–4 = disagree, 5–8 = neutral, 9–12 = agree.

practices than other conservatives.[3] Although their upbringing looks different from that of the Eco-Engaged, they share the sense that the environment played a prominent role in their early socialization. This is an important factor to pay attention to when understanding the divisive dynamics between the Optimists and the Eco-Engaged eco-types.

WHAT DOES AN OPTIMIST ECO-TYPE FEEL LIKE?

The Optimists have moderate scores on affinity, morality, and self-efficacy, but their scores on the items capturing perception of the severity of ecological decline is notably low (figure 4.1). They relate to an environment that is tangible and immediately in front of them.[4] When asked to picture the environment, Optimists discuss the fields, streams, and hills or mountains around them. They speak most reverentially about places that they imagine to be devoid of human activity. The possibility of spending time in a natural setting, uninterrupted by sounds of traffic or other people, is something Optimists seek out. They associate the environment with feelings of peace and contentment, whether that's a favorite river for fishing, a nearby area with hiking or ATV trails, or their own farm or backyard.

"I Yearn to Have That Connection to Nature":
Moderate Affinity for the Environment
When I interviewed Bill, we sat at his kitchen table while two of his kids were at school, his wife was at work, and a babysitter watched their youngest child. Bill is a conservative who works as a realtor in Pullman. This is a new career for him, and early in the interview he tells me that one of the most difficult things about having a young family and a busy job is that he's

limited in the time he can spend fishing and hunting. He only gets out to his favorite natural areas once a year now, and even that feels like a stretch for his family's high-paced life. But he tells me that it is essential for his mental health: "It's a longing, it's a yearning. I need to be out and have that connection." He describes himself as, "a true supporter of the outdoors." In fact, Bill moved from an urban area in California to rural eastern Washington precisely because of the proximity to natural areas the community offers.

The Optimists love the outdoors; it is a place where they feel calm and peaceful, and they perceive natural spaces as being healthy and resilient. Shauna, conservative and employed as a legal adviser at a university, tells me, "I really enjoy being outside and in the environment." She explains, "For me, it invokes a lot of happiness or serenity." This is such a consistent pattern—the Optimists experience the environment as a healthy, thriving place where they can get away from the hectic pace of daily life. Even those who live in more bucolic, rural areas, who we might not imagine as needing a respite from urban hustle, describe the environment as a kind of oasis. Sheri, a libertarian who lives on a farm in Whitman, offers a clear illustration of this: "Last night we put in the vegetables in our vegetable garden and spent two hours just out in our beautiful yard." Sheri continues, "That's what I think of as environment." Although, as she explains, "I know it's more than that, but I immediately think about the grass and the trees and the bushes and shrubs and flowers in my yard." Although Optimists prize nature, it is either a specific place that they visit or it's something that's around them all the time. In either case, it is tangible, and their knowledge of these spaces is based on their own sensory experiences. If they encounter published evidence that contradicts their knowledge, they are more likely to trust what they can see, hear, and smell with their own eyes, ears, and nose than the views of anonymous experts.

Optimists feel an affinity for the environment that exceeds their perception of the severity of environmental issues and their sense of moral responsibility to lower their environmental impact. The survey data reflect these patterns. Optimists agree that the natural environment is very important to them, and tend to fall in the range of neutral-to-agree with the statements, "I am very interested in issues relating to the environment," and "I often think about environmental topics" (see "Affinity" score in figure 4.1). When I examined variation in the affinity Optimists reported on the survey, I found that those with the highest scores were male, conservative, and lived in towns, suburbs, or urban areas. I believe this says something about the nature of affinity among Optimists, which I would characterize as a sort of nostalgia for an iconic rugged masculinity captured by archetypes like the self-sufficient homesteader or the adventurous explorer. I noticed that the men I interviewed were more likely to have an emotional, even reverential, connection to the environment, whereas female Optimists were much more matter-of-fact, and less likely to wax poetic about a favorite river or mountain. This pattern is also an important point to balance a more frequently shared association with conservative men: their tendency to deny climate change. Learning about the Optimists offers a novel way of understanding an eco-social relationship that many social scientists characterize as anti-ecological.[5]

"Mother Nature Has a Really Weird Way of Working Things Out": Ecological Decline is Exaggerated

One of the most unique features of the Optimists is this combination of having a great deal of respect and appreciation for the natural environment alongside the perception that environmental issues are not something to worry over. Immediately after Bill tells me about how he yearns to be in nature, I ask him if he worries about the impacts that people are having on the planet. He politely shares his view that "I think it's more, well, political. Like imposing restrictions and making it seem worse than it is." In this case, Bill is speaking to concerns about "running out of this or that species" and sharing his frustration that when hunting season is restricted, it becomes "crazy and dangerous." He sums up his views: "I think that there's great aspects to population control for the animals, and hunters play a big part of that. But I don't see the environment deteriorating." Bill agrees that the issues we do have are, in his words, "a man-made problem," but he doesn't think they are intractable or urgent. He explains, "I don't necessarily want to worry myself to death about the environment when . . . I think it's still going to be here when I die, and when my kids die, and when their kids die." In short: "Mother Nature has a really weird way of working things out."

The Optimists feel very confident in their knowledge of local ecosystems: they bear witness to ecological changes over time, and feel that there is nothing or little to worry about in the changes that they see. In their minds, the planet is not vulnerable; the planet is resilient and powerful. The Optimists look around them and feel good about the state of human-environment interactions. Where does this sense of optimism come from? Certainly, there are prominent thinkers whose optimism about environmental issues seems bolstered by a faith in technological innovation. Environmental social scientists often allude to the views of these so-called "techno-optimists" as an influential factor driving the denial of climate change.[6] Yet, I only interviewed one Optimist who conveyed this sort of belief in technology. Scott works in purchasing at a university, where his job entails introducing technological solutions to reduce greenhouse gas emissions. When I ask him how he feels about the state of the planet, he is optimistic: "I look at the environment in a positive way." This is because Scott is buoyed by advances in technology: "Look at the progress we've made with vehicles as far as pollution and gas economy. We use less fuels and we go farther and it pollutes less." Scott trusts that leaders in the corporate sector like, "Elon Musk and the guys at Apple and the guys at Google" are actively pursuing sustainability and will "make a big impact." The way things are going, in Scott's opinion, technology that doesn't harm the planet is, "just around the corner." I expected more Optimists to agree with Scott, since past literature emphasizes the centrality of techno-optimism to positive assessments of ecological decline. Yet Scott was an exception. Other Optimists were extremely skeptical of technological solutions. If faith in technology is not the root of Optimists' evaluation of environmental issues, then what is?

First, Optimists see nature as resilient. The time they spend in the outdoors bolsters their suspicions that claims of environmental demise are exaggerated and that "Mother Nature" will work things out. Shauna tells me that while she sees consumerism and materialism as threats to ecological integrity, she doesn't worry because, "in the long run, the environment does change over time, and it has different ebbs and flows, and I think it will withstand that." Shauna's faith is not based on a sense that humans are good for the planet, but that the planet has the capacity to withstand the destructive systems that humans have created. Optimists often tried to make sense of why others are so worried about environmental issues, and drew attention to their own familiarity with natural areas in order to understand this gap in responses to ecological decline. Jeff did so when he told me that he thought people in cities are the ones panicking about environmental problems. In his view, they are "out of touch with the environment." He explains, "They don't see—they can't go down to places like the Snake River and see the beauty there."

The second reason for Optimists' perception that ecological issues are not severe is based on their sense of a growing awareness in the population. Tina, a conservative who owns and manages a farm with her husband, tells me that while she still thinks, "we have a long ways to go to improve the environment," she feels hopeful because, "we have more people thinking about ways to do better." She points to growing awareness about recycling, which she hadn't even heard of when she was little, and is common now. Scott, the techno-optimist quoted above, tells me he puts himself in this increasingly aware group. He says five years ago he would have scoffed at the notion that the combustion of fossil fuels is causing the climate to change, but that he now trusts that information and has learned a lot about the environmental impacts of various energy sources. While he is not going to get a hybrid or electric car, because "that just doesn't make sense yet, financially," he is pleased to see how engaged the students at his university are in environmental issues. He says if he were younger and buying his first vehicle, he would buy a hybrid.

The Optimists do not worry about ecological decline. Survey respondents who fall into the Optimist eco-type report some of the lowest scores on measures of severity (see "Severity" score in figure 4.1). On the items, "Humans are using up the earth's resources," and "Environmental problems are much more serious now than they used to be," the Optimists' scores are only higher than those of the Indifferent. On the item, "Protecting the environment should be among our country's top priorities," Optimists' average scores are low and are similar to the Fatalists'. On average, they disagree with all of these statements. The only sociodemographic variable that can explain heterogeneity in the perception of severity is political orientation: conservative Optimists report lower scores on the severity measures compared with liberal Optimists.

In terms of their specific concerns over environmental issues, Optimists are most worried about water pollution and least concerned about climate change. This is consistent with Optimists' orientation toward an environment that is immediate and tangible, rather than something they have not seen with their own eyes such as an image of the earth from space or a photograph of a polar bear on an ice floe. This emphasis on the tangible dovetails with my Optimist interview participants' views about climate change. As Aaron McCright and Riley Dunlap's research shows, within the US, conservative white males are more likely than any other sociodemographic group to deny climate change.[7]

Among my interview participants, Optimists were most likely to challenge climate science. I did not ask all of my participants about climate change specifically, yet nearly one-third raised the issue. Of these, four were Optimists who expressed doubts that climate change is an urgent and pressing issue and relied on the argument that the earth's surface temperatures change naturally over time. Sheri told me that "every time I hear about global warming, I remember I took an astronomy class . . . actually, it was several science classes and I remember in the textbooks, seeing these graphs of the earth warming and cooling, warming and cooling." Sheri tells me, "The bulk of that graph happened before industrialization. The earth goes through cycles, the sun goes through cycles, and sometimes there's ice in places where we don't want it. Sometimes it's hot where we don't want it. But we adjust and the earth adjusts." As a climate scientist would point out, Sheri is right that there have been warming and cooling periods over at least the last million years. But she is overlooking overwhelming evidence that carbon dioxide emissions are now leading the current warming trend rather than simply being an indicator of changes in global surface temperatures.

What I want to highlight in Sheri's comments is her perception that *the earth adjusts*. This is central to an Optimist eco-social relationship. Also common among the Optimists I interviewed is a sense that the government cannot be trusted to relay scientific evidence. To Sheri and others, the government uses climate change and other environmental issues, "to ramrod legislation and other kinds of political decision making that have very . . . they have a glaze of environmentalism, but there's really something else going on." Across each of the issues I included in the survey, Optimists tend to be more concerned than the Indifferent, to have similar levels of concern as the Fatalists, and to be less concerned than the Self-Effacing and Eco-Engaged.

"Leave it Better Than You Found It": Moderate Moral Responsibility

Because the Optimists are so antagonistic toward the ideal environmentalist, and seem fairly unconcerned over evidence of ecological decline, it would be reasonable to expect that they feel no moral responsibility for environmental protection. Yet this would be inaccurate. Optimists had moral impulses that centered on stewardship and conservation. Their moral responsibilities were voiced in phrases they shared like, "Pack it in, pack it out," and "Leave it better than you found it." But while the Eco-Engaged and the Self-Effacing might take such expressions to refer to the entire planet, the Optimists applied this ethos to the ground beneath their feet. The Optimists I interviewed described these phrases as representing how they care for the environment, and they advocated for these efforts to be recognized as pro-ecological in mainstream culture. They were the only group to consistently tell me, "*I* should be considered an environmentalist!"

Optimists feel strongly that humans should "care for the land," as Sheri puts it, and they perceive individuals to have moral responsibility in this domain. When I asked Sheri what she thought were the most important things people could do to protect the environment, she says, "be a good steward on the land, educate yourself to do that, and raise awareness about it." For Bill, this is what he does as a hunter and fisher. He believes his fees for licenses serve as important tools for maintaining parks and protected areas, and tells me he is often picking up litter when he's outside and tells his children to do the same. In fact, he runs a "Green Club" at their school and litter clean-up is part of the Club's mandate. For him, this is a moral responsibility: "As a hunter, as a fisher, you respect the environment, you take care of the environment. That's part of the hunting code."

Although Optimists are neutral about their moral responsibilities, they are quite actively engaged in eco-friendly practices. The average Optimist survey respondent has moderate scores on the items, "I have a moral responsibility to reduce my impact on the environment," "I worry about my impact on the natural environment," and "I try to reduce the amount I consume in order to protect the environment" (see "Morality" score in figure 4.1). Although the Optimists' summed scores are higher than scores for the Fatalists and the Indifferent, they are much lower than those of the Self-Effacing and the Eco-Engaged. Within the Optimist category, women who grew up in environmentally active households and who currently have a high household income report the highest scores on items measuring the degree to which people feel morally responsible for reducing their environmental impact.[8]

The Optimists I interviewed and surveyed are engaged in environmentally responsible practices, such as buying local foods, reducing and recycling waste, and growing food in a garden. Optimists in the survey self-report engaging in sufficiency practices frequently (second only to the Eco-Engaged) and practice efforts to reduce consumption with the same frequency as the Self-Effacing (see figure 4.2). The survey data indicate that Optimists who grew up in environmentally active households report more frequent engagement in eco-friendly consumption than those who did not. With respect to reducing consumption, older and racially diverse Optimists report the highest frequency of engagement. Older Optimists who grew up in environmentally active families report the highest level of engagement in sufficiency practices. The Optimists that I interviewed associated many of these practices as pro-environmental, but rejected the premise that such efforts convey moral worth. I want to underscore that point: Optimists saw environmental practices as pragmatic and rejected the ideal environmentalists' view that they have a moral responsibility to engage in pro-environmental

consumption. This is not a disengaged group. But the Optimists
are far less likely than those with
other eco-types to use moral language to describe efforts to reduce
or green their consumption.

Although Optimists express a
sense of moral responsibility to
actively keep the land clean, they
tend to feel that this ethos is not
valued in the wider culture, particularly by urban, liberal, Eco-
Engaged environmentalists. Tina
argues that she and her husband

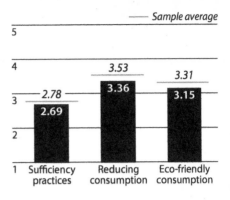

FIGURE 4.2. Optimists' engagement in
eco-friendly practices
Note: 1 = never; 5 = always.

should be considered environmentalists, because "we take care of the land
we have." Tina isn't necessarily opposed to the ideal environmentalist, but
she doesn't like what she sees as a tendency for the Eco-Engaged to tell
others what to do. In Tina's words, "I don't think I should be telling someone
else what they need to buy. You can educate, don't get me wrong, but I still
think I can't enforce my views and my thoughts on other people." Optimists
believe their eco-type is widely and frequently denounced in society, and
describe feeling that because they are not seen as caring about the environment, they are treated as inferior to the Eco-Engaged. Consider Bill's
relationship with his liberal sister who lives in Seattle and reflects the ideal
environmentalist. When Bill's sister visits, she reprimands Bill and his wife
for driving too much, for using plastic water bottles, and for not having a
composter for their food and yard waste. Bill says it feels like his sister looks
down on him because he doesn't do these things. As he explains, "She's not
really listening to what I say because according to the world, she's doing the
right thing. She's not going to listen to me." Optimists sense that their eco-
social relationship is overlooked and devalued, particularly by Eco-Engaged
liberals whose own orientation to the environmental reflects the prototypical ideal environmentalist.

Seemingly in response to feeling like their relationship to the environment is denigrated in mainstream culture, Optimists challenge the ideal environmentalist. Some of these critiques are about *access*. For example, Scott
and Shauna describe the uneven access to the sorts of amenities that make
it easier to bike, buy green products, and so forth. Scott points out that "the
organic line is always more expensive than the non-organic line." Shauna

notes that in addition to the income required to be Eco-Engaged, having a lifestyle in keeping with the ideal environmentalist is also more accessible to those living in a city: "A lot of the people I know who live in larger cities ride their bike everywhere and have more products available to them." Other critiques focus on the *limited material effectiveness* of green consumption. Tina tells me that someone she knows frequently drives long distances to buy organic products, and can often be overheard boasting of the environmental benefits of organic production. But Tina is skeptical: "Some people who buy all the green stuff are making a trip to the city every day to get it." Although she appreciates that "they think, 'doing this this makes me an environmentalist,'" she critiques their narrow thinking: "they're not thinking about the other impacts they have," referring to the greenhouse gasses emitted from traveling to stores with organic products. Finally, some Optimists are critical of the *culture of consumerism and status consumption* that eco-friendly shopping reproduces. For example, Sheri suggests she is skeptical of the altruism behind a lot of eco-friendly consumption, telling me, "A lot of the time it just seems like they're trying to impress their neighbors" In Sheri's mind, this is problematic because it doesn't challenge consumerism: "that's still 'keeping up with the Joneses,' it just has an environmental spin to it. It's still consumerism."

"You Can Only Do So Much": Moderate Self-Efficacy

I see the Optimists' perception of the severity of ecological issues as pragmatic in tone. This same spirit of pragmatism is also evident when Optimists discuss their own capacity to implement their environmental ethics into daily life. Although Optimists are generally quite confident about their contributions to environmental protection, they also don't compare themselves to an out-of-reach cultural ideal. For the Eco-Engaged and Self-Effacing, the ideal they aspire to emulate is someone who has drastically reduced their footprint, someone who grows their own food, has solar panels, and drives a hybrid or electric car. But the Optimists' ideal seems attainable: anyone who is aware of the land they live on and leaves it better than they found it. Interestingly, elements of the ideal environmentalist are also infused into Optimists' moral commitments, particularly eating locally, being conscious not to overconsume, and being mindful of waste. Although the Optimists I interviewed sometimes told me they would like to engage in these sorts of practices more often, they did not attribute their low level of engagement to either a moral failing or a lack of agency.

The Optimists expressed a relatively high level of self-efficacy, even though they weren't deeply committed to environmental practices. In our interviews, Optimists told me they felt like they did their part for the environment. For instance, Bill describes what he thinks a responsible citizen does to contribute to environmental protection: "I think we need to do our part and act responsibly. I believe in recycling." Likewise, Shauna says she feels good about her everyday practices, because, in her words, "I take steps to try and be aware of, you know, the energy that I am using and recycling and things like that." Optimists are aware of a more demanding model of ecological citizenship, but they aren't aspiring to meet it. As Tina explains, "I can only do so much. I guess you could worry yourself to death over it. But I think we are doing what we can to teach our children to improve, which is important."

Optimists' sense of self-efficacy is reflected by their responses to questions about the extent to which their lives are oriented to protect the environment. I asked survey respondents to indicate their agreement with the items, "I always do what I can to reduce my impact on the environment," "I am able to do what it takes to reduce my impact on the environment," and, "I have oriented my life around my desire to reduce my impact on the environment" (see "Efficacy" score in figure 4.1). Optimists tend to express neutral responses to these items. My interview data suggest this is not because they are critical of their capacity to act on their moral impulses, but because they do not see individuals as bearing the responsibility to protect the environment. The variation in these responses to the self-efficacy questions is only explained by eco-upbringing, as those Optimists who grew up in environmentally active households are more likely to express a stronger sense of self-efficacy. This makes sense, since having access to environmental practices during socialization should make their adoption more straightforward as an adult.

Capturing the Optimists' sense of efficacy to protect the environment also requires looking at how they evaluate the responsibility and trustworthiness of other actors and institutions. In the survey data, Optimists tended to see all actors and institutions as having roughly equivalent degrees of responsibility to protect the environment, from nonprofit organizations to businesses (figure 4.3). Compared to other eco-social relationships, Optimists had a relatively high level of trust in each of these groups, with the exception of governments and businesses. As I discussed earlier, in reference to climate denial, the Optimists that I interviewed often conveyed a

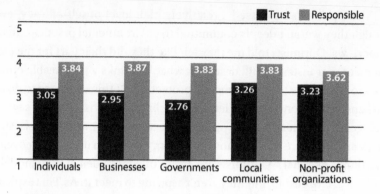

FIGURE 4.3. Optimist respondents' opinions of various actors' responsibility for environmental protection and trustworthiness
Note: 1 = not at all; 5 = very much.

sense that the government uses environmental policy as a Trojan horse to push an agenda.

"My Friends Are Environmentalists, But They Would Not Want You to Call Them That": Complicated Relationality

Earlier, I described how Optimists feel urban liberals misunderstand and deride their eco-social relationship. When it comes to looking at relationality among Optimists, this becomes important again. In the interviews, I asked people whether their friends and family felt the same way they did about the environment. The Optimists told me that, yes, their friends and family felt as they did. But the common ground they shared was a sense of frustration with "environmentalists" who feel their approach to protecting the environment is the only one that is honorable and virtuous.

In Optimists' social circles, calling someone an "environmentalist" is not a compliment. As I've already noted, Optimists don't like the ideal environmentalist. As Sheri tells me, "there's a lot of conversations that happen around the dinner table on Sunday afternoons about the 'damned environmentalists.'" Part of what the Optimists resent is their sense that this ideal environmentalist is the association many people have when they are imagining who cares about the environment. The Optimists were most likely to tell me that they and their closest friends and family are just as worthy of being considered environmentalists, and to suggest they want to reclaim the term. For instance, Tina thinks her father-in-law should be considered an environmentalist. She explains, "he would definitely tell you he's not environmentalist, but he is. He is committed to being a steward of the land."

Scott tells me that even though his friends wouldn't buy organic foods, they are "very attuned to the environment around them."

When I asked survey respondents whether most of their friends and family worried about environmental issues, Optimists had a fairly low average score. They tended to disagree with the statements, "Most of the people I'm close to try to reduce their environmental impact," or "I prefer to spend time with people who care about the environment." These statements make up a measure of relationality, and when I examined what sociodemographic traits were related to this variable, I found that political ideology and eco-upbringing matter. Politically liberal Optimists who grew up in environmentally active households are more likely to agree with the three statements above, especially compared with conservatives from less environmentally engaged backgrounds. This suggests that even within the Optimist eco-social relationship, higher cultural capital, politically liberal people are most likely to evaluate others based on their responses to ecological decline.

The Optimists' Environmental Impact

Although the overall footprint scores for the five eco-types don't differ significantly, Optimists have the among the largest average household and per person footprint estimates. The average Optimist household generates 18.7 tons of CO_2e each year (ranging from 2.5 to 95 tons), and the average individual Optimist generates 7.8 tons (ranging from less than one to 58 tons). These estimates are above the sample averages for both household (18.1 tons) and per person (7.1 tons) footprint. Forty-four percent of the Optimists I surveyed believed that their footprint was the same as the average American. Only a small fraction of the survey sample overall felt that their impact was likely larger than the average, and the Optimists are consistent with this pattern, with only 1.9% estimating that their footprint was above the national average. That is, like the Eco-Engaged, Optimists underestimate their impacts on the environment.

Optimists engage in a relatively large number of flagship behaviors. For instance, Optimists are second only to the Eco-Engaged for the percent having solar power for their home and not driving a gas- or diesel-powered vehicle. Optimists are also second only to the Eco-Engaged for the percent of respondents indicating that they eat a vegetarian or vegan diet. And while Optimists fly more than most other eco-types, they fly less frequently than the Eco-Engaged.

BOX 4.1. Examining the Composition and Sociodemographic Antecedents of Optimists' Carbon Footprints

The composition of an average Optimist's carbon footprint is much more similar to the Eco-Engaged than to the footprint of the Self-Effacing (figure 4.4). As you can see in figure 4.4, nearly half (45%) of the Optimists' footprint is comprised of emissions from ground transportation, and one-third is comprised of home energy use. The percentage of carbon emissions from flights is lower than for other eco-types. The only variation in household carbon footprint within the Optimists is explained by gender—female Optimists report lower carbon footprint scores than male Optimists.

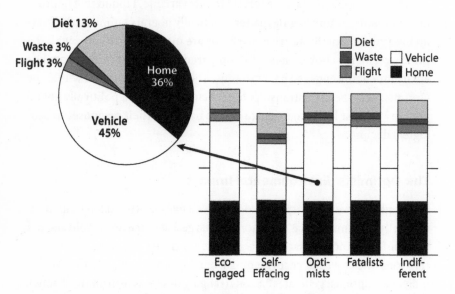

FIGURE 4.4. Composition of the average Optimist survey respondent's household carbon footprint against size and general composition of the footprint of other eco-types

Relating to the Optimists

When I've presented this research to academic audiences, I often lose people's willingness to cultivate curiosity and practice empathy when I get to the Optimist eco-type. My audiences may roll their eyes at the sanctimoniousness of Eco-Engaged judgments and sensibilities, but there is an implicit understanding that their hearts are in the right place. But when I describe an eco-social relationship predicated on a perception that climate change is natural, or not such a big deal, many people's hackles are up immediately. How could someone who doesn't accept climate science or feel intense concern about the state of the planet possibly care about the environment?

THE PERSONAL AND CULTURAL CONTEXT
OF THE OPTIMIST ECO-TYPE

Many of the Optimists I interviewed were raised in families that spent time in nature and engaged in environmental practices. Unlike the Self-Effacing, who struggle to feel the effortlessness of aligning with the ideal environmentalist, the Optimists express confidence in the moral worth of their eco-social relationship. The combination of being confident that they care about the environment, recognizing that they care in a way that is different from the ideal environmentalist and Eco-Engaged, and sensing that the Eco-Engaged denigrate the Optimists' way of caring for the environment are interconnected dynamics shaping this eco-social relationship. Most Optimists were raised to see humans as stewards of the earth and to evaluate their impacts with the mantras of outdoor enthusiasts: "Pack it in, pack it out" and "Leave it better than you found it." This is the belief system that feels right and natural for Optimists. While they wouldn't condemn anyone for driving a big diesel truck (since it leaves their immediate environment looking no worse for wear and may facilitate travel to a valued natural area), Optimists denounce those who litter, vandalize, or in any way render their environs looking worse than they found them.

The Optimists described their social networks as populated with others who shared their environmental beliefs and practices. However, while the Eco-Engaged were surrounded by people who were interested in low-carbon living, the Optimists seemed to be connected by a shared frustration with those "damned environmentalists" who denigrate the Optimists' eco-social relationship. Optimists spend time with people who share their sense of being excluded from environmentalism. Their close friends also know the experience of having what feels like a virtuous eco-social relationship denigrated in mainstream culture. The Optimists and their friends and neighbors rebut these critiques of their eco-social relationship by arguing that liberal Eco-Engaged environmentalists can't really *know* the environment from the vantage point of their condominium in the city.

With respect to the cultural context of the Optimists, I *first* note that the "environment" that the Optimists confront is local and immediate. The environment is something you can take in and evaluate with your senses: you can assess its vitality through seeing, smelling, and listening.[9] The environment cannot be captured in photographs of earth from space or graphs of carbon dioxide in the atmosphere. If Optimists look around at their local environment and feel that its issues can be fixed, or that the places they value are healthy and resilient, then they see no need to panic. Because I interviewed people in the midst of fire seasons so aggressive and severe that, in 2015, President Obama declared a state of emergency in Washington, I thought this might feel like evidence that all was not well in the immediate environments of my participants. Certainly, that was the case among most people I interviewed, but not among the Optimists. They interpreted these fires as part of a natural cycle that shows the planet is doing what it has always done to keep ecosystems in balance.[10] In short, the environment is resilient; it is tangible and close, and therefore knowable.

A *second* factor shaping this eco-social relationship is that Optimists perceive others, particularly urban liberals, as being critical and judgmental of their environmental beliefs and actions. They sense that political liberals and well-educated, wealthy urbanites look down on their relationship to the environment and they don't accept that judgment. More than any other eco-social relationship, the Optimists are constantly challenging the premise of the ideal environmentalist. I picture the Optimists as backed into a corner and swinging. A large part of their connection to the environment is a defense of their own impulses, in response to feeling devalued by broader society.

Finally, it's important to recognize the wider cultural context of climate denial, in which the Optimists certainly play a role. As a growing cadre of social scientists and journalists have demonstrated, fossil-fuel companies like ExxonMobil and BP have invested in think tanks designed specifically to spur doubt about climate science, acting directly and through these think tanks to propagate public mistrust of climate scientists and climate mitigation policies.[11] I am confident that many of the Optimists I interviewed had been on the receiving end of these efforts to dispel doubt, since many of the counter-climate-science arguments that Optimists posed mirrored those disseminated by fossil-fuel interests, such as the framing of climate change as "natural" or as a "risk," not a reality. Just as the Eco-Engaged feel an affinity with, for instance, marketing and television shows advancing the moral worth of the eco-conscious consumer, Optimists encounter a familiar and trustworthy cultural schema in archetypes of an independent thinker who questions scientific evidence shared by the government, and who trusts their own senses to evaluate ecological decline based on what is immediate to them.

Many environmental social scientists and political liberals express an aversion toward the Optimists' eco-social relationship. In some ways, this is understandable, in that this is a strongly conservative eco-social relationship, and content in polls, media, and academic studies shows that conservatives' opposition to environmental policy is a barrier to achieving sustainability and confronting climate change. But, in this chapter, I demonstrated common ground between the Optimists and other eco-types, and demonstrated how they care about the environment. Optimists vilify people they see as overconsuming—like Bill, who says he has little respect for "somebody who lives excessively. You know, they have their house and toys and cars and their X, Y and Z." And Optimists idealize many environmentally friendly practices. Shauna says, "I would like to have a space where I could do more gardening and just producing my own vegetable and things. I would ride my bike more or try to use, you know, walking or biking as means of transportation." For the Optimists, caring about the environment means spending time in sacred natural areas and intimately knowing those spaces, and their own communities. They argue that they too care about the environment, and advocate for their eco-social relationship to count as an "environmentalist" one. The Optimists relate to a tangible environment that is immediately surrounding them. They perceive this environment to be healthy and resilient and feel capable of addressing any ecological issues that arise. They reject the notion that ecological decline is urgent and catastrophic.

5

The Fatalists

If tomorrow we all were gone, another billion years from now, the earth will do just fine. No problems. It would redo itself, cleanse itself, be fine.
—TED, LOWER CLASS, CONSERVATIVE, 40 YEARS OLD

Ted is a 40-year-old truck driver who works for an agricultural company and lives in Whitman, a small, agricultural community in eastern Washington. We sat down in a local pizza restaurant to conduct the interview, and spoke for nearly two hours. Ted loves the natural world—his ideal leisure activity is a day of hiking or fishing, which he does whenever he has time off. In his words, "I just like being outside. Fresh air and clean water. Just love it. The joy of it. I love outside." The only television Ted watches consistently is programming about the environment, and this is his primary source of information about environmental issues. He is upset about the impacts humanity has on the world, voicing deep and diverse fears: "I think about the oceans. I think about all the garbage in them. I think about global warming and everything that's happening in the environment. It's not in a good spot."

Ted believes he should do something to help, but he feels both powerless and conflicted in his response to ecological decline. When he contemplates the sorts of actions he could take, he tells me it's just so depressing that he tries to take his mind off the environmental damage he sees instead. He says, "What can I do? I recycle. I cut my little plastic bands in the garbage. Recycling, really, is all I can do. It's like, 'let it go' kinda thing, because what am I gonna do? I'm not gonna change the government. I'm not." In the face of the severity of ecological decline, and Ted's diagnosis of how humanity has come to have such a deleterious impact on the planet, the sorts of individualized responses emblematic of the ideal environmentalist feel laughably ineffectual.

Ted and the other Fatalists have a critical and nuanced assessment of the political and economic landscape of our era. Ted refers to this landscape as, "the big picture," a term he uses throughout our interview to contrast with his own limited power and agency. The big picture refers to the degree of influence that governments and corporations have on the architecture within which individuals like Ted are forced to live. Ted sees the state and the corporate sector as deeply invested in using their power to create profits for already wealthy actors and institutions and to prolong their control over society. In his words: "It seems so much like corporations and government are so corrupted. The whole system is corrupted, so it's really hard to make anything happen." Ted's prognosis of the likelihood governments will protect the environment is bleak. He tells me, "I think governments are never gonna protect our interests. They're just gonna protect their own interests. And that means getting the funding from the corporations." In Ted's view, the market is far more powerful than the state: "Big corporations are gonna rule, and have for a long time, I think." In terms of his assessments of the political and economic landscape, Ted's views are fairly consistent with a sociological critique of contemporary democracy.[1] As the sociologist Stanley Lieberson wrote back in 1985, "Those who write the rules, write rules that enable them to continue to write the rules."[2]

In the Fatalists' diagnosis, ecological decline is a consequence of unchecked corporate power. As a result of how much power corporations have, and their vested interest in profiting from natural resource exploitation, Fatalists have little hope of societal transformations. Many elements of their views, though perhaps not the cynicism, can be found in scholarly discussions of the barriers to meaningful efforts to protect the environment.[3] In making sense of how it has come to pass that US residents have such egregious impacts on ecological integrity, Ted looks to what he perceives as the corporate-driven rise of consumer culture. He shares with me his opinion that corporations have turned America into a nation of consumers for their own profit: "these corporations want to make money, so they try so many ways to get people to buy stuff." And, he says, they're succeeding. They're creating "a little magical fantasy world. I see America as a giant shopping mall. I really do. I love America, love living here, but I see it as a giant shopping mall. That's all we are anymore. Shoppers." Ted is caught in an impossible quagmire. He sees "the big picture," which reminds him that as an individual, he has very little power to change anything, including environmental problems. He is familiar with the cultural ideal of an ideal environmentalist, but he is not assuaged by the promise of shopping his way to a greener future.

Ted doesn't trust the underlying theory of change that animates the practice of voting with your dollars, since it's premised on change starting with individuals choosing from options offered by corporations. As I noted above, Ted feels that the structure of daily life, from what's on the shelves in stores, to what's on television, to the availability of work, is all controlled by corporations via their relationship to the state. As he remarks, "I think individuals just kind of fit into whatever piece is there." Therefore, reversing ecological decline needs to start with corporations: "If corporations make a change, people will kind of gravitate toward it. I think that's where the change will happen. People are automatically already doing the little things. Recycle this, buy this, it's all good. Until big corporations make a big change, you're not gonna make a big impact."

Despite feeling that individual, consumer-based efforts are futile, Ted nonetheless thinks it's impressive when people purchase eco-friendly products. Describing green consumers, Ted believes, "They just care more about the environment, what they're doing, and what their impact is. Their footprint on the earth, they care more about it." Ted tells me he sometimes buys recycled paper towels, because, as he says, "I just think it's a better choice." But he's not convinced that he's actually making a difference: "I think I feel better about it, but I don't even know if I'm making an impact or not."

Ted has a number of insightful critiques of consumer-driven ecological reforms. First, he shares his observation that the number of products on the shelves of our retail spaces has grown exponentially over his lifespan, a point he makes to illustrate that the rate of consumption is overtaking any material benefits that green products might offer.[4] What Ted is pointing to here is that it is the actual rate of material production and consumption that matters—not how eco-friendly some of those goods may be. If production and consumption are increasing exponentially, he argues, spending money on an organic product to try to save the planet is a fool's errand. Ted's opinion seems to reflect what the environmental sociologist Richard York has proven through his research: that introducing cleaner, greener alternatives into a marketplace does not displace the older, less environmentally friendly options. The new green product or innovation is simply added to the existing array of choices.[5] One of the ironies about the Fatalists is that this eco-social relationship seems to have been overlooked by environmental social scientists, yet this is the group that makes sense of ecological decline in a way that is most consistent with arguments from environmental social science.

Ted's second critique of eco-friendly consumption relates to the expense and limited availability of ethical consumer goods—points made by Optimists as well. Ted's critique doesn't come from a social justice vantage point; it is driven by his suspicions of the theory of change underlying conscious consumption. He tells me that it's impossible for conscious consumption to save the planet because so few people can afford to shift all of their purchases to eco-friendly options. He argues that the ideal environmentalist model of eco-social change would only be materially effective if everyone engaged in it, which Ted doesn't see as probable. To reverse ecological decline, Ted suggests, corporations need to stop producing damaging goods altogether and slow the rates of production. Ted doesn't see this as a likely outcome since slowing production would affect corporate profit margins. The only other option he can see is for the government to use its regulatory power to limit corporate hegemony. This seems just as unlikely to Ted, given the influence that corporate elites have on the US political system.

The Fatalists confront ecological decline with a deep sense of powerlessness. They don't feel like they consume profligately—they don't have yachts, private jets, or second homes. But they are aware that the cumulative impact of American households is ecologically untenable. Our everyday lives collectively use a prodigious amount of resources and create air, water, and soil pollution, even though no single person wishes to have this effect nor has much capacity to impact service delivery or production lines.[6] For the Eco-Engaged, like Eileen and Nadine, actions such as growing food, driving an electric car, or eating a vegan diet offer the comfort that comes with taking what feel like meaningful actions. Confronting ecological decline while making small sacrifices to be a more ethical consumer offers the Eco-Engaged a sense of virtue and control. But Ted and other Fatalists don't see these actions as an effective approach to protecting the environment. So how do the Fatalists experience ecological decline?

Ted's approach is consistent with many other Fatalists. He finds solace in reminding himself about ecological resilience. As he tells me, "I think the earth will fix itself if we're gone." This doesn't let humanity off the hook: "Of course, we need to fix ourselves, I think that's very important." He just doesn't think we can do it: "Is it gonna happen? I doubt it." The only happy ending Ted can picture is the eventual demise of humanity: "If tomorrow we all were gone, another billion years from now, the earth will do just fine.

No problems. It would redo itself, cleanse itself, be fine." In the Fatalist's imaginary, the end of the story is when our species has undermined our own capacity to live on the planet. Like Ted, many of the Fatalists see this as a happy ending—for this is when the earth can start to regenerate.

Getting to Know the Fatalists

Only around 14% of the survey sample (and 8% of the interview sample) fit into the Fatalist eco-type. Compared with the Eco-Engaged, who are easy to spot, with their reusable mugs, cloth bags, and hybrid cars, the Fatalists have a lower profile. You are most likely to identify a Fatalist by talking with them. You would hear their frustration with overconsumption, concerns about overcrowding on the planet; they might tell you about their lack of trust in the government, their belief that in contemporary America corporations have all the power. Ultimately, you would hear that the Fatalists appreciate the planet and are upset with humanity's impacts on ecological integrity. But they don't have any faith in the ideal environmentalist. The only narrative that they draw on to offer a hopeful outlook is the belief that our species is nearing the end of our tenure on earth.

Do you know any Fatalists? In terms of their sociodemographic characteristics, they are likely to be conservative and are unlikely to have grown up in environmentally active households. They are also likely to be younger and to live in a rural area.[7]

WHAT DOES A FATALIST ECO-TYPE FEEL LIKE?

Fatalists share a sense that environmental problems are serious but they are skeptical of the efficacy of the ideal environmentalist. Fatalists worry that the environment is facing severe ecological decline, but they do not feel a sense of moral responsibility to address this decline in the way that the Eco-Engaged and Self-Effacing do. Like the Self-Effacing, they doubt their own efficacy to effect pro-environmental change (see figure 5.1).

"For Me, It's Everything": Complicated Affinity

The Fatalists I interviewed conveyed a range from moderate to strong affinity for the environment. Those with a strong affinity told me nature is the best thing about life. Many of the Fatalists I interviewed face struggles every day: uncertain employment, low wages, a lack of stable housing, loss and illness in their families. Amidst this chaos, the natural world feels like a haven—a

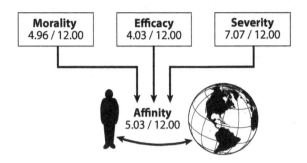

FIGURE 5.1. Eco-social relationship model for the Fatalists
Note: 1–4 = disagree, 5–8 = neutral, 9–12 = agree.

place to find peace and joy and comfort. I interviewed Charles, a liberal, in a local café in Pacifica. Charles is in his late 60s. Although he currently lives in a rented home with several roommates, he was homeless for several years, when the boat he previously lived on was destroyed in a storm. When I spoke with him, he had recently retired after a career of manual labor. After the loss of his boat, which was uninsured, Charles has had to go back to work as a night janitor for several local restaurants. The boat was his only significant material possession and his social security payments don't cover even his modest expenses, so retirement was really not an option for Charles. When I asked what he pictured when I said "environment," Charles closed his eyes and, in his soft-spoken voice, said: "For me, it's everything. It's the best of this life." Charles moved to the island where he now lives after visiting it once. As he tells it, "When they dropped the ramp of the ferry, I was overwhelmed with . . . (pause) . . . coming home. I'd never been here. That was it. I've been here for 26 years."

Fatalists don't think about the environment very often, although environmental issues are important to them. Darren is retired, a grandfather, and a conservative-leaning Vietnam War veteran living in Whitman. Darren tells me he'd like to be considered an environmentalist. He qualifies this: "Not, I guess, a flag-waving sort, but yeah, I do care. Anything I can do, I do." When I ask him what he does, he tells me, "Not much. I don't guess it really crosses my mind that often." Darren describes feeling, "Sadness. An overwhelming sadness," when he pictures the environment. This is because he can't stop noticing all of the damage humans have wrought on the planet. Like Ted, Darren primarily watches nature channels on television and has been concerned about the environment since his time in Vietnam. As he recounts, "We just nuked the environment over there. Just razed it. Terrible."

Don, a liberal who drives a taxi in Pacifica, tells me that he feels disgusted with what humanity has done to the earth and tries not to think of it too often. He has felt this way a long time: "I've been disturbed by the presence of humans in the physical environment since I was a boy of seven or eight." He explains this is "because it was obvious to me that humans were polluting the environment, with their automobiles, and their gasoline, garbage, and everything else."

The survey data suggest that the natural environment is important to the Fatalists, and that they feel somewhat interested in, but rarely think about, environmental issues. Overall, the Fatalists have among the lowest scores for affinity, higher only than the Indifferent (see "Affinity" score in figure 5.1). Of course, affinity varies, and variation among the Fatalists is shaped by their socialization. Fatalists who were introduced to environmental practices as children are more likely to self-report a higher level of affinity for the environment. This is a consistent theme across all eco-types—those who grew up immersed in environmental practices generally feel a stronger affinity for the environment than those who didn't.

"It's Not in a Good Spot": Ecological Decline Is Severe and Inevitable

The Fatalists have a grim diagnosis of ecological health and a pessimistic outlook on the future of eco-social relationships. As Ted says, about the planet, "It's not in a good spot." Whether it's pollution in the oceans, global warming, or plant and animal extinction—issues the Fatalists discuss at length and in detail—they are appalled at what our species has done and have no hope that we will turn things around. Don's comments on the future of eco-social relationships are particularly vivid. His perspective on humanity is that we are a greedy and violent species and that we have undermined our own capacity to survive. He sounds almost pleased by this—he doesn't feel that humans deserve to persist on the planet. He tells me, "I just think we are due for a real slap in the face, collectively, as a species." In his view, "We are a violent species and we are destroying the planet. And I don't care for it." As he puts it, "It's heartbreaking some of the things that are going on. It just breaks my heart."

Don's comments about the severity of ecological decline are consistent with the survey results, which showcase an eco-social relationship characterized by the perception that the environment is in a crisis as a result of human activities. The Fatalists report consistent agreement that environmental problems are more serious than they used to be, humans are using up the earth's resources, and that environmental protection should be one of the nation's top priorities (see "Severity" score in figure 5.1). Above, I noted that Fatalists who grew up exposed to environmental practices expressed stronger affinity for the environment. Interestingly, with respect to severity, I found those from eco-engaged homes diagnosed environmental problems as *less severe*. Conservative Fatalists and those with less education also perceived ecological decline to be less severe than did their well-educated, liberal counterparts. Many existing studies find that political conservatives and people with less education tend to be less concerned about the environment.[8] I argue that this is partly a reflection of efficacy and partly influenced by the prevalence of the ideal environmentalist. Environmental education researchers Harold Hungerford and Trudi Volk demonstrated that those with less education tend to feel less empowered to take meaningful actions generally and in the context of environmental protection.[9] In an article coauthored with Parker Muzzerall, I argued that the schema of the ideal environmentalist appeals to liberals more than conservatives, and that some conservatives react to the cultural hegemony of this schema by rejecting claims of catastrophic ecological decline.[10]

When I look to specific environmental issues, I find that Fatalists express low levels of concern, roughly equivalent to the Optimists. On a scale from one (not at all concerned) to five (extremely concerned), Fatalists are least concerned about climate change and most concerned about water pollution, but their average scores hover around "3." Why would Fatalists deem the environment to be in crisis, yet express such low levels of concern for specific environmental issues? My guess is that this is because Fatalists trust that the planet will be fine when humans are gone and because they feel powerless to effect any change. The Optimists also place hope in the resilience of the planet, although the two groups get to this conclusion from different starting points: Optimists think ecological crises are exaggerated and that "Mother Nature will work things out," while Fatalists agree with characterizations of the planet as suffering, and believe it will only recover once we are gone—a perspective that aligns with their experience that humans are violent and destructive. The second reason why Fatalists might express little concern for environmental issues lies in their low sense of self-efficacy and social efficacy more broadly.

"We Need to Wake Up": Moderate Moral Responsibility

The moral foundations of the Fatalists' eco-social relationship are interesting. On the one hand, this is a group that seems to take pride in their commitment to recycling and picking up litter, but on the other hand, they are also the only group whose theory of ecological destruction is not at all individualized. If you think back to the Eco-Engaged and the Self-Effacing, you might recall that those eco-types vilify individuals who they see as being greedy and overconsuming. A big footprint, to someone with an Eco-Engaged eco-type, is a household that buys more than they need—whether that's a pick-up truck as a status-symbol, or a yacht. But the Fatalists don't have consumers in their gaze: they look to corporations as the guilty party. When I asked Fatalists if they felt that people have a moral responsibility to protect the environment, they cautiously answered, yes, but qualified their answer, arguing that responsibility should be tied to impact and that corporations have far greater impacts than individuals. Yet blaming corporations and the state that permits exploitation doesn't mean Fatalists let themselves off the hook for their own actions.

Fatalists see corporations as highly immoral, pursuing profits at the expense of human and ecological well-being. When I introduced Ted, I described his analysis of corporations as embedded in natural resource exploitation for the purpose of maximizing profits. This diagnosis is highly consistent with the Treadmill of Production theory, developed by environmental sociologist, Allan Schnaiberg.[11] In the Treadmill model, the corporate sector undermines ecological health by extracting natural resources and generating waste and pollution from production processes. This is also how Darren understands ecological harm. When I asked him to picture a person with a big footprint, he told me he doesn't picture an individual, but thinks corporations fit that model more clearly: "it's the big corporations that dump their waste and pollution—that's where the big impacts are gonna be." And with respect to natural resources, "they're gonna take and take and take 'til there's nothing left to take." Treadmill theory brings together capital, environment, and labor—demonstrating how public and private investments in labor-saving technologies increase both the amount of natural resources used in production and the pollution generated by the production process. Ted's analysis of environmental issues is not dissimilar to this, though he doesn't integrate impacts on workers. Referring to corporations' never-ending pursuit of profits, Ted offers an example: "They create more coffee shops where you gotta go buy more coffee that you don't even need. And then they use that money to make more coffee shops. It's just ridiculous. It's like a snowball effect."

Why would society put up with a production cycle that benefits corporations and harms workers and the environment? The Fatalists address this conundrum in a similar way to Treadmill theorists. In the Treadmill of

Production theory, one reason why the state supports this cycle of exploitation is corporate lobbying.[12] Here is Darren again, sharing his theory of ecological decline: "Corporations slide all this money to these politicians to vote one way or the other." But what about civil society? In Treadmill theory, civil society is rendered blind to the effects of the treadmill because we have become dependent on the jobs and economic growth produced through the treadmill. Although Fatalists don't state this diagnosis in such stark terms, I often heard them tell me they think people need to wake up. Or as Don puts it, "People are asleep." He says this in the context of a critique of bottled water. Don describes the way that Nestlé has depleted groundwater stores across the country, "bottling it for their water business" and "claiming some corporate right to do this." Don thinks Nestlé should be shut down, but because the towns where they operate get "some jobs," people don't notice "that the corporation is doing very negative things to the planet." Fatalists demonstrated a stronger capacity for sociological critique than any other eco-type, yet this group has been overlooked by environmental social scientists.

Fatalists clearly see corporations as both morally responsible for ecological decline and as unwilling and unlikely to act with integrity. But despite rejecting the premise that if individual households reduce their consumption, we can effectively confront ecological decline, Fatalists still feel morally responsible for doing their part. Darren tells me, "Whenever I see trash, I pick it up." Even Don, who says, "I don't think it's our job to protect the environment," still recycles religiously, and makes art installations from discarded goods he finds in his community. He has a vegetable garden and composts his kitchen waste to make soil for it. Charles described his efforts at shopping in the bulk section and bringing his own containers in order to use less plastic. What is unique about these practices, in contrast to the Eco-Engaged and the Self-Effacing, is that the Fatalists do not see these sorts of individualized actions as a moral imperative for society. When it comes to the conscious consumer model at the heart of the ideal environmentalist, Fatalists are pretty derisive. As Don puts it, all the "Vote with your dollars, 'Save the earth' stuff is a lot of nonsense. We are the problem." In an almost understated turn of phrase, in light of the rest of our interview, Don says: "I don't have much hope for the future of human beings." Fatalists take on these actions as part of being a good person, but they remain unconvinced that their efforts are materially or culturally impactful. The moral contours of the Fatalist eco-social relationship are closely tied with their sense of efficacy, both personal and societal.

Fatalists in both the interview and the survey feel more strongly that they have a moral responsibility to protect the environment compared

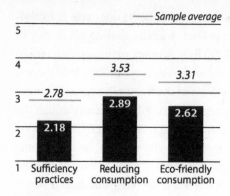

FIGURE 5.2. Fatalists' engagement in eco-friendly practices
Note: 1 = never; 5 = always.

with the extent to which they worry about their impact or try to reduce how much they consume (see "Morality" score in figure 5.1). Overall, this leaves Fatalists with the second-lowest level of perceived moral responsibility to protect the environment (above the Indifferent). Among Fatalist survey respondents, women who grew up in environmentally active households with university-educated mothers express the strongest agreement with statements about moral responsibility. These patterns suggest that cultural capital plays a role in shaping Fatalists' moral frameworks in the context of environmental protection. People who grew up in higher cultural capital households are more likely to feel a personal moral responsibility to protect the environment, even within the Fatalist eco-type.

Fatalists are relatively unengaged in environmentally relevant practices. They are only more engaged than the Indifferent in eco-consumption, reducing consumption, and are equivalent with the Indifferent for sufficiency consumption (figure 5.2). There is some variation in Fatalists' engagement in environmental practices. Making sense of this variation requires a look at cultural capital. Fatalists who currently practice eco-friendly consumption grew up engaged in these practices and in higher cultural capital activities like attending artistic performances. These patterns underscore the argument that green consumption is a classed practice associated with cultural capital. Even beyond eco-friendly consumption, Fatalists who grew up in environmentally active households are also more likely to try to reduce their level of consumption and to engage in sufficiency consumption. Fatalists in towns and suburbs report higher levels of engagement in reducing consumption than those in rural areas, indicating that there are place-based, community-level influences on Fatalists' engagement in these practices.

"It Just Feels Pointless to Worry": Low Self-Efficacy
The Fatalists evaluate their self-efficacy even more negatively than the Self-Effacing, as they incorporate a sense of doubt about the power of individual action writ large. The Self-Effacing convey a belief that if they could only

care about the environment as the Eco-Engaged do, then humanity would have a greater chance of reversing ecological decline. In contrast, Fatalists argue that their own ability to effect pro-environmental change is unimportant and that society as a whole is ill-equipped to protect the planet. Low self-efficacy is infused throughout my interviews with Fatalists—they feel strongly that there is nothing they can do to alter the course of ecological decline. They see this trajectory as so inevitable that they liken it to a law of nature. As Charles says, "It just feels pointless to worry about the environment." He tells me, "I don't carry anxiety about [environmental issues], because it's like the rain. You have to accept it. You can fight it, you can yell about it, you can do whatever you want. Nothing will change."

The Self-Effacing evaluate their own efficacy as low, but Fatalists evaluate the efficacy of humanity to be low. Fatalists tell me that because humans have created a society that is destructive, there is no way out. Right after Don tells me that he tries to be as environmentally responsible as he can, he follows up with a caveat: "well, as much as is possible given the restraints of our culture." When it comes to enabling responsible eco-social relationships, Don explains, "I don't think the system is set up that way." Ted's comments shed some light on the sort of structural constraints Don is describing: "the government isn't going to make the corporations do what they need to do, and the corporations just tell us what they need to so that we keep buying whatever they're selling."

There are two ways that this low efficacy emerges in the survey data. With respect to the three items measuring self-efficacy, Fatalists are higher only than the Indifferent. They report low levels of agreement with the statements, "I always do what I can to reduce my impact on the environment," "I am able to do what it takes to reduce my impact on the environment," and "I have oriented my life around my desire to reduce my impact on the environment" (see "Efficacy" score in figure 5.1). The variation in responses to these items can be partially accounted for by looking at age and eco-upbringing, as older Fatalists who grew up in eco-engaged households tend to express a stronger sense of self-efficacy than others. Or, in other words, younger Fatalists who did not grow up in environmentally active households feel particularly powerless to effect pro-environmental change. This points to the possibility of either a generational effect or an age effect. That is, it could be the case that younger Fatalists who did not grow up immersed in eco-friendly activities will eventually develop a stronger sense of self-efficacy as they age; it might be that younger people with a Fatalist eco-type have always felt relatively powerless. Alternatively, it could be that pressure to align with the ideal environmentalist is particularly acute in contemporary culture,

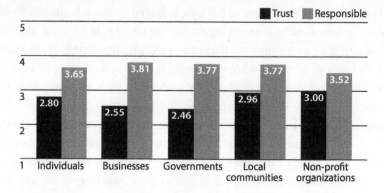

FIGURE 5.3. Fatalist respondents' opinions of various actors' responsibility for environmental protection and trustworthiness
Note: 1 = not at all; 5 = very much.

and that in this context, those who have a Fatalist eco-social relationship and who did not grow up in environmentally active households are at a unique disadvantage, and experience this as a lack of self-efficacy.

Second, I noticed this low level of efficacy when I asked survey respondents who is responsible for protecting the environment, and the extent to which they believe those entities will act on that responsibility. Fatalists see all entities as relatively equally responsible, ranging from individuals at the lower end to governments at the higher end, but they have very little confidence that any institution in society can be trusted to protect the environment (figure 5.3). Fatalists have particularly low levels of trust in governments and businesses, and have more trust in local communities and nonprofit organizations (figure 5.3). When Fatalists look around at the institutions that should be protecting the planet, they feel little to no hope that they will do so. This "trust" gap is especially large for governments, as Ted illustrated so emphatically. Given that Fatalists identify corporations and an acquiescent government as culpable for ecological decline, it is unsettling to see such low scores for "responsibility" in figure 5.3. Yet if we think about the question of responsibility as reflecting both what ought to be as well as what is likely to be, it becomes more understandable that the disaffected Fatalists would communicate their resignation to the status quo.

"Most People I Know Just Let it Go in the One Ear and Out the Other": Low Relationality

The environment is not a common topic of conversation in the Fatalists' social networks. When it does come up, it is often as part of an indictment that the world more generally is in dire straits. Ted tells me about a recent conversation he had at work. In his work as a truck driver, Ted is often on the road at the same time as his four colleagues. He explains that they have conversations over the radio about, "all kinds of stuff. Some of which I can't talk about here." When I ask him to recount the last conversation that was relevant to the environment, he told me he had recently read, "that the average American consumes more than 34 Kenyans." So, he brought that up on the radio: "Then they started talking about it." Overall, they all agreed on a few things. First, that there are, "Too many people on the planet." Second, "that America is a giant shopping mall." And third, that "you can't fix it, but it's a big problem."[13]

Although Fatalists recounted conversations in which they discussed the severity of human impacts on the planet, they rarely raised examples of people in their lives who engaged in practices they perceived as caring for the environment. As Darren said, when I asked if the people he knows try to reduce their consumption, "most people I know just let it go in one ear and out the other." Charles is an exception. Through his involvement as an actor in a local theatre group, he has met people who he perceives as caring a great deal about the environment. Describing a friend of his, Charles explains, "She's vegan, she's a naturalist. Very fanatical about the environment." He tells me that her home is, "full of gardens and everything, but also nature. She only cleared what she had to." Charles then tells me about friends who are homeless and sleep in the forest: "they do their own litter patrols, even where they don't sleep, making sure there's no litter, that it always stays clean."

It is uncommon for Fatalists to point to people in their social circle who are taking what they see as meaningful steps toward protecting the environment. On the survey, Fatalists' scores on the items measuring relationality are only higher than scores among the Indifferent. For each item, "most of the people I'm close to are very worried about the environment," "most of the people I'm close to try to reduce their environmental impact," and "I prefer to spend time with people who care about the environment," the Fatalists' average scores are in the "disagree" to "neutral" range. Are there Fatalists who do use evidence of environmental commitments to evaluate their social worlds? Yes, and those who do are likely to have grown up in environmentally active households. Once again, this pattern points to cultural capital and a mechanism for creating social networks comprised of people who share an orientation to the environment and ecological decline.

The Environmental Impacts of the Fatalists

The Fatalists have an above-average household carbon footprint (18.6 tons), which ranges from 2.7 to 95 tons. However, Fatalists often live in larger households, and when we look at per person footprint estimates, the Fatalists actually have slightly lower-than-average footprints (6.5 tons, ranging from less than one to 48 tons). The average per person footprint in my sample is 7.1 tons. Over 60% of Fatalists estimate that their household resembles the American average, in terms of their carbon footprint, and this is a fairly accurate guess. The Fatalists are among the least engaged of all eco-social relationships in flagship behaviors such as having a hybrid or electric car, recycling, and reducing their meat consumption. They are among the most likely to drive a gas- or diesel-powered car (second only to the Self-Effacing) and they are among the most frequent flyers (second only to the Eco-Engaged).

Relating to the Fatalists

Much existing research on human-environment relationships relies on dichotomies that contrast those who are "pro-ecological" or "biospheric" with people who are "anti-ecological" and "egoistic." These tidy distinctions blurred and disintegrated when I sat down to listen to a diverse array of people describe their perceptions of and responses to ecological decline. For example, looking at the Fatalists' scores on the survey gives the impression of a group of people who don't really care about the environment very much. They don't seem too concerned about climate change or air pollution, they are not engaged in efforts to practice conscious consumption, and their scores for affinity, morality, and efficacy are remarkably low. But to conclude that Fatalists don't care is inaccurate.

THE PERSONAL AND CULTURAL CONTEXT OF THE FATALIST ECO-TYPE

At the heart of the Fatalists' eco-social relationship is a sense that humanity has an overwhelmingly negative impact on the world. Fatalists believe that human impacts on the planet are undermining our own existence, but that when our species is out of the picture, the environment will recover. Fatalists don't want to feel as though they are making the problem worse. They try to take small steps in their own lives to improve the world—picking up

BOX 5.1. Examining the Composition and Sociodemographic Antecedents of Fatalists' Carbon Footprints

Looking at the breakdown of their carbon footprint (home energy use, ground transportation, air transportation, recycling, and diet), the Fatalists look most similar to the Self-Effacing: home energy use comprises just over a third of emissions, while vehicle use makes up just under half of emissions (see figure 5.4). Income is the only variable significantly related to Fatalists' carbon footprint, with wealthier Fatalists more likely to have a larger carbon footprint than lower-income Fatalists.

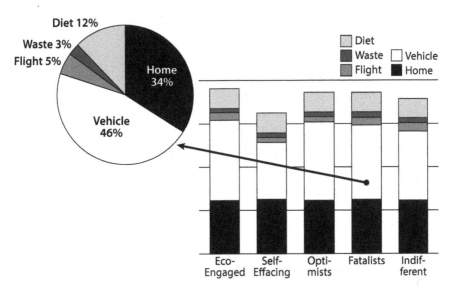

FIGURE 5.4. Composition of the average Fatalist survey respondent's household carbon footprint against size and general composition of the footprint of other eco-types

trash, recycling their cans. But their greatest strategy for accepting ecological decline without feeling debilitating sadness and remorse about it is to avoid thinking about changing it. Charles likened ecological issues to the rain. They just happen. There's nothing he can do about it. As Charles explains, that's "Because it's not like there are options. The situation exists. It's not going to change." The Fatalists approach ecological decline from a place of acute powerlessness, and this sense of powerlessness is not unique to environmental issues. In response to that sense of powerlessness, the only way to move forward with grace and dignity is to try not to think about human impacts on the planet and find some comfort in the possibility that things will improve when our species is gone.

The Fatalists' sense of powerlessness is infused throughout their social context. It is uncommon for Fatalists to know people who demonstrate self-efficacy in the environmental domain. When the environment is a focal point of conversation in their social circles, it is to share evidence of the failure of society to deliver an equitable and sustainable world. Not only do Fatalists and their friends and family perceive environmental problems as serious, they also perceive powerful actors as having no interest in ameliorating environmental issues. This leaves Fatalists further convinced of their own powerlessness and pessimistic about our common future. In the face of this level of powerlessness and pessimism, it is not at all surprising to me that Fatalists see little value in using their consumer choices or political voices to make the world a better place.

The cultural narratives about the environment that the Fatalists are attuned to are distressing. They read and watch accounts of human impacts on the planet that convince them of the severity of ecological decline, but they do not encounter any narratives of ecological reform that feel feasible and effective. Fatalists perceive their government as having failed to protect them and the people they know. In their view, the government exists to serve the interests of corporate America. They still feel strongly that we need the government on the side of the people, but have no hope of that happening.

Fatalists see corporate power as the root cause of eco-social problems. In their view, because corporations exist to create profits, and rely on exploiting workers and natural resources to do so, they will continue to harm people and the planet until they are restrained by the government. But as they observe corporate actors' success in influencing who runs for government and in lobbying elected representatives to favor options that sustain corporate power, Fatalists cannot imagine governments committing to the sort of regulatory frameworks that are needed.

The Fatalists are aware of the ideal environmentalist in their cultural milieus, but this schema is not as influential for them as it is for the Eco-Engaged and Self-Effacing. Fatalists feel that shopping for change and relying on individuals to fix the problem represents too weak a solution to confront the problems posed by a large and growing population that is constantly encouraged to consume beyond our needs and means. While they are dismissive of political consumerism as a tool for social change, Fatalists place more hope in collective action. Yet here too, they are resigned to inaction and a continuation of the status quo, as they perceive too few people to have the time, knowledge, money, and energy to engage in sustained activism, and perceive the state and market to be too powerful to be influenced by civil society.

For Fatalists, caring about the environment is depressing. They sense that humanity has come close to destroying the planet and see everyone as implicated in this decline, particularly governments and the powerful corporations who have a stranglehold on democracy. They see ecological decline as a further sign of the failure of society to uphold the common good. Fatalists don't feel a strong moral responsibility to engage in individualized actions to protect the planet and try to avoid thinking about environmental problems, because it's too painful. They make a minimal effort in their daily lives to effect eco-social change, either through the conscious consumer practices of which they are skeptical, or the sort of collective actions they see as more promising, but difficult. As they reconcile the tension between recognizing an environment in decline and encountering few feasible channels to meaningfully engage in reversing that decline, Fatalists conclude that the planet will be better off without humans. And in the meantime, they aim to do as little damage as possible within the confines of the cultural, political, and economic structures that shape their social worlds.

6

The Indifferent

My concern for the environment out of ten? I'm a four. I'm not too
concerned. I feel bad about the ice cap and the polar bears, but I don't
know . . . I wish maybe they would pass more laws; I suppose.
I don't know how that would be helped. I am not a lawyer. I'm not
a judge. I'm not any kind of fancy politician, so I don't know.
—AVERY, MIDDLE CLASS, LIBERAL, 45 YEARS OLD

Avery works as a librarian in Pullman, and we spoke in the library during her lunchbreak. When I asked Avery what she pictured when I said
"environment," she provides a stream-of-consciousness, word association
response: "I guess something like green, water, grass, outdoors, trees, Al
Gore, you know? Garbage, unfortunately. Conservation. The polar bears that
are dying, you know. It's very sad." The defining characteristic of the Indifferent eco-type, and one that distinguishes it from others, is a quality that
comes through Avery's comments—this sense of being a passive observer
of the environment, rather than an active participant. When the Indifferent
talk about their upbringing, they often mention things like growing up on a
farm, or camping with their parents, but while other people point to these
experiences to justify why they care so much, the Indifferent do not. Instead,
they point to their upbringing as they explain why environmentalism is not
for people like them. The Indifferent were most likely to try to convince me
it was a waste of my time to engage them in an interview about the environment, often by telling me how little they knew about ecological matters. My

interviews with the Indifferent were the shortest in duration and there were few subjects in our conversations that animated this group.

When sociologists James Jasper and Jane Poulsen sought to explain why some people join social movements, they suggested that experiencing a "moral shock" can be an important antecedent to movement participation.[1] In other words, if someone sees something terrible and devastating, such as witnessing animals in a feedlot, they can be motivated to take action to address that phenomenon. A compatible theory related to consciousness and social change exists in environmental sociology—people tend to become aware of their reliance on resources like clean air and water, when the provision of those services is disrupted in some way.[2] Might the Indifferent be able to be "shocked" into a different eco-social relationship? In the town where Avery lived, smoke from a nearby wildfire had recently ground daily activities to a halt. The streets were deserted, businesses were closed, and the sun was small and pink behind thick smoke. People were told to stay indoors and were advised of the risks of the smoke-filled air. I thought this event might have intensified Avery's concerns for the environment, or at least for her own health or the health of her family. But that's not what I heard. Avery did describe how the smoke disrupted her family's daily routine: "That was really hard for our kids, actually. We couldn't take them to the swim park, we kind of had to restrict their outdoor play, just because it was so smoky and hot." Not only was it hard for her two young children, "it was also really hard for us, being parents, having to keep your kids cooped up and entertained inside when you are trying to explain to a 6- and a 7-year-old why they can't go outside and play." But the fires did not deliver a moral shock to Avery, nor prompt her to reflect on the worsening frequency and severity of wildfires in the Pacific Northwest.[3] She explains, "it was, like, stinky and smelly but we ran a humidifier in our house to filter out some of the smoke."

Among the Indifferent, a possible link between a disruptive, potentially upsetting event and a heightened commitment to addressing or even acknowledging environmental issues remains unformed, even in the face of crisis. This link doesn't materialize because the identities of the Indifferent have virtually no tie to either the biophysical environment or the environmental movement, and the Indifferent feel incapable of effecting any change to the natural world. These twin themes—an identity that is unrelated to the physical environment or efforts to protect it alongside a sense of limited capacity to effect pro-environmental reforms—emerged frequently in my interview with Avery. In particular, Avery conveyed a sense of having limited efficacy. When I asked what it felt like to live in a smoky and, as she suggested, unhealthy environment, Avery's response conveys a dialectic of low concern and low efficacy: "Well, it makes me sad obviously, because I realized all those trees were burning down. But, you know (pause), I guess you can't (pause), that was a thing that you couldn't really control, so it's not like I blamed anybody." She summarizes her thoughts on the matter, "I guess it made me sad, but what can you really do? I can't go to volunteer and fight a fire (laughs). I don't even think I want to! That sounds too scary." On the one hand, it sounds like because the environment is not top of mind for her, Avery does not see herself as the sort of person who would be out there getting involved in environmental issues. On the other hand, it also sounds Avery attenuates her level of concern as she evaluates her ability to protect the environment. Put simply, Avery gives me the impression that she doesn't see engagement in environmental protection as something for people like her, even though she would like the environment to be protected.

Although the Indifferent have a low level of interest in the environment and cannot picture themselves engaging in environmental protection, they nonetheless recognize and admire the ideal environmentalist. Avery tells me several times how impressed she is by her neighbors who drive an electric car and eat a vegetarian diet. She describes this family with pride, as she tells me that people in her neighborhood are quite "environmentally friendly," which she knows because of their choice of vehicle and their dietary restrictions. But Avery cannot imagine taking these sorts of actions herself: "At this point in my life, I can't see it happening." This was a common refrain among the Indifferent: that it is impressive that some people take actions to reduce their environmental impact, but that such a commitment is not feasible for a person like them. Again, in addition to perceiving a gap between their own identity and the identity of an environmentalist, there is also an element of powerlessness to the Indifferent eco-type. Avery's ranking of her concern for the environment is a good example of this powerlessness:

> My concern for the environment out of ten? I'm a four. I'm not too concerned. I feel bad about the ice cap and the polar bears, but I don't know . . . I wish maybe they would pass more laws; I suppose. I don't know how that would be helped. I am not a lawyer. I'm not a judge. I'm not any kind of fancy politician, so I don't know.

Avery doesn't feel capable of contributing to environmental protection. She thinks it's important to protect the environment, but does not see herself as being at all influential in that fight. As she says, "I don't have time to do that, and I have no interest in doing that."

I recognized over the course of this research project that I have tried to cajole many of the Indifferent I've encountered in my life to care about the environment in the way that I do. Particularly when I was in my 20s, I felt passionately that my power to stop climate change was to reduce my footprint and get others to do the same. I felt a need and a license to convince people, one-by-one, that they should care about climate change in the same way, and as passionately, as I did. Perhaps unsurprisingly, this was not a very effective technique. For example, when I spoke with my mother-in-law, a nurse, about the threat of climate change, she would respond by sharing her opinion that a much more immediate risk to humanity was a flu to which we had no immunity. She wasn't trying to tell me not to care about climate change, just that she was more concerned about a global pandemic. But I experienced her response as a personal affront, and assumed it meant she didn't care about the environment. (Writing this book in the midst of Covid-19, not a flu of course, but nonetheless a pandemic, it's not beyond my notice that she had a point!) This is all to illustrate that there are some issues with which I don't identify. It doesn't mean I don't care about them. The same themes emerged in my interviews with Avery and other Indifferent participants: the Indifferent do not identify with environmentalism, but that doesn't mean they don't care about protecting the environment.

Getting to Know the Indifferent

Only 7% of the survey sample, and 17% of the interview sample, fit the Indifferent eco-type. The Indifferent share a low level of affinity for the environment and express little emotion about ecological decline. They also don't express any sense of personal responsibility to help protect the planet. Put simply, it isn't their issue. Their identity is in no way dependent on having a connection to nature, or climate change, or climate action, or environmental justice, or any other phenomenon related to human-environment interactions. They still see the ideal environmentalist as positive—they just cannot imagine themselves aligning with this ideal in the foreseeable future. In terms of their sociodemographic characteristics, people holding an Indifferent eco-type are likely to be older and politically conservative, and they are unlikely to have grown up in an environmentally active household.[4]

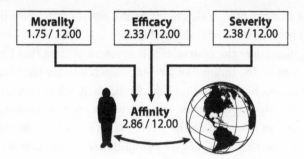

FIGURE 6.1. Eco-social relationship model for the Indifferent
Note: 1–4 = disagree, 5–8 = neutral, 9–12 = agree.

WHAT DOES AN INDIFFERENT ECO-TYPE FEEL LIKE?

The Indifferent have distinctly low scores on each element of eco-social relationships: affinity, severity, morality, and efficacy (figure 6.1). The most evocative image I can offer of the Indifferent eco-social relationship is of watching human-environment interactions from the sidelines. The Indifferent are not emotionally invested in environmental issues. Even when confronted with an environmental problem, from contaminated water to wildfires, the Indifferent respond with a figurative shrug. They don't get drawn into worrying about ecological decline and they don't feel like they are either strongly positively or negatively affected by the environment. This low level of affinity permeates all facets of their eco-social relationship, just as a low level of efficacy permeated the Self-Effacing and Fatalist eco-social relationships. The Indifferent cognitively accept that the planet is in a state of ecological decline, but they observe this as passive bystanders.

"It's Just There, You Know?": Weak Affinity for the Environment

The environment is a subject that the Indifferent rarely think about. Consider my interview with Christine, in the small farming community of Whitman, where she grew up. Christine is a 28-year-old conservative who does not vote and who works part-time as a home care aid. Her boyfriend was at work while I interviewed her and she was home with two of her children—both under three years old. Christine started our interview by trying to convince me I shouldn't interview her, because she didn't know anything about the environment. When I asked her what she thought of as the environment, she said, "I don't know, just what's around you. It's just there, you know?" Christine does not convey a deep emotional attachment to the environment, nor did she seem to be imagining any particular ecosystem or place of personal significance. The environment is just in the background. I interviewed Burt at a café down the road from where Christine lives. Burt, also conservative, is in his late 60s. He is trying to retire from his job as a farm laborer, but continues to need to work for financial reasons. My interview with Burt began in a similar way to my conversation with Christine—Burt stressed that he had little to offer in an interview about the environment, and this was a refrain he returned to often. When I asked what he pictured when he thought of the environment, Burt said, "I don't know. I'm not all up on all that."

The Indifferent participants I interviewed gave me the impression that the subject of environmental protection is very much in the periphery of their consciousness. When I asked Myra, a liberal in Pullman, what comes to mind with the word "environment," she laughs: "Well I picture, like, green things?" She then explains, "Like, I care, but I'm not really reading anything or being an activist. You know, like if it's right in front of my face I might do it but I'm not pursuing it, if that makes sense." Myra senses what someone who feels a strong affinity for the environment would do, and makes clear that this is not part of her lifestyle. The Indifferent convey this sense of having a degree of awareness that there are actions a person could take to protect the environment alongside a feeling that those actions are not feasible given the parameters of their lives.

The Indifferent not only perceive the environment as existing in the background of their lives, they also prefer this. Sarah is a recently retired English teacher and lifelong Republican voter who lives in Pacifica. Sarah's home is in the more affluent of the two neighborhoods in which I interviewed people. When I ask Sarah what she appreciates about the environment, she tells me she likes it when her surroundings are clean and tidy, and that she notices when this tidiness is compromised: "What I hate to see is trash on the side of the road. That's what I will notice when I'm out on a walk." I also notice this preference to keep the physical environment in the background when Sarah describes environmental tensions in the town where she lives. Many of the people I interviewed in Pacifica noted that there is a high level of conflict in the community between those who encourage more development and those who want to protect undeveloped areas. Sarah does not want to take a position—she simply dislikes the conflict. In her words, "I feel very sad about it. About the contention and the anger on the island." In her assessment, this is an instance where, "the natural environment is hampering the community environment." Sarah wants the environment to stay in the background—she dislikes when it looks unclean or becomes an issue of contention that divides her otherwise peaceable community.

This weak affinity for the environment shows up in the way the Indifferent describe their interest in environmental issues and subjects, and the importance they place on the environment. On the survey, the Indifferent consistently scored the lowest on the measures of affinity. They disagreed with each of the items, "I often think about environmental issues," "I am very interested in topics related to the environment," and "The natural environment is very important to me" (see "Affinity" score in figure 6.1). There was very little variation in this general lack of affinity, but Indifferent respondents with higher incomes tended to convey weaker affinity for the environment than those with lower incomes. If Sarah's experience applies for others, this might be because wealthier people have more capacity to adjust their living situations if the environment around them becomes contaminated.

"I'm Not too Concerned": Watching Ecological Decline from the Sidelines

Consistent with their tepid affinity for the environment, the Indifferent also have quite muted views on the severity of ecological decline. As Avery succinctly states, when I ask how worried she is about the environment: "I'm not too concerned." The unconcerned Indifferent extrapolate from their own experiences of ecological crises as they evaluate the severity of environmental issues more generally. For instance, Burt tells me he thinks that the Environmental Protection Agency is overreacting when they warn people about the impacts of pesticides on human and ecological health. Burt has had pesticides on his skin, and even in his eyes. But he was unphased by these experiences, since, in his words, "I'm still walking and breathing." This leads him to feel that, generally, people who worry about the environment are, "too negative, if I can put it that way. They don't understand."

The Indifferent also maintain a low level of concern simply because of the hectic nature of their lives. When I ask Amber, a conservative in Pullman, what she thinks about climate change, she tells me, "Sometimes we watch documentaries and things like that about it." She feels that "It [the environment] is really good to think about." But any concern it generates in her is ephemeral: "Twenty minutes later, the kids need something, and your mind goes back to that." The Indifferent evaluate environmental issues as not warranting alarm. This evaluation seems to rest on two things. First, evaluating the local environment as healthy, as Amber says, laughing, "We are in our little bubble here and everything grows and it's green and we have healthy drinking water and so the concerns are not directly affecting me." In this tendency to align their environmental concerns with their perception of the health of their immediate surroundings, the Indifferent are similar to the Optimists. Second, the Indifferent have a distinct tendency to think of environmental topics infrequently, and even then, to have those thoughts washed away by the tide of everyday responsibilities.

Some might suspect the Indifferent simply reflect environmental privilege. Environmental privilege is a form of environmental inequality that describes inequitably distributed access to healthy and beautiful ecosystems versus toxic or dangerous environments.[5] Those with environmental privilege are situated in safe and picturesque settings, while those without environmental privilege live or work in ecologically unhealthy settings. Is it possible that the Indifferent are apathetic because they have never known what it is to live and work in a toxic or dangerous environment? After analyzing the data to explore this possibility, I can confidently say, no, the Indifferent are not disinterested in environmental protection because they feel protected by privilege. Only one Indifferent interview participant, Harriet, a Republican, seems to clearly reflect the notion that indifference can be borne from privilege, aside from Sarah. Harriet grew up in a wealthy agricultural family. She is in her 70s and her primary residence is in Pacifica. In our interview, she is terse and her answers are to-the-point, and she often expresses a sense of annoyance at being asked about her feelings for the environment. When I ask her about any environmental problems that she may have experienced, she tells me she has only been aware of pollution when she traveled to the Global South. Like Sarah, Harriet tells me that she takes pride in the cleanliness and tidiness of her local environment.

Harriet's experience of strictly encountering environmental contamination as a tourist was not common among the majority of the Indifferent interview participants. In fact, of all the people I interviewed, the Indifferent shared some of the most challenging experiences with human-environment conflicts. Above, I talked about Burt, who got agricultural chemicals in his eyes. This happened at work—Burt was sprayed in the face with a chemical pesticide. He just got in the shower and washed out his eyes. Burt recounts, "I wasn't really that worried until, like, the manager showed up when I was in the shower." His manager kept asking him if he was okay. Burt continued insisting, "They're fine, I can see just fine." In fact, he says, "It was basically the people talking that probably scared me the most. I knew that if I got it washed out quick enough, I wouldn't have no damage done." Sure enough, he tells me, his eyes are fine now. For the Eco-Engaged or Self-Effacing eco-types, this could have been a turning point—having chemicals in their eyes might prompt them to reflect on what these chemicals do to insects, soil, water. For Burt though, this was an experience he just wanted to move past.

There are several examples like this. Consider Amber, who grew up in a town where nuclear waste is stored—and which is frequently in the news in Washington because of accidents and spills. Amber tells me that recently, "the ground on top of one of the containers with all the hazardous material sank," and as a result, there were reports in the news that "there could be some leakage of hazardous material." Amber has friends and family who are employees at the nuclear waste facility and I ask if they are worried, or if she worries about them. "Everybody is fine," Amber tells me. She explains that stories like this are routine where she grew up, and companies have response protocols in place to deal with risks, "It's kind of just a part of life being there. Everybody has their emergency procedure, and nobody is overly concerned." Myra, who runs a daycare out of her home in Pullman, also grew up in a contaminated environment. When I ask if she's ever been affected by environmental problems, she lists the close family members who have died from or been diagnosed with cancer. In Myra's view, this is a direct result of growing up in an agricultural area where heavy pesticide use is the norm. Later, when Myra associates caring about the environment with buying organic foods, I ask if she buys, or would like to buy, organic products. She answers, "No. I'm sure it'd be better if we ate organic stuff. Especially with my family getting cancer from pesticides but I think I'd choose not to worry about it. I mean, I can't really control it so I just don't worry about it."

If the Indifferent seem unphased by events in their own lives that could threaten their health and safety, it shouldn't be too surprising that they are unconcerned about environmental issues more generally. On average, the Indifferent disagree with the three statements on the survey that measure perception of severity. They disagree that "Environmental problems are more serious now than they used to be," that "Humans are using up the earth's resources," and that "Protecting the environment should be one of our country's top priorities" (see "Severity" score in figure 6.1). Those Indifferent who grew up in environmentally active households tend to rate the severity of environmental issues even lower than those who did not. This may be because their concern is attenuated by a feeling that people are at least aware of environmental challenges, since their families demonstrated this sort of awareness. However, the Indifferent are the least likely of all eco-types to have grown up in a household that was involved in environmental protection.

Although the Indifferent are generally unconcerned about environmental issues, they do tend to be relatively more concerned about water and air pollution and the impacts of toxic chemicals on human health than they are about climate change and plant and animal extinction. Nearly half of the Indifferent (45.4%) are concerned or very concerned about health risks from toxic chemicals, and a similar proportion are concerned about water pollution. But only 20% are concerned or very concerned about the environment in general, and roughly the same percentage worry about climate change. This suggests that the Indifferent sense that air and water pollution are most likely to disrupt their everyday lives, and that they don't see climate change or biodiversity as being so directly connected to their own well-being.

"It's Not Like I Get an Emotional Reaction if I Throw Away Something and It Could Be Recycled": Weak Moral Responsibility

On the one hand, the Indifferent are aware of the ideal environmentalist and (unlike the Optimists) they tend to admire that ideal. Some even suggest they wish they could emulate the ideal in their own lives. Further, the Indifferent I interviewed made a point of noting that they recycle and pick up litter in their communities. Yet on the other hand, the Indifferent do not seem to see any sort of engagement beyond waste management practices as relevant to them. When they acknowledged that their practices diverge from the ideal, they seem in no way bothered by that, unlike the Self-Effacing. As Amber explains to me, "We recycle. Sometimes." But when she doesn't recycle something, she doesn't dwell on that action or berate herself for it, even though she recognizes that others might: "It's not like I get an emotional reaction if I throw something away and it could be recycled. I should, but I don't."

The Indifferent admire the ideal environmentalist. Earlier, I mentioned that Avery noted several times in our interview that her neighbors had an electric car and ate no meat. The Indifferent often associate environmentalism with the ideal environmentalist. Like Amber who, when I asked what an environmentalist is in her mind, tells me: "I would say in everyday life they are more conscious about their decisions, maybe as far as purchasing food, water, and then how they dispose of their trash." Myra, who stays at home with her five children and runs a daycare out of her house, explains that she pictures environmentalists as people who are, "a lot more careful about, like, food and organic stuff and they're going to the farmers' market." In contrast, she says, "I tend to get lazy and buy junky food for my kids." Sarah describes the images that come to mind for her as associated with being an environmentalist: "walking to work, or riding your bicycle, not using gas, buying products that don't have as many wrappers, that sort of thing."

But the Indifferent participants' admiration for the ideal environmentalist is also accompanied by critique. Primarily, the Indifferent sense that those who align with the dominant ideal are elites who look down on everyone else. Louise, a 57-year-old conservative woman, describes seeing eco-friendly consumers at the grocery store: "they're better-dressed people and just fancy, with everything else. They get the organic stuff." But she bristles at her impression that these shoppers look down on her: "that's fine if they have the money to do that. A lot of people don't. So, you can't look down on the people that can't afford that." Christine has experienced the same feeling, telling me, "Wealthy, fancy people just buy stuff that looks nice. Organic. They just pull it off the shelf without looking at prices. It makes them feel like they're smarter or something." Louise tells me she thinks lower- and middle-class people are probably more environmentally responsible than the wealthy, eco-chic, explaining, "I see more [concern for the environment] in the poor and middle class because they have to preserve resources and they seem to care a little more. They're not wasteful, like the rich."

When justifying their orientation to the environment, the Indifferent explain that they don't see themselves as having the resources, knowledge, or authority to contribute to environmental protection. Sarah is aware of household-level environmental practices. She says, "My understanding is that if we all ate more of a vegan or a vegetarian diet, there would be less of an impact on the planet." But she doesn't do so. She explains, "I try to make better choices but not always. Sometimes the wallet becomes more important than health or anything else. I don't go to the grocery store with the environment in mind. I go to the grocery store with my budget in mind." Although Sarah owns her home and collects a pension that places her in the middle class, she is retired and on a fixed income. Sarah conveys to us that being a savvy consumer is much more central to her identity than being an eco-consumer.

This doesn't mean that the Indifferent don't ever integrate environmental practices into daily life, but it does imply that none of the narratives about who cares about the environment fit the Indifferent. Like Amber, who tries to recycle when she can, others describe picking up litter in their communities and buying foods they see as being better for the environment. Christine tells me, "When I have my oldest, if we see garbage we'll stop and we'll pick it up." And Avery said that she and her husband, "try to shop at the farmers' market," but that they usually "end up fulfilling the rest of the grocery list at [a much cheaper grocery store]." Louise, who grew up in a farming family, tells me that she hangs her laundry to dry because she likes the smell of the clothes afterwards, and uses a root cellar to preserve food from her garden because she likes the taste of home-grown vegetables. It is not an affinity for the environment that makes these practices feel appealing; instead, it seems almost incidental to the Indifferent that any of these actions might be associated with caring for the planet.

Overall, the survey results reflect the characterization of the Indifferent as feeling—and exercising—a weak level of moral responsibility toward the environment. Specifically, the Indifferent disagree that they "have a moral responsibility to reduce their environmental impact," "worry about their impact on the environment," and "try to reduce how much they consume to protect the environment" (see "Morality" score in figure 6.1). There is remarkably little variation in these responses among the Indifferent and the small variation that exists is not associated with any of the sociodemographic measures I collected.

Consistent with their low levels of agreement about having a moral responsibility to be conscientious consumers, the Indifferent also self-report the lowest average engagement in environmental practices. They engage the least frequently in eco-consumption, reducing consumption, and sufficiency consumption (figure 6.2). The variation in engagement in these practices is largely related to eco-upbringing. Across all forms of environmental practices, those from environmentally active households report the highest levels of engagement. That is, even among the Indifferent, there is a high cultural capital variation that is more engaged in eco-friendly practices.

"It's Just Not Realistic for the Life that I Have": Low Self-Efficacy

The Indifferent know that their own practices don't align with those of the ideal environmentalist but, in contrast to the Self-Effacing, they express very little remorse or discomfort about this. They acknowledge that the high standards of the ideal environmentalist demand more time, money, and power than they have. As Amber says, "Would I like to be super environmentally friendly in all the choices I make? Sure. But that's just not realistic for the life that I have." Amber has three children under seven years old, a demanding job, and is recently divorced. Christine faces similar constraints. As she describes it, "I try to buy stuff green, but I also have three kids to take

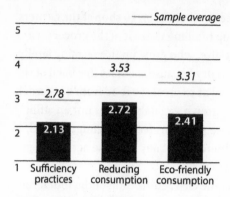

FIGURE 6.2. Indifferent engagement in
eco-friendly practices
Note: 1 = never; 5 = always.

care of. It's like sometimes I can do it and other times I can't." But even those with more time and discretionary income feel unable to meet the demands of the ideal environmentalist. Avery tells me that she certainly feels sad about environmental issues but, in her words, "what can I really do?" As I quoted earlier in the chapter, Avery doesn't see herself as having the sort of knowledge or occupational prestige required to contribute to environmental protection. This sentiment comes across clearly in Burt's remark, "there's only so much a guy like me can do to make it better."

Even when the Indifferent express an interest in environmental protection, they suggest that taking efforts to protect the planet is too out of sync with the ordinary flow of their day-to-day life to be achievable. In their everyday lives, they want to live in a place with a clean and tidy environment—beyond that, they are nonplussed. When I asked Amber how important she feels it is to protect the environment, she laughs, "Well, I think we should protect it." But then she stops laughing: "What that looks like though, I don't really have an answer." Louise tells me she can't imagine how society would reverse the damage we've done to the environment or live in a way that doesn't somehow damage the planet: "I don't care what you do, you're going to affect the environment."

The survey results paint a picture of a group that feels disconnected from efforts to reduce their own environmental impacts and generally suspicious of other actors and institutions in society. The Indifferent survey respondents had the lowest levels of agreement with the items measuring self-efficacy. These include: "I always do what I can to reduce my impact on the environment," "I have oriented my life around my desire to reduce my impact on the environment," and "I am able to do what it takes to reduce my impact on the environment" (see "Efficacy" score in figure 6.1). Generally, the Indifferent who grew up in environmentally active households express greater self-efficacy than those who did not. Indifferent respondents in urban areas convey lower self-efficacy than their rural and suburban counterparts, but beyond these patterns, there are no significant

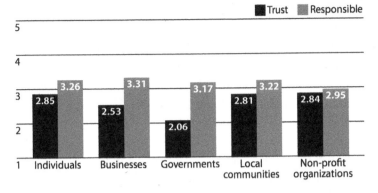

FIGURE 6.3. Indifferent respondents' opinions of various actors' responsibility for environmental protection and trustworthiness
Note: 1 = not at all; 5 = very much.

sociodemographic associations with self-efficacy. That is, Indifferent who have been socialized to engage in environmentally friendly practices are more likely to feel capable of protecting the environment. Those who live in urban areas, where pressures to emulate the ideal environmentalist may be more ubiquitous, perceive a larger gap between their own actions and the ideal efforts an individual would take to protect the environment.

The Indifferent respondents' views on trust and responsibility for environmental protection suggest a bleak outlook on society's capacity to address environmental problems. The Indifferent perceive individuals and businesses to have the greatest responsibility among the various actors and institutions, and while they have a moderate level of trust in individuals, they have little trust that businesses and governments will act pro-environmentally (see figure 6.3). Their levels of trust are the lowest across all eco-social relationships. The "trust gap" among the Indifferent is greatest when it comes to governments and smallest for nonprofit organizations, though the Indifferent place little responsibility to protect the environment on the shoulders of nonprofit organizations.

"I Don't Know Anyone Who's Totally Outraged": Low Relationality

The Indifferent have neighbors, colleagues, and acquaintances whom they would characterize as aligning with the Eco-Engaged, but no one in their family or close circle of friends would fit this description. In general, the Indifferent I interviewed described a social circle where the environment is never a subject of interest and where people feel they have too much going on to worry about the ecological effects of their consumption choices. Avery tells me she doesn't "know anybody who is like, you know, totally outraged" about environmental issues. Amber says most people she knows "don't have the resources or time to be very environmentally friendly." Myra, who runs a daycare, describes one of the parents as caring a lot about the environment. She elaborates, "he's a lot more informed and aware than I am about the environment. And he has a hybrid car and all that." Although there are people in their social worlds who align with the ideal environmentalist, and they respect those people, they're not close to anyone who embodies the ideal. Many of the Indifferent I interviewed described growing up in frugal and pragmatic families whose orientations to the environment reflect their own. Amber grew up on a farm, which she thinks left her with a practical perspective on human-environment interactions: "I've seen sort of how the land is managed for farming. We grew alfalfa. So, when I hear about people getting so concerned about the environment, I don't know. Nobody in my family ever did. Which I think is just kind of life on a working farm."

The Indifferent are not using evidence of people's eco-social relationships to organize their social networks. Indifferent survey respondents had the lowest relationality scores of all five eco-types on each of the items: "Most of the people I know are worried about the environment," "Most of the people I know try to reduce their impact on the environment," and "I prefer to spend time with people who care about the environment." This suggests both that the Indifferent are unlikely to have close friends and family who resemble the ideal environmentalist, and that a person's orientation to the environment is not important to the Indifferent. However, consistent with patterns in previous chapters, the Indifferent who grew up in environmentally active families report higher scores when asked about how important eco-social relationships are in their judgments of others. In other words, again, there is a high cultural capital subset of this eco-social relationship that uses evidence of how much a person cares about the environment in order to evaluate them.

The Environmental Impacts of the Indifferent

The Indifferent have a carbon footprint that is just slightly below the average for my survey sample, although they are the least likely of all eco-social relationships to believe their impacts are below the American average. Their average household footprint is 17.9 tons, which is below the average of 18.6 tons. The Indifferent household carbon footprint ranges from less than one ton to 96 tons. The per person footprint of the average Indifferent

BOX 6.1. Examining the Composition and Sociodemographic Antecedents of Indifferent Carbon Footprints

The average Indifferent household footprint is very similar to that of the Eco-Engaged and the Optimists (figure 6.4). The largest share of emissions is from vehicle use (making up 44%) and home energy use (35%), although the relative weight of vehicle use is slightly lower than for most other eco-types. My analyses of the survey data suggest that those Indifferent who are wealthier have larger footprints than others. Other sociodemographic variables, such as political ideology or eco-upbringing, have no bearing on the greenhouse gas emissions resulting from the daily practices of the Indifferent.

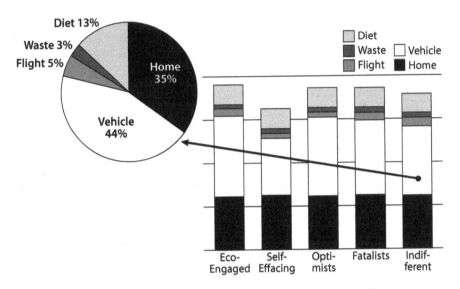

FIGURE 6.4. Composition of the average Indifferent survey respondent's household carbon footprint against size and general composition of the footprint of other eco-types

respondent is higher than the average—at 8.1 tons it is the largest per person footprint of any eco-type (the sample average is 7.1 tons). The per person footprint of the Indifferent ranges from less than one to 48 tons. In terms of their own estimate of their environmental impacts, the Indifferent stand out for having the smallest share (36.6%) of respondents who believe their impact is lower than the average US household.

Of all the eco-social relationships, you're least likely to see the Indifferent engaging in the sorts of flagship behaviors that can bring down a household's carbon footprint: few have solar panels or drive an electric or hybrid car, most report eating a heavily meat-based diet, and they are not recycling much of their waste. However, they are also among the most likely, second to the Self-Effacing, to not have a vehicle at all.

Relating to the Indifferent

For readers who care deeply about the environment and feel responsible for doing everything they can to protect it, the Indifferent eco-social relationship could verge on offensive and could probably come across as anti-ecological. Yet if we attend to their personal history, social context, and cultural context, we can shift our attention from a sense of frustration with individuals who fit in the Indifferent eco-type, toward a deeper understanding of the contextual factors shaping this eco-social relationship.

THE PERSONAL AND CULTURAL CONTEXT OF THE INDIFFERENT ECO-TYPE

This is an eco-social relationship characterized by low levels of affinity, perceived severity of ecological decline, and personal moral responsibility to address that decline. But it is also characterized by low self-efficacy. The Indifferent I interviewed are harried! Many have young children, demanding jobs, aging parents that they need to care for, and mental and physical health issues of their own. Any thoughts they have about environmental problems are fleeting—these thoughts are quickly crowded out by more immediate responsibilities. They have a sense that their lack of interest in eco-consumption and low-carbon lifestyles puts them on a lower tier than those who effortlessly integrate these activities into their lives. But the chasm between their current life and the ideal environmentalist feels too great to bridge.

The ideal environmentalist does not resonate at all with the Indifferent, even though they admire those who emulate the cultural ideal. They don't have close social ties to people who are passionate about the environment and since the Eco-Engaged are likely to eschew people like the Indifferent, this is not particularly surprising. The Indifferent are surrounded by friends and family who share their pragmatic orientation to environmental issues. Some Indifferent participants spoke of fathers who loved camping, but this love of the outdoors did not instill in them a strong affinity for the environment. In general, the family and friends that the Indifferent connect with regularly share their lack of interest in environmental subjects and their belief that as long as daily life unfolds in a predictable way, the environment must be fine. The Indifferent know people who align with the ideal environmentalist and they are intrigued by this lifestyle. But they don't feel that those eco-conscious people are close-enough contacts to ask questions of. They keep their curiosity private.

If they were to express beliefs and engage in practices common among Eco-Engaged, the Indifferent would likely not fit in with their friends and family. If they spoke passionately and fearfully about environmental issues in their social circles, they might be mocked for overreacting. If there is one word to describe the way that the Indifferent experience ecological decline, it would be "dispassionately." This is how environmental issues were approached in their families growing up, and this is how most of their friends and coworkers orient themselves to the environment. The Indifferent do not have close friends and family who discuss the urgency of ecological decline and the virtues of reducing consumption. This point calls to mind the way in which we, as individuals, exist in community and rely on our social connections to sustain our sense of identity, belonging, and self-worth.[6]

The cultural context within which the Indifferent eco-social relationship is reproduced is one where the environment is seen as the backdrop of everyday life. Every now and then, events happen that might cause you to take notice, but it's easy to downplay the severity of those events as long as you and your family are not seriously injured or harmed, and everyday routines soon return to normal. The Indifferent agree that the environment needs to be protected and they are grateful that there are people working to protect it. They don't convey a strong anti-environmentalist stance—they just don't think about these issues much at all. They do associate environmentalism with the ideal environmentalist, and this is the expression of concern that they see most frequently in their surroundings. They can't picture themselves ever following suit, but they're mostly respectful of conscious consumers, even though they sometimes resent the wealth that accompanies an eco-conscious orientation to the environment.

As the Indifferent explained to me, environmentalism just isn't their fight. It doesn't resonate with them, and they don't feel as though they have any skills or resources they could put to use to have an influence or become involved. This lack of identity with the mainstream cultural depiction of an environmental movement exists alongside a sense that environmental issues in their lives are not that bad. They might be elsewhere, but the Indifferent feel baffled by the notion that there would be something they could, or should, do to effect any change with respect to issues in distant places.

I shared stories from Amber, Burt, and others about events and experiences that might have served as a moral shock for some readers, but that failed to motivate the Indifferent to take action. I'm hesitant to say that the Indifferent are actively constructing denial of the severity of environmental problems, because that presumption seems to require me to contradict how the Indifferent understand their own experiences.[7] But I can comfortably say that the Indifferent are aware that others are alarmed, and reject the basis for that fear. My suspicion about the Indifferent is that their own relationship to the environment is unclear, even to themselves. I sense that because they associate environmentalism with the ideal environmentalist, and because they cannot see themselves adopting the sort of practices that they envision "environmentally concerned" people doing, they move on, concluding the story by dismissing the nature of their own connection to the planet.

When political liberals picture people who are apathetic about ecological decline, they may well be picturing the Indifferent. Of all the eco-social relationships, it is, admittedly, the hardest to make the case that the Indifferent care about the environment in their own way. Yet still, while they are particularly unconcerned with environmental problems, it is not accurate to say they don't care. It's more accurate to say that they are assured that others are caring more actively than they are. They can feel comfortable in their own practices as long as they are not making their local environment look unclean, and as long as their own lives maintain the security of routine—if you get up each day, and clean water comes out of the tap, and you can drive to work and fill up your car with gas, and send your kids out to play at the park, then how could claims of an ecological crisis be true?

7

Confronting Political Polarization

Imagine you're hosting a group of neighbors for a potluck dinner. The first of your neighbors arrives by bike, towing their young children behind them in expensive bicycle chariots. From the back of the bike carriers, they pull out a small plate covered with a sheet of beeswax wrap from a cloth bag. They lift a corner of the beeswax, revealing artfully arranged, cut vegetables, as they explain that they bought the vegetables at the local farmers' market earlier in the day. After you smile and tell the couple how delicious their food looks, they go on to say that their children helped them make the hummus and baba ghanoush dips that are in the cloth tote bag.

Behind the young family comes a neighbor who works in construction. You often see him leaving the neighborhood early in the morning in his big pick-up truck and he's driven it here tonight, though he only lives a few blocks away. He's carrying two different flavors of Doritos and several bottles of pop in plastic grocery bags and sets these on the counter. Overhearing the young couple talk about shopping at the farmers' market, he chimes in: "What a rip-off! Everything is so overpriced there." The young couple frowns.

Next, a middle-aged woman shows up in an older car. As she walks in, carrying a jar of organic salsa and a paper bag of corn chips from the same store the construction worker shopped at, she starts chatting to the young family. The woman begins to look visibly uncomfortable as the young parents ask why she drove to the dinner. The construction worker rolls his eyes, muttering, "who cares?!" under his breath, but the middle-aged woman explains that she just got off work and raced over so she would be on time. In an effort to ease the awkwardness of the situation, she asks what sorts of dips the young family brought.

Soon after, the next family arrives. They each seem to be wearing something in a camouflage print. As they set down a plastic container filled with meat, they tell everyone it's jerky made from moose that they hunted themselves and cured in their backyard smoker. The bicycling family looks appalled when asked if they want to try some, and the parents explain that their family is vegetarian. It's another awkward moment, and everyone seems relieved by the interruption of the last guests arriving—a single mother with three young kids. The oldest child is holding a box of cupcakes from the local grocery store and happily accepts a piece of the homemade jerky.

This scene is a fiction: it is fairly unlikely such a diverse group would be found in the same room or even the same neighborhood. But this story, which uses impulses of the Eco-Engaged, Fatalists, Self-Effacing, Optimists, and the Indifferent to draw the cast of characters, illustrates some of the tensions and misunderstandings that can obscure important common ground. Each of these fictitious households showed up to an event because they wanted to connect with their neighbors. They each brought some food to the party—and likely the food they saw as a treat and thought others would enjoy as well. But these good intentions and desires for social solidarity were negated and undermined by competing views on the moral significance of dietary, transportation, and shopping practices. An event intended to bring people together ended up in hurt feelings, irritation, embarrassment, a sense of dread for the evening ahead, and perhaps more divisiveness than existed before the potluck. This could be the last neighborhood gathering for a while.

The foundational premise of this book is that we all care about the environment, which I substantiated through interview and survey data. The social context of our life and our biography culminate in different ways of caring for and connecting to the planet. Yet there is a widespread sense that one way of caring about the environment has a cultural monopoly on what constitutes a moral eco-social relationship—and this is best reflected by the orientation of the young, bike-riding family from the potluck.

The Role of Eco-Social Relationships in Political Polarization

Environmental social scientists have offered compelling explanations of the reasons behind the significant wedge between liberals' and conservatives' views on environmental protection generally, and climate action more specifically. This body of research points to disagreement over what people feel is the ideal balance between economic growth and environmental protection, and politically polarized views on the merits and weaknesses of various environmental policy tools.[1] In other words, these studies identify polarization as driven by conflicting views on how best to address environmental issues, with liberals more likely to support environmental protection policies regardless of the costs or effects on the profit margins of polluting industries. Conservatives, in contrast, are more likely to oppose costly state regulations and more apt to favor market-led solutions.[2]

However, individuals are rarely confronted with situations where their views on economic and environmental trade-offs are solicited and evaluated against someone else's opinions on the matter. In contrast, people are constantly perceiving and evaluating others' eco-social relationships, and this is a significant reason why our orientations to the environment play such an influential role in political polarization. Attending to these dynamics complements existing research to work out how it is possible that civil society can essentially agree that we need to protect the environment yet express so much animosity toward one another's position on how best to do so.

At a time when high cultural capital people feel strongly that we each have a personal responsibility to fix structural problems, it is common to evaluate others based on what we perceive to be their commitment to saving the planet.[3] This is a significant point to pay attention to in the context of political polarization because such judgments and evaluations often take place imperceptibly in everyday, routine interactions. My interview data offer many examples of how these evaluations unfold in daily life, and showcase why these evaluations influence political polarization.

The Eco-Engaged and Self-Effacing liberals I spoke with made a point of describing close friends and family they were proud to know. These social contacts were people who resemble the ideal environmentalist—people who take pains to respond to ecological decline by meticulously reducing particular elements of their environmental impacts.[4] Elena (Eco-Engaged, liberal) tells me, "On the whole, the friends that we talk to share our concerns about the environment." When I ask who she pictures as an environmentalist, Elena names a couple she and her husband are friends with, offering an anecdote to demonstrate their commitments to the planet. Elena tells me that whenever these friends fly, they "take a little cup with them. And every time [the flight attendant] would offer coffee or water, our friends would put a mark on their cup to count how many Styrofoam cups they didn't use." She is so impressed: "Isn't that smart!" This example illustrates the way that a flagship behavior like avoiding disposable cups can feel meaningful as a cultural practice. Her friends' story of rejecting additional cups felt significant enough for Elena to share with me as an illustration of environmentalism, even though the story itself is set in the context of air travel. Lexi, who is a Self-Effacing, liberal undergraduate student, tells me about a friend who she looks up to, because of this friend's knowledge of environmental issues and commitment to ethical consumption. Lexi says her friend, "really cares about the bees. Oh, she loves the bees!" Lexi tells me that "one time, she walked into my house and I had a thing of honey from [a discount grocery store] and she damn-near slapped me. She's like 'Uh-uh. There is a farmers' market right there and you will go and you will get *that* honey.'" Lexi isn't put out that her friend chastised her. She's impressed by her friend's knowledge of and dedication to the environment.

Cheryl (also Self-Effacing and liberal) comments on the reasons why she admires the Eco-Engaged: "They're much less impulsive, that's part of it. They're really thinking about what they're buying and how it's affecting things. I kind of admire them. I think there's more space between them and their stuff. It's not as, maybe not as impulsive or materialistic or something." While some might be put off by the sanctimoniousness of counting Styrofoam cups while on an airplane or telling others where to buy honey, people who align with or admire the ideal environmentalist see these actions as evidence of moral worth in a time of catastrophic ecological decline. The Eco-Engaged are the most likely of all survey respondents to focus on a person's relationship with the environment when evaluating their morality and potential value and suitability as a friend. The survey data show that this pattern extends beyond the Eco-Engaged and Self-Effacing, as liberal Optimists also use evidence of environmental commitments to determine who is and is not suitable for friendship.[5] The way that liberals intuitively evaluate the people around them can play a role in exacerbating political polarization over environmental protection when the criteria for earning moral worth are not agreed upon across the political spectrum.

Many of the conservatives I interviewed wanted to distance themselves from the ideal environmentalist, but broaden the label "environmentalist" to include themselves and their friends and family. James, a conservative Fatalist, told me that his mental association with the word "environmentalists" is "stinky, non-bathing hippies." Yet, despite this pejorative view, James also told me he thought some of his friends and family should be able to call themselves environmentalists, because of their commitments to land management and stewardship. Bill, the Optimist, tells me, "I would say I am an environmentalist," and that "we all need to be." But he believes most people would associate his sister, and not him, with caring about the environment. Bill's sister lives in an urban area and focuses on the sustain-ability of her consumption choices. In his view, people like her look down on conservatives who seem unconcerned by their environmental impacts. Later, Bill draws a parallel between the dynamics he senses among eco-social relationships and conflicts over religion: "You have your Catholics and then you have your Seventh-Day Adventists. You see the divide and the difference between how they go about things. Each group wants you to join their club." But, Bill says, they should just leave each other alone, and this is similar in the environmental arena: "You have your environmentalists who only want you to be like them. You get this 'looking down on us' from the left, pointing the finger. And on the right, we're just like, 'what?!' "

There is an underlying pattern in James' and Bill's comments that was common among the conservatives I interviewed: a sense that dominant con-notations of who counts as an environmentalist do not reflect conservative eco-social relationships, and further, that liberals unfairly look down on con-servatives for not caring "the right way" about the environment. In response, conservative Optimists endeavored to reclaim the label of environmentalist for themselves and the people in their social network, and conservatives with various eco-social relationships expressed anger and frustration at what they perceived as virtue-signaling and self-righteousness from liberals. I inter-pret these patterns as evidence that some conservatives react to the cultural authority that the ideal environmentalist wields at this time and place, par-ticularly because, in some ways, this ideal seems predicated on opposing the moral worth of quintessentially conservative eco-social relationships.

The absence of widely recognized, socially valued, conservative eco-social relationships in mainstream culture contributes to political polariza-tion. Some of my conservative participants described relationships to the environment that they observed in their social contexts and felt were over-looked in mainstream culture. For instance, Jenny (Optimist, libertarian) says she thinks an environmentalist should be someone "who really cares about their surroundings. That's me! I really do care about my surround-ings." Jenny is referring to all elements of her environment—the physical, the built, and the social. Generally, conservatives were much more likely than liberals to make inclusive statements such as, "we're all environmentalists because we're all being affected by our environment and affecting it" (Sheri, Optimist, libertarian). Conservatives often challenged what they viewed as the ideal environmentalist's cultural monopoly by arguing that there are other ways of caring about the environment beyond scrutinizing consump-tion choices. It is significant that they didn't see any conservative eco-types respected and admired in popular culture.

When liberals express disgust toward people who don't align with the ideal environmentalist, they intensify the dynamics that lead to political polarization. The Eco-Engaged and Self-Effacing liberals who I interviewed spoke angrily and scornfully about people who they saw as acting in opposition to the foundations of the ideal environmentalist. They focused on stereotypically rural and conservative practices and characterized these practices as reflecting a lack of moral worth. Lexi, Self-Effacing and liberal, tells me, "You know what really pisses me off? Big freaking diesel trucks, like regular people driving these trucks with their black exhaust. It makes me so sick to my stomach because they obviously don't care about what it's doing to the environment." For Lexi, this feeling of disgust is visceral and immediate. It is not something she reflects on; she feels confident that someone driving a big diesel truck doesn't care about the environment.

Jerry, a retired, liberal and Eco-Engaged eco-type, loves spending time at his cabin but despises those who litter on the forest roads in the area. It was tricky scheduling an interview with Jerry because he and his wife regularly drive to their cabin, which is a few hours away. They have this cabin in order to enjoy "nature in its pristine state," but Jerry is visibly upset when describing the sound of ATVs around his cabin and feels angry at the people who drive them. He assumes that these are the people responsible for leaving beer cans on the forest service roads he loves to walk on, and he expresses his incredulity: "Those ATVers, they tear up property, they litter. Why on earth would you throw a beer can on a beautiful forest service road? I don't think I'll ever get my head around that." Jerry isn't noticing that being in the forest, on an ATV, is what it looks like for some people to care about the environment. The politically conservative Optimists I interviewed put their appreciation for the planet into action by getting outdoors, into areas with few human settlements. Jerry is judging the ATV-riders' actions by his own moral impulses, rather than cultivating curiosity about the perspective of the ATV enthusiast.[6]

Jerry focuses on the environmental impacts of the ATV and litter, but he does not seem to notice the impacts he has from owning a second home and driving back and forth to it. This tendency to vilify the sorts of environmental impacts others have and to overlook one's own impacts is particularly common across my interviews with the Eco-Engaged. In another example, Laurel, Eco-Engaged and liberal, critiques households that "have bought into that throw-away lifestyle." She assumes that "a great many of them would say 'who cares about the environment?'" Laurel tells me she has recently flown to Texas and to Kentucky (predominantly conservative states), and in each of these places she's seen the sorts of people who don't care about the planet. They, "are throwing cigarette butts on the floor, leaving their beer cans on the roadside." Although the carbon footprint of her air travel has a more significant environmental impact than cigarette butts and beer cans, what Laurel is offended by is her sense that the people she saw, "had no consciousness that these things they're doing are derogating the environment and not even aware that they're impacting the people around them." Like Jerry, Laurel's own environmental impacts (air travel) are out-of-focus—it is the litter that is in sharp relief. When liberals perceive conservatives to be flagrantly violating the moral framework of the ideal environmentalist, they tend to conclude that conservatives are anti-ecological people who don't care about the environment. This judgment plays an important, and underrecognized role in driving political polarization over environmental protection.

The cultural prominence of the ideal environmentalist generates, to borrow a phrase from sociologists Jonathan Coley and David Hess, "reactive effects" that accelerate political polarization. When conservatives perceive the moral worth of their eco-social relationship to be under attack from liberals, they challenge the competence and moral consistency of politically liberal orientations to the environment. Conservatives characterized liberal environmentalists as hypocrites, as aggressive, and as uninformed. Sarah (Indifferent, conservative) described "left-wing environmentalists" as "people who lobby for a cause in an aggressive way and maybe not always a smart way." Tina, an Optimist and conservative whose family runs a large farm, tells me that the sort of people we often assume are environmentalists are "not all that knowledgeable or realistic. They're aggressive." Greg (Optimist, conservative) labels activists who were protesting an oil refinery in his area as "hypocrites" because they showed up to protest in kayaks made from oil products, as "aggressive," and as impractical: "You know what? We need gas. If the semis in this country stopped running for 30 days, this country would be toast. It would collapse. You wouldn't have food; you wouldn't have medicine."

It bothers many conservatives that their knowledge of the environment is devalued. Louise, Indifferent and conservative, challenges whether people who drive "70 miles roundtrip just to get their organic stuff" are really doing much for the environment, given the emissions from their drive. Louise's comments cast doubt on the competence of green consumers. Tina questions the competence of people working at the Environmental Protection Agency. She explains that "none of them are actual farmers" but that they impose rules and regulations on her family's farm. Tina challenges their authority to do so, arguing "That would be like me moving into an urban area and me saying, 'you need to do this, this, this, and this.'" Jenny, a libertarian, says that she resents having her perception of ecological decline challenged: "The 'judgmentalness' that you hear from the [urban and liberal] westside of the state, well, I have to I laugh. 'Cause I think to myself . . . if you were to come over here and actually truly experience life here, you would find it is so much different than you think." And Bill (Optimist) expresses frustration that he's told not to have a plastic water bottle by people who "fly all over the place, for work and vacation and whatnot." He says Leonardo DiCaprio comes to mind as someone with a negative impact on the environment. As he explains, he doesn't want to be told to drive less or not have a plastic bottle by someone who flies in a private jet. Many of the conservatives and libertarians that I interviewed sensed that some liberals look down on them because of their eco-social relationship. They react by challenging liberals' moral consistency and competence.

Although I heard attacks on eco-social relationships from both sides of the political spectrum, only conservatives argued that the distribution of cultural power is highly uneven and, in their view, favors liberals. I observed some evidence of uneven cultural power in the way many liberals could evocatively describe their negative judgments of the role of conservatives in causing ecological decline, but fail to consider their own impacts on the environment. I also observed inequality in cultural power through the absence of comments from liberals that conservatives might implicate them as culpable for environmental issues. It was easy to prompt conservatives to describe their judgments of liberals—judgments that took aim at the foundational beliefs and practices of the ideal environmentalist. The difference is that conservatives could also easily identify the sorts of judgments liberals make of them. The conservatives I interviewed assumed that urban liberals look down on them. For instance, Sheri tells me she thinks that in the minds of liberals in Seattle, "You guys are just uneducated." Other conservatives tied this more directly to the realm of environmental practices. For example, Jeff said he felt that just because he didn't buy "organic foods and all that," people assumed he and his family were "rednecks." While Sheri is referring to her politically conservative town, Jeff is referring to his conservative family—but in both cases they assume that liberals have more cultural power and authority than do conservatives.

The ways in which these dynamics play out at multiple scales in contemporary American life manifests in political polarization over environmental protection. Across the political spectrum, many of the people I interviewed blamed individuals for complex problems such as climate change. This tendency to individualize ignores history and the involvement of powerful actors. There is a history of corporate investment in campaigns calling out "litterbugs" and framing those who want to protect the environment as not caring about the livelihoods of the working class.[7] Participants like Laurel and Bill did not have a hand in these campaigns, but in pointing the finger at individuals they inadvertently reproduce the social structures such campaigns have created.

Overall, the everyday judgments and misconceptions of eco-social relationships across the political spectrum culminate in a divided landscape. For conservatives, antagonism toward environmental protection is partly a reactive effect against the hegemony and liberal orientation of the ideal environmentalist. When liberals engage in character attacks against conservatives, it can exacerbate the conditions for these reactive effects. Conservatives' reactive effects serve to confirm, for liberals, that conservatives are anti-ecological—and in this way, differences in how people care about the environment become politically polarized and polarizing.

Why Do These Patterns Drive Divisiveness?

Why do the patterns above exacerbate political divisiveness and divisions along lines of social class? In short, because the ideal environmentalist occupies so much of our cultural space, has so much cultural power, appeals most strongly to upper-middle-class liberals, and captures relatively little of the diversity of eco-social relationships that exists in the United States. As a result, caring about the environment has become a high-stakes exercise. It is more than a debate over what proportion of gross domestic product is appropriate to spend on environmental protection, or over the merits and drawbacks of a carbon tax. The political polarization over environmental protection that I captured in my research is a debate over belonging and moral worth in the face of ecological decline.

The way the ideal environmentalist is portrayed and venerated contributes to political polarization. This is because many conservatives reject the moral authority of the ideal environmentalist, and liberals tend to rebuke those who oppose this cultural ideal. In other words, liberals have constructed and accept a status hierarchy that many conservatives reject. Sociologists Cecilia Ridgeway and Sandra Nakagawa conducted an experimental study to try to understand why people defer to status hierarchies.[8] Why do people with less power consent to a status hierarchy that may be punitive and unfair? Ridgeway and Nakagawa argue that low-status members of a group accept status hierarchies because they are rewarded with the modest prize of being seen as reasonable when they assent to the group hierarchy. Put more simply, by assenting to a status hierarchy that places them at the bottom, people with low status are accepted into the group—and it is this incentive that motivates their cooperation. I suggest a similar pattern is unfolding in daily interactions and conflicts over the ideal environmentalist. When conservatives challenge the cultural authority of the ideal environmentalist, they are disdained by those who accept the hierarchy. Even the Self-Effacing, who are not at the top of the ladder, nonetheless enforce moral sanctions on conservatives who they see as questioning the value of the ideal environmentalist. In fact, calling out beliefs and practices that conflict with the moral ideal may be one way that the Self-Effacing compete for recognition within the hierarchy. The Eco-Engaged, who most closely resemble the culturally ideal environmentalist, convey pity, not anger, toward those who they see as lacking the capacity to live up to the standards of the ideal, but they openly question the moral worth of conservatives.

Strong cultural support for the ideal environmentalist can obscure the way that reflecting this ideal requires a particular set of tastes that are associated with cultural capital and liberal values. Obscuring these associations exacerbates polarization because it can leave people with a sense that living up to the standard of the ideal environmentalist is universally accessible. It is not. Taking on an awareness of ecological decline requires a scientific literacy that many people don't have, not to mention trust in experts that many don't feel. Uncritically accepting that some industrial activities, such as fossil-fuel extraction, should stop is going to be far more complex and difficult for those whose livelihoods depend on that extraction. Feeling personally responsible for putting fewer greenhouse gasses into the atmosphere is easier for those in social circles that reward such efforts, and those who grew up in households that instilled the virtues of environmental protection. Implementing a commitment to reduce environmental impact in our contemporary context is likely to require spending more money on eco-friendly products than one would spend on their conventionally produced counterparts, which favors households with more disposable income who live in places where green goods are easy to access. And, importantly, the impulses of the ideal environmentalist resonate more strongly with liberals than with conservatives.

The ideal environmentalist, my participants observed, reflects politically liberal values. This does not suggest that liberals care more about the environment than conservatives, but that liberals care about the environment in a way that is reflected by the ideal environmentalist and widely recognized as indicating a commitment to the environment. When I asked my interview participants who was most likely to reflect the ideal environmentalist, they inaccurately made assumptions that this ideal is wealthy, female, and white, and they accurately noted that this person would be politically liberal. Liberals are more likely to reflect (Eco-Engaged) or admire (Self-Effacing) the ideal environmentalist than are conservatives and libertarians. They are also more likely to suggest that this is the best way to care for the environment. The Eco-Engaged and Self-Effacing are also the eco-types most likely to be politically liberal. When I read Jonathan Haidt's book, *The Righteous Mind*, the political differences I was seeing in my data became clearer. Haidt draws on extensive experimental and survey evidence to argue that liberals and conservatives have different moral foundations. In other words, some issues and problems that feel morally charged to liberals may not be felt the same way by conservatives, and vice versa. Haidt identified five moral foundations: fairness, care, authority, loyalty, and sanctity. Each of these foundations resonates with conservatives, but the latter three more strongly than fairness and care. Liberals primarily connect to the foundations of fairness and care.

Although these moral foundations may seem abstract and distant from the specific case of environmental issues, follow-up research using Haidt's theory demonstrates its applicability in studying political polarization over environmental protection. In a survey experiment, social psychologists Matthew Feinberg and Robb Willer found that conservative respondents were more likely to support environmental protection after they read a vignette stressing the need to preserve the *purity* of ecological resources than they were after reading a vignette stressing the need to *care* about and reduce harm to a vulnerable planet.[9] The narrative about reducing harm more closely reflects the impulses of the ideal environmentalist. Interestingly, liberals were moved to support environmental protection regardless of the way the appeal was framed. Research on moral foundations tells us how liberals and conservatives understand their own moral intuitions, but it says little about how they understand moral frameworks different from their own.

The ideal environmentalist reflects the sensibilities and lifestyle of upper-middle-class liberals, but is being promoted in cultural spaces in a way that implies it is the ideal we should all pursue. In the US context, the impulses of the ideal environmentalist are common to encounter, whether on popular television shows like *The Good Place*, novels like *The Good Neighborhood*, documentaries like Leonardo DiCaprio's *Before the Flood*, or in school curricula.[10] These cultural representations of caring for the environment resonate with high cultural capital political liberals, and affirm their own eco-social relationships and perceptions of what constitutes a moral response to ecological decline.[11] When teachers, scholars, writers, artists and marketers reinforce the idea that the ideal environmentalist is what it looks like to care about the environment without recognizing a range of eco-types, they narrow the possibilities for cultural membership in environmentalism.

The ideal environmentalist is ubiquitous and widely venerated, yet there are few places in popular culture that respectfully depict eco-social relationships beyond this ideal. There are so many ways of caring about the environment: appreciating time spent outdoors; farming land with an eye to sustaining productivity and economic livelihoods; hanging laundry to dry and trying not to throw away anything of use; reading about and discussing environmental issues; voicing concerns about climate change at Fridays for Future protests. But it is the ideal environmentalist that connotes caring for the environment in mainstream culture. The lack of more diverse eco-types being portrayed in mainstream culture restricts the appeal of many environmental practices to high cultural capital liberals.

We have the opportunity to confront politically polarized views on environmental protection by recognizing the moral worth of eco-types that look unfamiliar to us. One of the reasons that American civil society is so divided over environmental protection is because too many of us believe that only people who feel and act the way we do truly care for the environment. I see this pattern among environmental social scientists and in the general public. Environmental social scientists have good intentions. We want to make the world more sustainable and equitable. But for many of us, when we study the social world, we come to that work with a very specific view of how we think people *should* interpret and respond to evidence of ecological decline. We too often fail to scrutinize our own ideals and practices the way we scrutinize others' ideals and practices. We assume that people like us are good for the environment, and people unlike us are thwarting the sort of world we want to bring about. Beyond environmental social scientists, I also observe these patterns in the general public. I commonly encounter people who assume that, based on the vehicle a person drives, or the food they buy or bring to a party, they can determine how much that person cares or knows about the environment.

This is the irony and the tragedy of how we experience ecological decline: too many of us are so convinced that our own way of interpreting and responding to environmental issues is the right way that we fail to recognize how others care about the environment. This creates a social context rife with misunderstandings and accusations and vitriol as civil society attacks itself out of a desire to be better for the planet. But while we do so, corporations carry on using the environment for profit and governments continue letting them do so. Denigrating someone else's character or moral worth on the basis of our assumption of how much they care about the environment weakens the solidarity of civil society. Judging how another person cares about the environment also obscures the environment itself, which is particularly problematic since this is a site of common ground.

What Do We Have in Common?

Much of the emphasis of what I have written in this book so far is on differences in how people relate to the environment and to the ideal environmentalist. Importantly, there are also areas of common ground across the five eco-types, and these areas of common ground can point to similarities that span political ideology. These areas of overlap offer hope and direction for engaging civil society in collaborative efforts to confront ecological decline.

Many of the liberal and conservative Eco-Engaged, Self-Effacing, and Indifferent participants I interviewed value the ideal environmentalist. They admire flagship behaviors, even though they vary in the extent to which they adopt these behaviors and see them as impactful. For the Eco-Engaged, the ideal environmentalist is familiar—the behavior of the ideal environmentalist mirrors their own way of experiencing and responding to ecological decline, and is how their close friends and family understand their moral responsibilities to the planet. The Self-Effacing aspire to resemble the ideal environmentalist. They know people with an Eco-Engaged relationship to the environment in their social networks and admire these people. They also know people who don't resemble the ideal environmentalist at all, and they can empathize with both impulses. The Indifferent, who are more likely to be conservative, encounter the ideal environmentalist in their neighborhoods, at work, or in popular culture. They aren't close to these people, but they admire them from a distance. The Indifferent are curious about flagship behaviors and they sense that these behaviors come from a place of caring about the environment and may offer other benefits, like better health and greater well-being. This suggests that if policies and neighborhood design choices were aimed at removing barriers to accessing eco-friendly practices such as cycling, gardening, and owning solar panels, there would be much greater engagement in these practices across the political spectrum.

The Fatalists and the Optimists, who tend to be politically conservative, are suspicious of flagship behaviors and picture the environment as resilient (either in the long term or currently). I would be surprised to see either of these groups make personal investments in metal straws to substitute plastic straws, but I believe both would be happy to see the plastics industry curb production and reduce its environmental impacts. There is no point in trying to cajole or shame the Fatalists and Optimists into being greener consumers, as this is not a model of environmental engagement that resonates with them and doing so is likely only to generate reactive effects. Yet many of the Optimists I interviewed and surveyed reported having (or wanting to have) solar panels, recycling their household waste, and even reducing meat consumption. Although the Fatalists did not report similarly high levels of engagement in these behaviors, I imagine these two eco-types would find common ground in rejecting the premise of shopping for a better world, and could creatively imagine alternative paths to addressing ecological decline.

Even the liberal Eco-Engaged and the conservative Optimists have something in common. These are the two groups who seem to be most diametrically opposed and most disrespectful toward one another's eco-social relationship. Yet there is nonetheless an area of overlap in their impulses and experiences. These are groups that are confident about their relationship with the planet and feel a strong affinity for the environment. They feel a strong sense of self-efficacy and tend to evaluate social efficacy more positively than do those with other eco-social relationships. While the Eco-Engaged and the Optimists may not agree on the right ways to go about protecting the environment, they both place great value in the natural world and their place in it.

I'm wary of sounding like a broken record, but the final area of common ground is that we all care about the environment. Everyone appreciates the earth and sees protecting the planet as important, even though we disagree on who is responsible for environmental problems and how such problems should be addressed.

Humans have not only drastically altered the planet we live on, but for many of us, our connections to the environment and each other seem to be overshadowed by a cultural schema (the ideal environmentalist) that is out of reach for, or beyond interest to, people who nonetheless care about the planet. Liberals tend to feel an affinity toward those who reflect the ideal environmentalist and antipathy toward those who don't. They often make judgments of the moral character of people who do not seem to be conscious, caring, and committed to reducing their impact on the environment. Conservatives resent these characterizations and attack in turn. They lob claims of hypocrisy at those who engage in sustainable consumption and question the knowledge and competence of liberals who perceive ecological decline to be urgent and severe. A study published in 2021 by an interdisciplinary team of psychologists and political scientists concluded that people who believe that those who are like them care more about democracy than those who are not like them tend not to act in a democratic way.[12] A conclusion of the study is that one of the most significant barriers to strengthening the solidarity of civil society is our misjudgments of others' values. In my research, I identified significant misunderstandings of eco-social relationships, particularly across lines of political ideology. These misunderstandings are a notable driver of political polarization.

Judgments of how much others care about the environment certainly make for awkward neighborhood gatherings, but we can try to respond differently when we find ourselves confronted with unfamiliar eco-types. We can begin by assuming the other person appreciates and cares about the environment, and that their eco-social relationship makes sense for them. If we want to better understand that eco-social relationship, we might respectfully ask the other person to explain where they're coming from. We are unlikely to ever convert anyone to our way of thinking (just as others are unlikely to convert us to their way of thinking), but we can each contribute to mending our fragile social solidarity by granting respect and recognition to other individuals and remembering that their eco-social relationship makes sense for them because of the circumstances of their life.

8

We All Care About the Environment

The Great Pacific Garbage Patch washes up in my memory in banal moments. Receiving takeout with plastic cutlery I don't need, rinsing a yogurt container for recycling, or weighing the cost of eco-friendly diapers . . . So as geeky as it feels to bring Tupperware on dinner dates when I know I'll want leftovers boxed up, I only need to imagine the restaurant's plastic packaging breaking down into edible shards, joining the toxic soup that whales swallow and birds unknowingly feed their newborns. I need only send my imagination back out to sea . . . and let the blunt truth of oceanographer Sylvia Earle ring hard through me: "There's no 'away'" to throw to.

—COLLEEN KINDER, "HOW SAILING ACROSS THE PACIFIC CHANGED MY THINKING ABOUT PLASTIC" *BLOOMBERG BUSINESSWEEK*, JUNE 26, 2020

The story above popped up on my newsfeed at the end of June, 2020. This is the sort of account I hear frequently, whether in the media or in my class-room. A person describes their experience confronting some manifestation of ecological decline and how it led them to rethink their personal use of resources.[1] I have read the same sort of story about people changing their thinking about eating meat, using plastic water bottles, purchasing fast fashion, and so on. For me, these accounts are moving. But what I have demonstrated in this book is that emotionally charged narratives like the one above appeal to some people, but not everyone. Specifically, this sort of narrative speaks to those who emulate and admire our cultural ideal of an environmentalist, namely the Eco-Engaged and the Self-Effacing. The narrative above would likely not resonate with Fatalists, Optimists, and the Indifferent—not because they don't care about the environment, but because they don't care about the environment in the way that is endorsed and codified in this story. The author of the excerpt above learned to contemplate the implications of her consumption choices after seeing islands of garbage in the ocean. What can we learn about human-environment relationships from the information I've described in this book so far?

Lessons Learned from Studying Eco-Social Relationships

Much has been written about people and the environment. Yet, by spending two summers talking to Washington State residents in four different communities, people representing a range of political ideology, education, and income, I came away with new knowledge about contemporary Americans' relationships with the environment.

LESSON #1: REFLECTING THE IDEAL ENVIRONMENTALIST IS A FORM OF CULTURAL AUTHORITY

The first lesson is that there is considerable cultural power in having an affinity for the beliefs and practices that resemble those that people associate with the ideal environmentalist. This lesson builds on previous work that suggests people with more cultural capital are likely to engage in these practices.[2] Shyon Baumann, Josée Johnston and I developed this line of thinking by showing that in the world of food, high-status people prefer foods that signal aesthetic sophistication *and* moral commitments.[3] For instance, while being "high-status" a few decades ago would have meant going to the ballet, or listening to classical music and jazz, those at the top of the social hierarchy now are also likely to be sensitive to the racial politics of art and music, and—as I show in this book—the environmental politics of everyday consumption.

It is not only the Eco-Engaged who reproduce the hegemony of the ideal environmentalist through their practices, but also the Self-Effacing, as they castigate people who appear to reject this prototype. That is, even though the Self-Effacing denigrate their own efforts to protect the planet, they also actively police opposition to the ideal environmentalist. On the other side of this dynamic, I heard from many participants who felt judged by people because of their eco-social relationship. This suggests to me that alignment with the ideal environmentalist is becoming a criterion on which a large group in society categorizes and stratifies the people around them. This happens because the Eco-Engaged see their tastes as "natural" and assume that people who don't share their beliefs and practices are either selfish or ignorant. Because of the liberal orientation of the ideal environmentalist, these character judgments divide people on the basis of economic and cultural capital in ways that are also politically polarizing.

These dynamics are more apparent in the model of eco-social relationships I described in the introductory chapter than they are in the models of environmental values and pro-environmental behaviors that are common in many studies of household-level environmentalism. In particular, by bringing in the ideal environmentalist (see figure 1.1), I was able to demonstrate how this cultural ideal shapes our judgments of one another's relationships to the environment. At this moment in time, reflecting the ideal environmentalist is a form of cultural authority—and challenging that ideal generates conflict and divisiveness. Across all eco-types, the Eco-Engaged are the most likely to use evidence of a person's relationship with the environment as a basis for choosing whether or not to befriend them. The Eco-Engaged are also most likely to have grown up in the types of environmentally active households that inculcate a commitment to making efforts to reduce individual environmental impacts. This leaves high cultural capital liberals with the most culturally dominant eco-social relationship—an important and overlooked form of power and moral authority.

LESSON #2: THE PRICE OF CHALLENGING THE IDEAL ENVIRONMENTALIST IS TO BE JUDGED AS IMMORAL

Lesson #2 builds on the previous lesson, focusing on evidence of the animosity that conservatives express toward the ideal environmentalist in order to contribute to a deeper understanding of political polarization. Research on political polarization has overlooked the subcultural dynamics I discussed in this book. Environmental social scientists have demonstrated how fossil-fuel elites who invest in fomenting doubt about climate science and fear about climate mitigation affect political polarization. Others have attributed political differences to conservatives' support of free-market capitalism.[8]

BOX 8.1. What Does an Ideal Environmentalist Look Like?

I have a long-standing interest in how a person's gender affects their relationship to the environment. For decades, ecofeminist scholars have argued that patriarchy underlies the oppression of women, minorities, and the planet though a shared logic of domination.[4] Yet the insight that women and men may be unevenly burdened by environmental problems and their solutions has been slow to find traction in environmental social science. I want to reiterate a few points about gender in this research: the ideal environmentalist that my interview participants imagined is often female, and, among my survey respondents, women tended to report stronger feelings of personal responsibility to protect the environment. Taken together, these patterns suggest that women are expected to uphold a higher standard when it comes to exercising a personal responsibility to protect the environment. This means that our cultural pattern of implicating individuals in environmental protection is tied to more intense emotional investment and a higher moral bar for women than for men.

Some of the same patterns exist for racialized minorities as for women. For instance, just as people stereotype the ideal environmentalist as female, they also stereotype her as white. And yet, race had very little to do with explaining membership in each eco-type or variation within eco-types. While the Eco-Engaged would be stereotyped as white, this is in fact the most racially diverse eco-type I identified. This means that the environmental impulses and commitments of people of color are overlooked among the public. A recent survey of Americans demonstrated this as well—survey respondents assumed environmentally concerned people are white and highly educated, and significantly underestimated levels of environmental concern among low-income Americans and racial minorities.[5] Race is only significantly associated with membership in the Self-Effacing eco-type, not in any other eco-social relationship. And within eco-types, there are no consistent patterns associated with race. The stereotype of the ideal environmentalist as white acts as a barrier to a more inclusive and diverse environmentalism.

Regarding the distribution of eco-types in the population, I want to note the prominence of the Eco-Engaged and the Self-Effacing. These groups, who accept the ideal environmentalist, represent nearly 60% of the people I surveyed. In contrast, the Optimists and Fatalists, who reject that ideal, comprise only one-third of the national survey sample. Although Optimists and Fatalists do not share the Eco-Engaged and Self-Effacing environmentalists' commitment to personal actions to mitigate environmental issues, they nonetheless place great value in the natural environment and seek a place in civil society to share and cultivate their ecological worldviews. These numbers point toward the likelihood that conservatives feel their eco-social relationship is somewhat of an "underdog" in part because, at least numerically, it is.[6] Their views are in the minority compared to a large proportion of the population who accept the ideal environmentalist.[7] Finally, I want to point out that the Indifferent are the only group who seem largely uninterested in environmentalism, yet they only make up 7% of my survey sample. In short, there is no evidence to suggest that we lack a civic foundation to repair humanity's impacts on the environment.

These arguments help, but they do not explain why the liberal Eco-Engaged I interviewed are more engaged in market-based solutions to ecological decline than the conservative Optimists, Fatalists, and Indifferent. Neither do existing explanations show why the conservatives I interviewed reject liberals' embrace of conscious consumerism.

Part of what drives polarization is the wedge between conservatives who do not support the ideal environmentalist and liberals who interpret this lack of support as evidence of a failure to care. Liberals approach those whom they see as not having an ability to engage in eco-friendly consumption with pity. But many liberals are hostile toward those whom they perceive as having the capacity to reduce their environmental impacts but seem not to do so. Conservatives challenge the ideal environmentalist, and many Eco-Engaged and Self-Effacing see that challenge as evidence of moral bankruptcy. Lexi, the Self-Effacing 21-year-old, said people who don't recycle and who drive pick-up trucks disgust her. These responses create a defensiveness among conservatives who react by lobbing charges of hypocrisy at the ideal environmentalist and challenging evidence characterizing ecological decline as catastrophic. Rather than defer to the ideal environmentalist, many conservatives question the legitimacy and authority of this cultural schema and those who endorse it.[9]

The price of challenging the ideal environmentalist is to be judged as immoral. To take this a step further, the Eco-Engaged and others who malign those who do not emulate the ideal environmentalist are an important and overlooked driver of political polarization. Overcoming polarization requires acknowledging the ways in which people who don't align with our cultural ideal nonetheless care about the environment. The Optimists and many Fatalists told me how important it is for them to spend time in natural areas. Many environmental social scientists are critical of what they see as white, male settlers' tendency to romanticize vast tracts of wilderness devoid of human activity. These critiques are important and justified—Dorceta Taylor tells us that when environmentalists concern themselves primarily with nonhuman elements of nature and not the people who experience those elements, they reproduce an environmentalism of whiteness and disregard how racialized groups make sense of nature (see box 8.1).[10] Likewise, Jules M. Bacon's work shows how wilderness preservation efforts make Indigenous peoples' existence invisible and erase the impacts that settler colonialism has had on Native American peoples and the planet.[11] These are extremely important critiques. And yet, we should make room to acknowledge that spending time in wild places is also an important way for some people to cultivate and sustain a relationship with the planet.

**LESSON #3: YOU CAN'T JUDGE (THE IMPACT OF)
A BOOK BY ITS COVER**

The Eco-Engaged are motivated to leave as small a footprint on the earth as possible. Many of the Eco-Engaged I surveyed and interviewed felt proud of their ability to lead a low-impact lifestyle, yet on average, the Eco-Engaged footprint is somewhat larger than that of other eco-types. Nonetheless, the Eco-Engaged are self-assured about the moral worth of their response to ecological decline. Why is the Eco-Engaged footprint not smaller than the footprint of others?

The more someone's lifestyle resembles that of the ideal environmentalist, the harder it is for them to accurately evaluate their own environmental impact. In chapter 2, I introduced the term "flagship behaviors." These behaviors (like recycling, using cloth bags, eating less meat, and cycling) are promoted ubiquitously in our classrooms, on social media and in popular films and books, and in stores and product branding. These are the practices that connote caring about the environment. Because the Eco-Engaged participate in these practices more frequently than others—and they know that—they evaluate the impact of their lifestyle as far below the American average. But because these flagship behaviors are not materially significant compared with practices like limiting travel and home energy use, engaging in them does not significantly reduce a household's environmental impact. In other words, "caring" about the planet in the manner of the ideal environmentalist doesn't necessarily translate into having a smaller footprint.[12]

I will use myself as an example to illustrate how this might happen. For most of my life, I haven't owned a car. Now, I have an electric car. I often eat vegetarian meals and I compost and recycle much of my waste. My family and I live in a relatively small apartment in a temperate climate, so our home energy use is negligible. But I also normally fly to at least two conferences per year and with family living in various parts of the country, and discretionary income that allows us to afford to visit them, my family and I take at least a couple flights to see our relatives. I live in Canada—it's cold! So, I also like to fly at least once every couple of years to a warmer climate. This is a huge carbon footprint—one that is far bigger than those of the farmers I interviewed in eastern Washington who use plastic bags and drive pick-up trucks and haven't been on a flight in years. It also adds up to a larger footprint than does leaving beer cans and cigarette butts behind at a campsite. When I was analyzing the survey data on flights, I had to recode quite a few responses, because in the space intended for people to type in how many flights they took in 2019, many people typed in an answer like "2009" or "2013." The respondent who wrote "2009" didn't take over two thousand flights—they last flew in 2009. In fact, only 5.6% of the people I surveyed take more than three short-haul flights each year, only 7.5% take more than three medium-haul flights in a year, and only 4% take more than three long-haul flights annually.

Are the Eco-Engaged generally aware of their environmental impacts? No, not as a rule. It would be tempting here to dismiss the Eco-Engaged as smug and hypocritical. But instead, we can focus on the evidence that allows us to understand why this makes sense: the Eco-Engaged have such a strong affinity for the environment and the last thing they want is to feel that they are harming it. They truly are trying to do the right thing and often make significant compromises to their leisure time, income, comfort, and convenience in order to do so. But because of the cultural prominence of the ideal environmentalist, an ideal that endorses conscious consumer choices in domains like eating and waste management, it is difficult to accurately judge the impact of an eco-social relationship.

LESSON #4: LOOK BEYOND THE INDIVIDUAL

One of the most enduring and foundational concepts in sociology is C. Wright Mills' notion of a sociological imagination.[13] Mills noted how common it is for individuals to lay the blame for their struggles and failings on themselves. He invited sociologists to correct this tendency by studying the social world in a way that calls attention to the social structures and relationships that shape the phenomena we study. I don't think environmental social scientists have done a very good job of using our sociological imaginations to study eco-social relationships, even while we have done so to study other topics such as environmental inequality.[14] I believe that, like the Eco-Engaged, many environmental social scientists feel an affinity for the impulses of the ideal environmentalist, and that this blinds us to the ways that our relationship with the cultural ideal reflects our own power and privilege. In fact, the only eco-social relationship in which the primary impulse was to focus on social structures as shaping people's experience of ecological decline is the Fatalists. Yet this is likely the most overlooked eco-social relationship in both academic literature and the public imaginary.

Believing that those in civil society should feel a moral responsibility to be conscientious about their consumer choices is central to our cultural conception of the ideal environmentalist. Many sociologists have critiqued this so-called "individualization of environmental responsibility."[15] Critics suggest that the conscious consumer might "crowd out" civil society's capacity to engage in collective action, although sociologists Margaret Willis and Juliet Schor rightly argued that there's no reason to assume that individual actions are either more selfish than, or mutually exclusive from, collective action.[16] Regardless of how effective an individualized response to ecological decline may or may not be, this is a response that reflects the tastes of relatively privileged liberals, creating a class of environmental citizenship that is out of reach for many. If we follow the Fatalists' view of the ideal environmentalist, we recognize on the one hand the good intentions behind the green consumer, and on the other hand the limitations of a practice associated with greenwashing and status distinctions. Maybe demoting cloth bags and farmers' markets from their moral pedestal could open up space for a greater diversity of eco-social relationships; perhaps even an expanded societal capacity to envision ways of confronting ecological decline.[17] The Fatalists' rejection of eco-friendly consumption may be a "canary in the coalmine" situation, signaling the decline of several decades in which society placed hope in consumer-driven reforms to make the world a better place.

The Fatalists' views on ecological decline reflect prominent theories in the environmental social sciences. They experience ecological decline as something beyond their power—they don't blame themselves for a changing climate, species extinction, or air and water pollution. They see evidence of ecological decline as an outcome of a capitalist system that pursues and rewards profit. The Fatalists have a grim view of society—they see us as "asleep," as Don the taxi driver put it, but not because we haven't been educated, as an Eco-Engaged participant might argue. The Fatalists see the lack of civic action to protect the environment as an extension of corporate power. Ted, the Fatalist truck driver who lives in Whitman, described what he saw as the "mall-ification of America." He believes that consumer pleasures are a big, shiny distraction that keeps Americans happy and entertained as they form an integral part of the engine of capitalism. Ted is not blaming individuals for being greedy, nor does he feel positively about capitalism and industrialization. Instead, he is pointing to the political and economic system of capitalism to identify structures that encourage people to find their sense of well-being and satisfaction in the marketplace. Ted's diagnosis is almost seamlessly consistent with how many environmental sociologists explain ecological decline. From Allan Schnaiberg's articulation of the Treadmill of Production, to John Bellamy Foster and Brett Clark's Marxist analysis of the drivers of environmental harm, social scientists tend to theorize ecological decline in a way that focuses very strongly on political and economic structures.[18]

Making space for the political talk of Fatalists and others who identify structural causes of ecological decline can sharpen our sociological imaginations and highlight the limitations of individualizing the responsibility to protect the environment. As I pointed out in chapter 5, the Fatalists raise a number of incisive critiques of conscious consumption, and they do not perceive their own distance from the ideal environmentalist as a personal failing; they see it as a socially structured outcome. In this way, the Fatalists help us to identify the many barriers preventing civil society from significantly reducing its impact on the planet—from infrastructure, to advertising, to the structure of work. They also help us remember that it is the state and the market, not civil society, that has the most egregious impact on the natural world. Listening to the struggles that the Self-Effacing describe in trying to align with the ideal environmentalist, I am also struck by an under-recognized cost of shopping our way to a better future: this model of change leaves so many people adrift, without access to a concrete set of practices that can forge a connection to the environment, to their communities, and to environmental protection at a time of ecological decline.[19] The Fatalists in particular act as a reminder of the need to implement our sociological imagination when we study and evaluate people's eco-social relationships.

However, the Fatalists are also profoundly disengaged and resigned to ecological decline. They express a weak affinity for the environment, shaped by their low levels of personal moral responsibility and efficacy to protect the environment. Despite making sharp critiques of systemic barriers to confronting ecological decline, the Fatalists are not a shining example of the emancipatory power of a sociological imagination. In a context where the ideal environmentalist dominates our cultural imaginary, there is seemingly little discursive or behavioral space for Fatalists to experience a feeling of harmony between their beliefs and their actions.[20] In fact, one of the relatively invisible benefits of adopting flagship behaviors uncritically is the sense of comfort and purpose this can afford. In our current moment, among the people I interviewed, a sociologically critical perspective on ecological decline and individualizing environmental protection can result in a sense of anomie or nihilism.

LESSON #5: WE DON'T ALL NEED TO CARE ABOUT THE ENVIRONMENT THE SAME WAY

The last lesson I want to draw out is that we don't all need to care about the environment in the same way. Just as there is no single recipe for a good relationship between two people, there is no single, best eco-social relationship.

Consider another example: it is common to encounter people who value the stunning diversity of ecosystems in the United States, from the mangroves of Florida, to the tundra of Alaska, and the deserts of New Mexico. And people generally understand that these diverse ecosystems emerge from unique climates, geological histories, and land uses. In the same way, eco-social relationships emerge from distinct interactions between biophysical landscapes and biography. Yet, as I listened to people talk about others' eco-social relationship and read environmental social scientific accounts of human-environment relationships, I rarely encountered an appreciation for the cultural diversity of eco-types that exists in the United States. Instead, it was common among both liberals and conservatives to express alarm and frustration that other people don't care about the environment the way they do.

By introducing five eco-social relationships, I have shown that people have very different ideas about their moral responsibilities to protect the planet and relate to distinct images of the environment. Some people relate to a powerful and resilient planet, while others relate to a planet that is gasping for air and suffering under the weight of human impact. Some people integrate a deeply felt responsibility to protect the environment into every decision they make—from the paid and unpaid work they commit their time to, to the location and design of their home, to how many children they have, to where they buy things and what they buy; other people hardly think about the environment at all.

Although my instinctive impulse is that everyone needs to embrace the idea that climate change is an emergency and take immediate measures to reduce our emissions, I try to challenge myself to interrogate that feeling. By interviewing people who described an Indifferent eco-social relationship, I came to understand why that response to ecological decline makes sense for them. One of the most relatable examples for me is Amber. Amber grew up on a large, working farm in a part of Washington dedicated largely to storing nuclear waste. Her family and friends in the area all made light of the risks of nuclear waste to human and ecological health. Now living in Pullman, Amber has three children under seven years old and is the breadwinner in the family. Her youngest has a chronic illness, and keeping him healthy requires Amber to purchase costly foods and household cleaners. Amber is not at all opposed to the practices associated with the ideal environmentalist. In fact, she tells me she wishes she could cycle, grow a vegetable garden, and shop at the farmers' market. But she doesn't have the middle-class resources to afford to make these changes to her routine: she doesn't have the time to stop at multiple stores for food or take her children to school and then bike to work, let alone grow a garden. She cannot justify the additional costs of buying local foods—she runs her household on a tight budget.

I want to return to an anecdote I shared earlier about my mother-in-law, Doris. Doris worked as a nurse for decades, and since I first met her in 2002, I would talk about the perils of climate change and tell her why she should eat less meat and recycle (I know, I know. I was insufferable!). She graciously tried tofu and would ask me for recipes for stir fries and salad dressings, but this was largely because she saw the health benefits of doing so. While I was trying to convince Doris that she needed to care about the environment in the way I did, she was telling me she thought a much more immediate threat was a global pandemic. She wanted me to wash my hands and use hand sanitizer. "How short-sighted," I thought; "How anthropocentric." Well, after Covid-19 turned the world upside down, shutting down schools, universities, and much of the economy, it is clear that what was extremely pressing and urgent for Doris but not for me has come to pass. She never says, "I told you so." Even though Doris agrees we should be protecting the environment, that is not the issue that keeps her up at night. And that's okay. What I am suggesting is that we should try not to assume that because someone does not look like the ideal environmentalist or care in the same way we do, that they don't care about the environment. We do not all need to care about the environment in the same way.[21] But we do need to have respect for one another's relationships to the world around us.

The Broader Implications of Contemporary Orientations to the Environment

When our cultural ideal of an environmentalist is premised on the interconnected themes of severity, individual moral responsibility, and daily conscious consumption, the market seems to become further entrenched as a centerpiece of society and daily life. Despite environmental activism's history of targeting the fossil-fuel industry, the forest industry, and various other resource extraction sectors, the ideal environmentalist actually places considerable trust in the market to deliver eco-friendly options, and considerable responsibility on individuals to purchase those products. Our cultural ideal not only obscures the role of corporate actors in escalating rates of using up environmental goods, it also creates opportunities for market expansion. Companies are easily able to distract from otherwise environmentally damaging or ethically dubious practices by offering green products and technologies. And public knowledge of environmental impacts seems to overstate the effects of individuals and underestimate how the market and the state contribute to ecological decline.

Idealizing individuals' efforts to reduce their consumption also sidelines the state from conversations about environmental protection. In my interviews, I heard most participants blaming other individuals for contaminating the environment, rather than focusing on the laws, policies, and (lack of) public infrastructure that inhibit equal access to pro-environmental practices, or on the state's role in escalating the rates at which the US uses up water, fuel, food, and forests. In his book, *Running Out,* anthropologist Lucas Bessire describes the way in which state representatives in charge of managing the Ogallala Aquifer give primacy to economic growth over groundwater. Interviewing a representative of the Groundwater Management District, Bessire discovered the agency knew they were overdrawing from the aquifer, but in the interests of propping up the agriculture industry, had adopted a policy of "controlled decline."[22] Controlling the decline of the aquifer meant accepting that humanity is using up the water faster than it can be replenished and choosing not to problematize that in order to sustain profits for the agriculture industry. Our focus on judging other individuals' eco-social relationships does little to open up important conversations about the limits we want our governments to impose to protect the environment.[23]

Across the various actors and institutions that make up society, from households and communities, to nonprofit organizations, to corporations and governments, environmental impacts are caused primarily by the state and the market, although very wealthy individuals have a large impact as well.[24] What these patterns indicate is that if, as a society, we are going to tackle environmental problems, governments and businesses need to make the most substantial reforms. The survey respondents for this study voiced this view when sharing the gap between trust and responsibility. Across all but the Indifferent eco-types, respondents saw either governments or businesses as most responsible for protecting the environment. Across all eco-types, respondents perceived governments and corporations as the least trustworthy sectors of society. As is well documented elsewhere, Americans have extremely low levels of trust that the government will act in a way that protects the common good.[25] This lack of trust also extends to the corporate sector. As much as powerful entities have sought to instill the notion that individuals are to blame for systemic problems and distract attention away from their own practices, a wide cross-section of Americans nonetheless sees the state and the market as failing to uphold the common good. In fact, this gap between responsibility and trust is a significant example of common ground across diverse eco-social relationships.

Although my respondents are clearly aware of the state's failure to adequately protect the environment, there is still a common pattern of blaming individuals for ecological decline. This tendency to individualize creates tensions and discomfort for everyone's relationship with the environment. Even though the Eco-Engaged are in a privileged position when it comes to their eco-social relationship, it is still a painful one. The Eco-Engaged I interviewed feel a deep sense of doubt that there are enough people committed to conscious consumption to make their theory of change effective. They care so deeply about the planet and are invested in an approach to eco-social change that seems doomed to fail. Embodying the other eco-social relationships also looks painful. The Self-Effacing never feel like they can do enough; the Optimists feel unfairly excluded from environmentalism; the Fatalists' only sense of hope is the extinction of the human race; and the Indifferent feel sidelined from mainstream cultural discussions of the environment and environmental protection. When we point a finger at other people's relationships with the environment to make sense of ecological decline, rather than focus on powerful institutions, we undermine social solidarity and exacerbate polarization.

Ultimately, one of the most important implications of the patterns I documented in this book is the way that environmental protection is stymied. Elected officials have to confront the reality of climate change and our current pace of production cannot continue. This is where I see civil society as having power and moral responsibility. One of the great gifts of conducting interviews with strangers is being reminded of the capacity that so many people have to be reflective and creative when it comes to critiquing cultural, political, and economic systems. This capacity is overshadowed and weakened when people focus their energy on attacking how those unlike them experience ecological decline. Many of the people I know and whose opinions I read see apathy as a clear and present danger in the fight against climate change. I challenge that impulse, instead suggesting that observing apathy is an opportunity for expressing empathy. Not doing so is perhaps even more dangerous than apathy itself, because we fail to make a connection to strengthen the fragile bonds holding civil society together.

Conclusion

Climate change is nothing but a bunch of computer models that attempt to tell us what's going to happen in 50 years or 30. Notice the predictions are never for next year or the next 10 years. They're always for way, way, way, way out there, when none of us are going to be around or alive to know whether or not they were true.
—RUSH LIMBAUGH, FOX NEWS, FEBRUARY 17, 2019

The GOP may soon become the party that destroyed the planet. They are the zombies who ask no questions. They are The Walking Dead who blindly follow a monster without scruples or morals.
—*ROLLING STONE*, APRIL 2020, P.13

In this second decade of the twenty-first century, the divisions across political lines in America are apparent every day. Conservative talk shows rouse and affirm the virtues of nationalism and express suspicion of those who do not, while liberal late-night shows convey both moral outrage at the politics of the day and a sense of disdain for those who do not share their indignation. Taking place simultaneously are unprecedented changes to the natural environment. The Intergovernmental Panel on Climate Change (IPCC) reported in 2018 that we surpassed 450 parts per million (ppm) of carbon dioxide (CO_2) in our atmosphere. In 2021, United Nations Secretary-General António Guterres described the recent IPCC Working Group 1 report as "code red for human-driven global heating."[1] At one point in the not-too-distant past, aims to stay below 350 ppm (the namesake target of the grass-roots environmental organization, 350.org) felt achievable. Now, we have far exceeded this limit at the same time as we have come to learn that those earlier targets actually underestimated the impacts of a changing climate on ecosystem functioning.

Environmental protection, including climate change mitigation and adaptation, has been swept up into the maelstrom of political polarization. There exists a conservative impulse—demonstrated in the late Rush Lim-baugh's statement above—that scoffs at evidence of a changing climate or claims about the urgency of the problem. The iconic liberal response, captured in the quotation from *Rolling Stone* magazine, is to take aim at the moral worth of those conservatives who allow the planet to be destroyed and those who "blindly" follow such "monsters." In such a polarized context, it can be extremely difficult to respect or trust points of view that are different from our own.

I detected the same notes of anger, name-calling, and finger-pointing in my conversations with Washington State residents. Across those interviews, I was also deeply struck by the way in which people misunderstand and malign others' relationships to the environment, and by the intrinsic value that my participants hold for the forests, fields, mountains, rivers, and ocean around them. The grand purpose of this book is to share those two insights with a broad audience. Ultimately, my aspiration is that reading this book might have evoked moments where you felt common ground with someone you previously thought you had nothing in common with, and moments where the experiences and perceptions of strangers piqued your curiosity.

Cultivating Curiosity

In the hopes that this book becomes part of a larger effort to correct misun-derstandings about the beliefs and orientations to the environment of people different from us, I want to share some insights I gained from listening to people from each of the five eco-types.

Conducting this research made me aware of a pernicious, subtle, and confrontational dialogue that implicitly and explicitly takes place between the liberal Eco-Engaged who want everyone to share their commitment to environmental protection, and the conservative Optimists who want to be recognized as environmentalists. Here is a stylized representation of this dialogue:

ECO-ENGAGED: "Anyone who drives a pick-up truck or an ATV
    doesn't care about the planet."

OPTIMISTS: "You think we don't care about the planet, but we do!
    We should be considered environmentalists. We use those vehicles
    to actually get out and see the world around us. We know the
    environment better than you do."

ECO- ENGAGED: "Know it? You don't know the environment at all.
    If you did, you would know that ecological issues are serious and
    urgent and require all of us to make personal sacrifices and be
    conscious about our own environmental impacts."

OPTIMISTS: "How dare you say I don't know the environment? You're
    up in your fifteenth-floor condo. You don't know anything. And
    don't tell me to watch my impacts while you fly all over the world."

This dialogue has come to feel so heartbreaking to me. Rather than the Optimists recognizing that the Eco-Engaged are acting out of a deep love for the planet, and the Eco-Engaged feeling energized, knowing that Optimists think being an environmentalist is a positive thing and want to co-construct what that label means, they are pitted against one another. This is a dialogue many people might encounter in daily life. My hope is that the accounts in this book provide some tools to disrupt these barriers to identifying common ground.

Speaking with Washington residents also showed me that there is a tendency for high cultural capital people to assume that lower-income people lack the capacity to care for the environment. This observation reminded me of environmental studies scholar Manisha Anantharaman's argument that the sustainable consumption practices of the working class are overlooked and devalued by self-identified environmentalists.[2] I found this tendency to denigrate lower-income people's contributions to sustainability when my participants referred to someone living frugally and consuming very little as an "accidental environmentalist."[3] The cultural ideal of an environmentalist is so strongly associated with behaviors like using a reusable water bottle and buying organic food that it seems to give many people license to exclude others from environmentalism if they cannot afford these choices.

Getting to know the Fatalists also had a major impact on how I understand environmental politics and those who engage in efforts to protect the environment. The Fatalists seem to have the sharpest diagnosis of why the environment is threatened. Their doubts about the practice of voting with our dollars usefully creates a space to focus on how corporate marketing and greenwashing can sustain ecologically untenable rates of production and consumption. I wonder if spaces of environmental activism might develop a thicker democratic imagination, that is, a deeper capacity to generate ideas for how to confront ecological decline, if there were more Fatalists involved. In our current context, I worry that Fatalists would be looked down upon in these spaces. Sociologist Dave Horton's research with environmental activists suggests that in order to belong in those groups, people had to adopt the sorts of practices that people associate with the ideal environmentalist. For instance, when someone drove to a meeting, they were quick to explain that they only drove because they lived on a farm, on which they grew food and harvested rainwater, and so forth.[4] A Fatalist might attend an environmental meeting eating a fast-food burger and wearing a sweatshirt from the Gap, and if others could cultivate a sense of curiosity for what brought them to the meeting, the collective effort might benefit from a sharper focus on holding government accountable and taking power away from corporations. In the absence of big or small moments of engagement in social change, I worry that the Fatalists' critical diagnoses of ecological decline will evaporate into despair and hopelessness.

I hope this book serves as a compassionate suggestion to the Eco-Engaged that judging other people for not caring enough about the environment undermines social solidarity at a time when we desperately need it. For example, instead of sanctioning her acquaintance for buying chips instead of organic food, Eileen could recognize that her friend has a lot on her plate. She could offer to babysit for her, or bring her some food, organic or otherwise. I would love to go back to 2002 and be less self-righteous with my mother-in-law—ask her for advice on how she grows a prolific vegetable garden each year and wait to be invited to do so before foisting tofu on the family. For those with an Eco-Engaged orientation, cultivating curiosity in how others care about the environment likely demands a concomitant focus on the incredible luxury and privilege that is both reflected and reproduced by aligning with the ideal environmentalist. Perhaps the Eco-Engaged could deploy their cultural power to make a bigger tent, spending more time listening to other people's experience of ecological decline instead of using a cultural megaphone to reiterate that their own views and experiences are the right ones.

Overall, the key observations here are that most Americans share something extremely important—caring about the natural environment and wanting to feel that our actions and our life benefit the world around us. Picture a Venn diagram with five circles, each of which represents an eco-type.

The area where these five circles overlap may be small, but it exists. Amidst distinct and at times conflicting eco-types, that area of overlap serves as a reminder that recognizing that people have different ways of caring about the environment should not blind us to important areas of common ground. Recall that fewer than 50 years ago, there was strong and bipartisan support for environmental protection legislation in the US. In fact, consensus on environmental protection was a rare moment of coalition-building in an era where liberals and conservatives held starkly different views on the Vietnam War. Even in our recent, polarized era, there are many academic studies that show support across the political spectrum for renewable energy.[5] There are examples of conservatives and liberals working together to protect the environment, as Justin Farrell documents in chapter 5 of his book, *The Battle for Yellowstone*. Even though liberals and conservatives may report different reasons for their interest in renewable energy or wilderness preservation, the important lesson is that there is a precedent for collaboration across party lines to advance environmental protection. These historical and current patterns hint at the possibility that there is common ground here, although what that looks like and feels like is not always apparent.

Future Research

I hope this book has activated an empathetic and critical perspective on eco-social relationships among those who study such relationships. I believe this sort of critical perspective is needed since much of our foundational literature places a blind faith in our assumptions and impulses as scholars. I invite my colleagues to approach the social world with less judgment and more awareness of the social structures that contour our own (and others') orientations to the planet. Our tendency to critique people that we deem to be anti-environmental creates the conditions for the sorts of authority relationships (i.e., "I know better than my subjects do") that lead to faulty explanations of the social world.[6] Rather than follow our subjects' lead to understand their experience of the world—something they are undoubtedly the experts on—we too often evaluate others according to the things that matter to us. By recognizing the privileged life experiences afforded to us by our education, our communities, the support of our family, friends, and colleagues, the opportunity to work in a field we are passionate about, and in particular the privilege of having the cultural authority to define what a "good" eco-social relationship is, we might approach our fields of study with a more open and empathetic gaze. Part of checking our privilege demands listening; if we are studying a phenomenon that we think might be obscured by an authority relationship, wherein academics have constituted the field of study without first considering people's diverse experiences, we can commit to reshaping that area by listening extensively before speaking or theorizing.

We can implement that open and empathetic gaze in our classrooms and public presentations as well as in our research. I have taught an undergraduate class on environmental sociology for almost a decade now. And every year, I admit, I find it easier to relate to students who want to save the planet. Once, while lecturing on Allan Schnaiberg's theory of the Treadmill of Production, I saw a student buying shoes online. I cried inside. How could someone shop for shoes while learning about the way that capitalist systems of production harm workers and the planet? As I plan my course, I feel like it is my job not just to teach environmental sociology, but also to cultivate in my students a deeper commitment to the sort of engagement and outlook that I believe will bring about justice and sustainability. And yet, if I'm honest, I didn't actually make the effort to ensure that students felt welcomed even if they spent class-time buying shoes, or, more commonly, if they only took the class because it fit their schedule or if they thought it would be easy. I created a classroom that was inclusive of anyone who agreed that ecological issues are severe and who was outraged at environmental inequality, and who wanted to play a role in reversing those trends. After writing this book, I can see that I didn't create a space for the Indifferent and I wasn't exactly welcoming toward the Optimists. One way to make a pedagogical atmosphere more welcoming is to think of speaking to as broad an audience as possible, not just to those who share our impulses and know our jargon. This does not mean ignoring empirical evidence, but exactly the opposite—it demands taking a critical view of the evidence at hand and being mindful of how our positionality shapes the subjects we examine and the interpretations that resonate with us.

I hope others improve on this research. I would like to see how conducting the same, or a similar interview with different people would shape the results. For example, I only interviewed in one state and am curious about how other regional contexts might condition eco-social relationships.[7] I also constructed my sample to maximize variation on the demographic characteristics that consistently prove to be most significant for capturing variation in ecological worldviews—political ideology, type of community, and social class. If I were initiating this research right now, I would also try to interview a large sample of people who identify as Black, Latinx, and Indigenous.

Interviewing in different subcultures of environmentalism would be generative. I worry that someone could read this book and think that I am saying there is not an eco-type reflecting those who tirelessly stand up for the health and vitality of ecosystems, like the activists protesting the Dakota Access Pipeline. The five eco-types that I focus on in this book emerged from my interviews in Washington State, where I deliberately recruited "ordinary" people rather than those at the vanguard of environmental movements. If I had instead interviewed dozens of activists, I may have identified eco-social relationships where strong affinity for the environment was not coupled with a belief that our primary responsibility is to reduce our individual consumption of natural resources, but instead, responsibility to be part of systemic change. An open question is whether dedicated environmental activists would engage in the same practice of maligning individuals for their eco-social relationships. For instance, would a passionate climate protester intensely resent individual climate deniers, failing to recognize the structural conditions that make skepticism in the face of ecological decline feel right for that person? Anecdotally, having attended many climate protests, I worry that the same pattern of making moral judgments of individuals based on their eco-social relationships exists in activist spaces as well. But I hope to be proven wrong.

How Can We Save the Environment?

At the start of my career, I wanted to know what motivated people to reduce their carbon dioxide emissions through actions like riding a bike, eating locally produced food and less meat, and being mindful of home energy use. As I adopted these practices, I also enthusiastically recommended them to others, even when they didn't ask. If these are the sorts of actions you are interested in adopting, I highly recommend a paper by Thomas Dietz and several coauthors published in the *Proceedings of the National Academy of Sciences*.[8] Their research identifies the material impacts of various household actions to reduce emissions, from carpooling or getting a fuel-efficient vehicle, to weatherizing your home or adjusting your thermostat. Regardless of whether you adopt any of the practices Dietz and his coauthors identify, or which ones you adopt, I recommend not making it an individual practice. Talk to neighbors and friends and family about what is working for you, and what behaviors are more difficult to practice consistently. Research suggests that these sorts of efforts at creating a community play an important role in changing the social norms that shape individual behavior and corporate strategy, while also helping to motivate your ongoing engagement.[9]

After a few years of studying what drives people to try to consume sustainably, I started learning more about the range of carbon footprints people have, and then about the size of the residential carbon footprint compared with the footprint of other sectors in the economy, like transportation and electricity generation. I felt duped! I felt like I had been spending time, money, and my family's comfort on practices that were not even making a difference. After this, I embarked on a phase of more political actions—attending protests, campaigning for environmentally committed political candidates, and speaking to media and decision makers about my research. But in these spaces, I often felt uncomfortable with the us/them discourse that pitted individuals against other individuals. For people wanting to get engaged through political actions, there are many options—movements such as Extinction Rebellion and Fridays for Future and organizations such as Ducks Unlimited and the Audubon Society are good examples—but there are many other local organizations that might be a better fit. For some, a local organization may speak more directly to the cultural values and context of their community.

After this project, I now perceive polarization and divisiveness as the most dangerous threats to the environment from civil society because they play a role in preventing institutions that should be taking serious steps to protect the environment from doing so. As a result, I now try to practice what I've been preaching in these chapters: to recognize that when I feel an aversion to someone's environmental practices or beliefs, that that person and I likely have different eco-social relationships and undoubtedly have had different experiences in our lives. I have no intention of trying to convince them to adopt my eco-social relationship, but I do seek opportunities to try to understand why their actions make sense for them. I don't see this work as negating material truths about the ecological untenability of many North Americans' lifestyles—it is true that the daily consumption patterns of most well-off people in the world collectively exceed the planet's carrying capacity. But more transformative change can be found in understanding the conditions that give rise to highly consumptive lifestyles rather than morally condemning people for driving big trucks or paddling a kayak to attend a climate protest.

From each phase of research that I described, some practices stick and others fall away. I still cycle, minimize home energy use, and try not to use air travel too often, but, gradually, my family's meat consumption has risen, we bought a car, and we buy exotic treats such as French wine and strawberries in the midst of winter. I still go to climate protests and communicate my research to the media, but not with the same frequency that I did before. All this to say, depending on the conditions of our lives, we will have a greater or lesser capacity to realize the sort of lifestyle we aspire to practice, and varying degrees of affinity for a range of environmentally relevant actions. In the same way, our ability to observe different eco-social relationships and respond with curiosity rather than condemnation will depend on broader political conditions (e.g., which party is in office, what policies they're pushing, what environmental crisis is unfolding). And it will depend on the context of our own lives—what else we are struggling with, what services our neighborhoods offer, who our friends are, how much free time and extra cash we have available, and so on.

Concluding Thoughts

At the most general level, I hope this book has demonstrated that the structures shaping our lifestyles and life outcomes also shape our experience of ecological decline. If high cultural capital liberals can challenge the assumption that some individuals have an anti-environmental worldview and that they must "educate" them to see the world as they do, civil society will be in a better position to build on the many ways that we all care about the environment.

I wrote this book because I want civil society to be a more powerful force to demand ambitious and effective environmental protection, and I believe one way to do this is to show people that debates over environmental protection rest on a foundation of ideological common ground (we all care about the environment) and that there is a great deal of diversity in how we relate to the environment. My goal for this project is that it will allow those who engage with its arguments to come together over their shared interest in the environment while disagreeing on the particulars in a more constructive and empathetic way.

The ultimate extension of my argument is that one way to narrow the political divide in support for environmental protection is to ensure that both conservatives and liberals feel their eco-social relationship is understood and validated in mainstream culture. Right now, liberals see their eco-social relationship reflected back to them in many cultural institutions, but sense conservatives' opposition to that eco-social relationship. Conservatives don't see their eco-social relationship reflected in mainstream culture and wish they did. This means that both liberals and conservatives misunderstand the eco-social relationships of those unlike themselves. Making an effort to understand how people across the political spectrum relate to the environment is worthwhile because we will be more interested in collaborating and cooperating with people who understand where we are coming from than with people who misjudge us.[10] In the context of eco-social relationships and environmental protection, this means we cannot expect people to join us in our efforts to protect the environment if we denigrate their connection with the environment.

In the preface, I wrote about the sense of peace and gratitude I feel when I spend time in the forest near my home. As I was completing this project, I had the good fortune to read forest ecologist Suzanne Simard's book, *Finding the Mother Tree.*[11] This eye-opening account of how forests work upends decades of research that characterizes forests as sites of competition for resources, with coniferous trees battling against fast-growing deciduous trees and shrubs for light and water. Simard conducted meticulous experiments, demonstrating how wrong this characterization of forests is: the species in a forest share resources, they pass nutrients through underground networks of mycorrhizal fungi, and trees have better survival outcomes when they are in a diverse forest, even if they are shaded by upstart shrubs. Simard likens forest ecosystems to human communities, and that comparison prompted me to consider her efforts to ask ecologists and other readers to look at the forest and observe cooperation rather than competition. My aspiration is similar: to ask environmental social scientists and other readers to look at society and observe a multitude of ways of caring about the environment rather than engage in a battle over who cares more or less, or better or worse. Our diverse eco-social relationships are a strength, and if we can cooperate rather than compete to define the "best" eco-type, civil society will be better able to confront ecological decline.

I recently walked through the forest to the clothing-optional beach that I described in the preface to this book. It was a chilly October day; the sky was a bright blue, the sun was out after a week of rain, and the wind was blowing. Waves crashed on the beach. It was breathtaking. As I was taking in the view, a man with no pants on waved to get my attention. When we made eye contact he smiled and called out: "Do you like my picture?" pointing to the sand, where he had used a branch to outline a flower with a smiley face, about 20 feet in diameter. It was impossible not to smile. Pants or no pants, it felt in that moment that we were both taking in the exhilarating beauty of the morning. I smiled back and told him: "I love it!" In that setting, I didn't even have to use my "Huh. How interesting" prompt to stop me from judging his sartorial choices. I sensed a shared connection that was more important than our different orientations toward being naked in public.

The animosity of political talk, the vitriol present in so many posts and stories on social media and television, and the obvious differences in tastes, opinions, and lifestyles can make daily life feel like a battle for belonging and dignity. Yet focusing on such differences obscures important common ground and significant ways that we cooperate with other humans and other species every day. Our shared appreciation for the natural environment offers a powerful foundation to find this common ground and has the potential to serve as a place where we can more readily witness humanity's powerful capacity for cooperation. There is no doubt that an enormous amount of work needs to be done to sustain ecological vitality. But politically charged battles within civil society over who cares more or better about the environment are not a productive use of our time, energy, and passion. We all want to exist in this beautiful world without destroying it. Recognizing that we share an appreciation for the environment is the first step to beginning to work together to protect it.

Appendix A: Interview Methodology

I began collecting interview data in Washington State. In part, this is because I lived in Washington and this was therefore the most straightforward place to begin interviews. But this state is also a meaningful place to start given that it is where early environmental sociology began.[1]

I collected data over two years and relied on valuable help from several research assistants. Because I wanted to interview people in urban areas, rural areas, and towns, and because I had no criteria other than this to select sites, I randomly selected one community from each of these categories. Then my research assistant, Darcy Hauslik, used data from the American Community Survey to identify several high-income neighborhoods, and several low-income neighborhoods. We were seeking a maximum variation sample, particularly for social class, and this was an effective way to achieve that goal. Next, we used satellite imagery from Google Maps to ensure that the areas across all sites were ones where we could solicit engagement by going door-to-door (i.e., not a large concentration of apartment buildings), and we sought some common attributes, such as walkability and access to green space, across the various sites. Because the rural sites are such small communities, I use pseudonyms for these places.

In the first summer of data collection, in 2016, I worked with graduate students Darcy Hauslik and Jacobs Hammond to interview 45 people in three sites: Olympia, Pullman, and Pacifica. In each site, we spent several days walking around the two neighborhoods and the downtown to get a feel for the place (see the Place Descriptions in appendix C). In the second summer (2017), we visited an additional rural community, because our first randomly selected rural area was so politically liberal. The second rural community (Whitman) is an agricultural area with a strongly conservative voting base. In the first three sites, we recruited participants by knocking on doors and leaving a recruitment letter with our contact information. In Whitman,

I was fortunate to have the assistance of Mark Billings, a hockey teammate and WSU graduate student. Mark was able to recruit people in Whitman to participate in the interviews. Research assistant Jesse Mendiola joined me and Darcy Hauslik to conduct those interviews.

The interviews were largely held in participants' homes, though some were held at the participant's workplace, or a café. Interviews ranged in length from 45 minutes to three hours and were structured around a semi-structured interview guide (see box A.1, below), with a brief amount of time allotted at the end for participants to ask questions of the research team and complete the follow-up questionnaire needed to gather sociodemographic information (see appendix B, interview sample).

The qualitative analysis for this project began immediately after the interview, when the interviewer would complete a memo summarizing the themes of the interview. The memo began with general impressions of

---

BOX A.1. Interview Guide*

Environment, emotions, and identity

1. To begin with, when I say the word "environment," what do you picture? What comes to mind?
2. Generally, would you describe your reactions to those images as positive or negative? In what way?
3. Are there any environmental problems that have had or currently have an impact on your quality of life? *[Prompt: wildfires, drinking water quality] (Probe: Can you try to describe what that felt/feels like to experience an unhealthy environment?)*
4. If 10 = extremely concerned and 1 = not at all concerned, how concerned are you about environmental issues? *Can you explain your answer? (Probe: What issues concern you the most? The least?)*
5. Overall, how important do you think it is that we protect the environment, if 10 = extremely important and 1 = not at all important? *(Probe: Do you feel the environment is currently well-protected? Whose job do you think it is?)*
6. Thinking about most of the people you know, do you think they would generally answer the last two questions [can repeat] the same way, or differently? *(Probe: Is it important to you that the people you spend time with feel the same way as you about these issues?)*
7. What sorts of things come to mind when you think of someone who has a positive impact on the environment? *(Probe: What sorts of things do they do and believe? What do they look like?)*
8. When I say "environmentalist" does anyone in particular come to mind? Someone you may or may not know, or even yourself? *(Probe: How positively or negatively do you feel about that person? Why?)*

*Note that the interviews did not always proceed in the order listed below as my intention was to structure the interview to resemble a conversation.

9. Who do you picture when you think of someone with a very large impact on the environment? What are your feelings toward that person? What sort of a person might they be?

10. What about the opposite? Someone who has the smallest impact on the environment—who comes to mind? What are your feelings toward that person? What sort of a person might they be?

11. In an ideal world, what would you do differently to change your impact on the environment? What sort of activities would you engage in? What stands in your way?

Green consumerism

I want to ask you a few questions now about what you buy and how you choose to buy things.

1. There are a lot of products out there that claim to be better for the environment, some people call these "green products." How do you feel about these sorts of products?

2. Take me back to the last time you went grocery shopping. Did you find yourself noticing what other people have in their carts? What sort of thoughts went through your head?

3. Still at the grocery store, how would you feel about the person ahead of you in line at the checkout counter if their cart were full of green products? *(Probe: Could you make any assumptions about how much money that person made? What about how good a person they are? What about how smart they are, or how much they know?)*

4. What about if their cart had no green products in it? Would you feel any differently about that person? *(Probe: Could you make any assumptions about how much money that person made? What about how good a person they are? What about how smart they are, or how much they know?)*

5. Do you know anyone who really tries to cut back on how much they consume? Like say, not driving much or not using much energy in their household? What do you make of someone like that? *(Probe: Could you make any assumptions about how much money they make? What about how good a person they are? What about how smart they are, or how much they know?)*

Citizenship

The last few questions I want to ask are about what you believe are our responsibilities to protect the environment

1. Thinking broadly, do you think individuals should be trying to help the environment? How do you think people should do that?

2. What do you think is the single most important thing you can do to try to protect the natural environment?

Wrapping up

1. Are there any questions you wanted me to ask or expected me to ask? Do you have any questions for us about the research?

the participant and the interview and proceeded through nine additional questions. The memo questions are included in box A.2, below. The research team transcribed the first 44 interviews. I transcribed the 15 interviews that I did not conduct, which allowed me to compensate for the lack of familiarity that can come with hands-off data collection. Next, I read each of the transcripts, noting themes and concepts of interest. I had the remaining 19 interviews professionally transcribed and noted connections to existing

---

BOX A.2. Analytic Memo (list of questions)

1. How would you characterize this participant's relationship to the environment?
2. What are the participant's primary emotions in relation to the environment?
3. How does the participant evaluate, judge, or assess others in the field of environmental protection?
4. What, in the participant's view, constitutes a *good person*? Is there an environmental axis to this "goodness"?
5. Are there tensions between this participant's normative ideals and their practice? How does the participant make sense of those tensions?
6. How does this participant understand their environmental impact (positive and/ or negative; problematic or not) in relation to their personal world, and the larger civic realm?
7. What tools, practices, skills, habits does the participant describe as ways to reduce his or her environmental impact?
8. Does the participant accept a moral responsibility to protect the environment? Challenge it? Feel angered by it? Protected by it?
9. What similarities and contrasts to other interviews are evident?

BOX A.3. Codes for Qualitative Analyses

Relationship with environment (10 themes)		*Environmental Responsibilities (3 themes)*
Eco-Engaged	Affinity	Moral responsibility
Self-Effacing	Severity	Dominant cultural ideal
Optimists	Morality	Counter-ideal
Fatalists	Relationality	
Indifferent	Efficacy	

Symbolic boundaries (4 themes)	*Social boundaries (5 themes)*
Perceived as: outside the boundary/ inside the boundary	Gender: women nurture the planet; women are natural green consumers; masculinity and resource-dependence
Moral boundaries	Class: the poor can't care; the rich are selfish
Cultural boundaries	Race: The Ecological Indian; eco-ignorant minorities
Economic boundaries	Conservatives don't care
	Urbanites don't get it

---

themes and added new themes as I cleaned these transcripts. This process took several months, at the end of which I uploaded the 63 transcripts into a software program (NVivo 11 for Mac). I created nodes for each of the themes I had identified in earlier rounds of analysis and narrowed down a full list of 46 themes to a final list of conceptual themes. I created parent nodes (in bold, below) and child nodes (beneath italic lettering) to use to organize additional rounds of line-by-line coding. These are included in box A.3.

Appendix B: Interview Sample

After each interview, participants completed a brief follow-up questionnaire that allowed me to collect sociodemographic information. This information is provided in table A.1, below, for each respondent (using pseudonyms for participant names and rural place names). The interview participant information is summarized by eco-type. To determine a participant's eco-type, I worked with two research assistants to code the data specifically for this task. I coded all interviews and each research assistant (RA) coded half of the sample. Thus, each interview was coded twice. I instructed the RAs to code labels for affinity, severity, morality, and efficacy and to characterize these excerpts as low/ weak or high/strong throughout each participant's interview transcript. Of all labeling codes (i.e., affinity, severity, etc.), only 6% had a mismatch across the two coders. For instance, an excerpt of text reading "I don't think there's any point in worrying about the environment" was coded as low affinity by one coder and as low efficacy by another coder. In these instances, the RAs and I would discuss the code and look closely at what the participant said immediately before and after (e.g., we ultimately coded this example as low efficacy, since the participant next said, "It's not like there's anything I can do about it"). Of all codes characterizing intensity (i.e., low or high), 8% had a mismatch across coders. We followed the same process that we used for labels to resolve these mismatches. After summarizing the strength of each facet of eco-social relationships for a participant, I then used the modal characterization for affinity, severity, morality, and efficacy to categorize participants into eco-social relationships. For instance, in Addy's interview, nearly 85% of her affinity statements were coded as "high/strong," 90% of her severity statements were coded "high," nearly 90% of her morality comments were coded as "high," and 75% of her efficacy comments were coded as "high/strong." Thus, Addy was categorized as Eco-Engaged.

Other sociodemographic variables included in Table A.1 include age, gender, whether the participant has children or not, their political ideology,

TABLE A.1. Sociodemographic Characteristics of the Interview Sample

Pseudonym	Age	Gender	Has Children	Political Ideology	Education	Income	Home Ownership	Employment Status	Occupation	Social Class	Site	Eco-Type
Addy	40	Female	Yes	Liberal	Bachelors	50–75K	Own	Part-Time	Book Keeper	Middle	Pacifica	Eco-Engaged
Angela	39	Female	Yes	Moderate	Bachelors	120+	Own	Childcare	Reporting Analyst	Upper-Middle	Pullman	Eco-Engaged
Annie	59	Female	No	Liberal	Masters	75–119K	Own	Fulltime	Realtor	Upper-Middle	Olympia	Eco-Engaged
Betty	85	Female	Yes	No Response	PhD	120K+	Own	Retired	Retail	Upper-Middle	Pullman	Eco-Engaged
Dave	32	Male	No	Liberal	Some College	31–49K	Own	Fulltime	Computer	Lower-Middle	Pacifica	Eco-Engaged
Denny	44	Male	No	Liberal	Bachelors	50–75K	Rent	Fulltime	Fireman	Middle	Olympia	Eco-Engaged
Eileen	59	Female	No	Liberal	Masters	31–49K	Own	Part-Time	Teaching	Upper-Middle	Pullman	Eco-Engaged
Elena	82	Female	Yes	Liberal	PhD	120K+	Own	Retired	Social Work	Middle	Pullman	Eco-Engaged
Eloise	47	Female	Yes	Liberal	PhD	75–119K	Own	Fulltime	Judge	Upper-Middle	Olympia	Eco-Engaged
Hank	90	Male	Yes	Liberal	PhD	50–75K	Own	Retired	Teaching	Middle	Pullman	Eco-Engaged
Ina	64	Female	Yes	No Response	Bachelors	120K+	Own	Part-Time	Teaching	Upper-Middle	Pullman	Eco-Engaged
Ivan	66	Male	Yes	Liberal	Masters	120K+	Own	Retired	IT Manager	Upper-Middle	Olympia	Eco-Engaged
Jake	71	Male	Yes	Liberal	MD	120K+	Own	Retired	Doctor	Upper-Middle	Pullman	Eco-Engaged
Jerry	63	Male	No	Liberal	High School	75–119K	Own	Retired	Utility Designer	Middle	Pullman	Eco-Engaged
Kyle	45	Male	Yes	Conservative	Masters	120K+	Own	Fulltime	Military Recruitment	Upper-Middle	Pullman	Eco-Engaged
Laurel	67	Female	No	Liberal	PhD	120K+	Own	Fulltime	Attorney	Upper-Middle	Olympia	Eco-Engaged
Linda	68	Female	Yes	Liberal	Bachelors	31–49K	Rent	Part-Time	Teaching	Upper-Middle	Pacifica	Eco-Engaged
Nadine	47	Female	No	Liberal	PhD	50–75K	Rent	Part-Time	Counselor	Upper-Middle	Olympia	Eco-Engaged

Name	Age	Gender		Politics	Education	Income	Housing	Employment	Occupation	Class	City	
Rachel	41	Female	No	Liberal	Less Than Elementary	120K+	Occupied, No Rent	Part-Time	Painter	Middle	Pacifica	Eco-Engaged
Ben	77	Male	Yes	Liberal	Bachelors	75–119K	Own	Retired	Investment	Upper-Middle	Pacifica	Self-Effacing
Brian	48	Male	Yes	Liberal	PhD	75–119K	Own	Fulltime	Instructor	Upper-Middle	Pullman	Self-Effacing
Caitlyn	38	Female	No	Liberal	High School	50–75K	Own	Fulltime	Bartender	Lower-Middle	Pacifica	Self-Effacing
Carissa	37	Female	Yes	Liberal	PhD	50–75K	Rent	Unemployed	Health Technician	Middle	Olympia	Self-Effacing
Cheryl	61	Female	Yes	Liberal	Bachelors	50–75K	Own	Retired	Social Work Assistant	Middle	Olympia	Self-Effacing
Ellen	33	Female	No	Liberal	Bachelors	Less Than 15K	Rent	Fulltime	Author	Lower-Middle	Pacifica	Self-Effacing
Janet	55	Female	No	Liberal	Masters	50–75K	Own	Part-Time	Volunteer Coordinator	Middle	Olympia	Self-Effacing
Jim	29	Male	No	No Response	Some College	13–30K	Rent	Fulltime	Chef, Prep cook	Middle	Pullman	Self-Effacing
John	71	Male	No	Liberal	Bachelors	31–49K	Own	Retired	Mail-Carrier	Lower-Middle	Pacifica	Self-Effacing
Judy	52	Female	No	Liberal	PhD	75–119K	Own	Fulltime	School Counselor	Middle	Olympia	Self-Effacing
Kim	38	Female	Yes	Liberal	Some College	31–49K	Rent	Fulltime	Associate Director	Lower-Middle	Pullman	Self-Effacing
Lexi	21	Female	No	Liberal	Some College	Less Than 15K	Rent	Fulltime	Nanny/Barista/Student	Lower-Middle	Pullman	Self-Effacing
Sharon	59	Male	Yes	Conservative	Masters	75–119K	Own	Fulltime	B & B Manager	Middle	Pacifica	Self-Effacing
Shelby	32	Female	No	Liberal	Masters	31–49K	Rent	Fulltime	Adviser	Middle	Pullman	Self-Effacing
Tom	29	Male	No	Liberal	Bachelors	15–30K	Rent	Part-Time	Bike Technician	Lower-Middle	Olympia	Self-Effacing

Continued on next page

TABLE A.1. (*continued*)

Pseudonym	Age	Gender	Has Children	Political Ideology	Education	Income	Home Ownership	Employment Status	Occupation	Social Class	Site	Eco-Type
Travis	38	Male	Yes	Liberal	Some College	75–119K	Own	Childcare	Concrete Finisher	Middle	Olympia	Self-Effacing
William	65	Male	No	No Response	Some College	50–75K	Own	Retired	Cabinetry	Middle	Pacifica	Self-Effacing
Bill	34	Male	Yes	Conservative	Bachelors	75–119K	Own	Fulltime/Childcare	Realtor	Middle	Pullman	Optimist
Ed	82	Male	Yes	Conservative	Masters	50–75K	Own	Retired	Regional HR	Upper-Middle	Olympia	Optimist
Jeff	48	Male	Yes	Conservative	Some College	50–75K	Own	Fulltime	Technician	Middle	Pullman	Optimist
Greg	66	Male	Yes	Conservative	Some College	50–75K	Own	Retired	Sales	Lower-Middle	Olympia	Optimist
Hannah	40	Female	Yes	Conservative	Bachelors	75–119K	Own	Fulltime	Manager	Middle	Whitman	Optimist
Jenny	44	Female	Yes	Libertarian	Bachelors	75–119K	Own	Fulltime	City Administrator	Upper-Middle	Whitman	Optimist
Scott	57	Male	No	Conservative	PhD	50–75K	Own	Fulltime	Technology	Middle	Pullman	Optimist
Shauna	63	Female	No	Liberal	Some College	120K+	Own	Fulltime	EEO Coordinator	Upper-Middle	Pullman	Optimist
Sheri	40	Female	Yes	Libertarian	Masters	50–75K	Rent	Fulltime	Preschool Teaching	Middle	Whitman	Optimist
Tina	47	Female	Yes	Conservative	Some College	50–75K	Own	Part-Time	Farm Owner	Middle	Whitman	Optimist
Charles	66	Male	No	Liberal——	Some High School	Less Than 15K	Rent	Part-Time	Janitorial/Construction	Lower-Middle	Pacifica—Fatalist	
Darren	67	Male	Yes	Conservative	Some College	Less Than 15K	Rent	Retired	Foreman	Lower-Middle	Whitman	Fatalist
Don	66	Male	No	Liberal	Bachelors	15–30K	Rent	Fulltime	Taxi Driver	Lower-Middle	Pacifica	Fatalist

Name	Age	Gender		Political	Education	Income	Housing	Employment	Occupation	Class	Town	Outlook
James	33	Male	Yes	Conservative	High School	31–49K	Own	Fulltime	Manager/Maintenance	Lower	Whitman	Fatalist
Karen	56	Female	Yes	Conservative	Some High School	31–49K	Own	Part-Time	Daycare Worker	Lower	Whitman	Fatalist
Ronald	60	Male	Yes	Conservative	High School	31–49K	Own	Retired	Farmer	Lower	Whitman	Fatalist
Ted	40	Male	No	Conservative	High School	50–75K	Rent	Fulltime	Truck Driver	Lower-Middle	Whitman	Fatalist
Amber	33	Female	Yes	Conservative	Bachelors	75–119K	Own	Fulltime	Investigators	Middle	Pullman	Indifferent
Avery	45	Female	Yes	Liberal	Masters	120K+	Own	Fulltime	Librarian	Upper-Middle	Pullman	Indifferent
Burt	55	Male	No	Conservative	High School	15–30K	Occupied, No Rent	Retired	Farm Laborer	Lower	Whitman	Indifferent
Christine	28	Female	Yes	Conservative	Some College	Less Than $15K	Occupied, No Rent	Part-Time/Childcare	Home Care Aid	Lower	Whitman	Indifferent
Harriet	72	Female	Yes	Conservative	Masters	120K+	Own	Retired	Teaching	Upper-Middle	Pacifica	Indifferent
Josh	59	Male	No	Liberal	Bachelors	31–49K	Own	Part-Time	Videographer	Middle	Pullman	Indifferent
Lindsay	28	Female	No	Liberal	PhD	Less Than 15K	Rent	Fulltime	Clinical Psych	Lower-Middle	Pullman	Indifferent
Louise	57	Female	Yes	Conservative	Some College	50–75K	Own	Fulltime	Caregiver	Middle/Lower-Middle	Whitman	Indifferent
Myra	45	Female	Yes	Liberal	Bachelors	31–49K	Own	Childcare	Teller	Middle	Pullman	Indifferent
Sarah	60	Female	Yes	Conservative	Bachelors	75–119K	Own	Retired	Teaching	Middle	Pacifica	Indifferent

and several measures used to estimate social class (education, income, home ownership, employment status, and occupation). My approach to estimating social class is detailed in a separate article.[2] A summary of these statistics shows that the average and median age of the sample is 52, while the modal age is 40. Forty-four percent of the sample is male and the remainder is female. Nearly 60% have children in the home. I asked people whether they leaned liberal or conservative, also giving options to describe their views as moderate or libertarian. Over 55% of the sample is liberal, 33% conservative, roughly 5% are moderates or libertarians, and 6% did not respond. Looking at social class, roughly 30% are lower class, 40% middle class, and 30% upper class. Note that I don't report on race here in order to protect participants' confidentiality, since only four participants are people of color. This is a limitation of the research, although the quantitative data oversample racial minorities and, in separate quantitative analyses, I note that racialized respondents are 60% more likely to be categorized as Eco-Engaged and 18% less likely to be in the Indifferent category.

Appendix C: Place Character Profiles of Interview Sites

Place character is a concept articulated by Krista E. Paulsen.[3] The approach is intended to serve as a tool for understanding how it is that the qualities of a place cohere and give sites specific identities. By defining a place's character, the analyst has an additional piece of information to draw on to make sense of residents' social meanings, beliefs, and actions. Following Paulsen's approach, I created a site observation template and hired two research assistants to work with me to document the character of the four study sites.

The template begins with naming the place and recording the date and time span of the observation. Next, I offered the following instructions:

1. Begin by walking downtown, enter shops, cafés, libraries.
2. Take notes: What is it like? What signs are posted? What are the people there doing?
3. Then walk away from downtown. What do the residential neighborhoods look like? Who do you see?
4. Is there a park or natural area nearby? If so, what's it like?
5. If possible, along the way, ask a few people how they would describe their community to an outsider.

The observer would repeat this pattern until they could fully answer the following questions: What stories are told about this place? What is it like to live here? What draws people here? What politics are evident here? What cultural practices are evident? What is the place of the natural environment here? Finally, each observer would complete the following sentence: "This is a place where people. . . ." Each of these themes is derived from Paulsen's description of how to document place character. Differentiating whether places shape the people who live there or whether residents create places is somewhat of a chicken-and-egg puzzle, but based on general agreement in the sociology of place literature, I understand places and residents to be mutually constitutive. Below, I offer a place description of each study site. Note that rural place names are pseudonyms.

OLYMPIA, URBAN HUB OF PROGRESSIVES

Olympia is a place where people foment mistrust of mainstream culture and politics and insulate themselves from the wider world, while remaining up to date on what is going on out there. This is a place where you talk about dismantling the patriarchy or decolonizing your yoga practices over a latte at the local, independent café. This is a place where you went for college as a misfit teenager and found people who were unique and just like you! You never left because the rent was cheap enough that you could work in a coffee shop and still have time to devote to activism. It's a place where you use gender neutral pronouns just to be safe. It is a safe haven for queer and trans teens who have been kicked out of their homes.

Olympia's unofficial slogan seems to be, "Stay Weird, Oly," which is printed on bumper stickers, t-shirts, and stickers plastered throughout downtown. Olympia certainly celebrates its weirdness. The local college's mascot is a Geoduck, which is not a duck at all, but a phallic-looking clam. The college itself is known for its radical left-wing politics. Walking through the downtown streets, I feel out of place without a tattoo and punk-rock clothing. My students and I are referred to as "normies" and it doesn't feel like a compliment. In Olympia, the age of grunge and Riot Grrrls doesn't feel like the past. To be in Olympia involves a lot of loitering. No one ever seems to be in a hurry. Despite being a large city, people often seem to know and recognize one another. This is a place that is diverse in seemingly every way except political ideology. While we imagine that a transgender person of color would be embraced and treated with dignity, we imagine a person with strong conservative views may not be.

This is a very progressive political place. There are Black Lives Matter posters on nearly every café and shop, and the pride flag is ubiquitous. We also see signs reading "Education Matters" and a lot of support for Bernie Sanders on bumper stickers. There are pro-union posters in many shops and the local paper had several stories about a move to raise the minimum wage in Olympia. A local, independent paper called *The Power and Light* seems to be in every café and restaurant we look in. At the time of our visit, the cover page reads, "ALL WATER IS HOLY." The content is strongly pro-environmental and anti-capitalist.

The consumer culture here is, paradoxically, against consumerism. A local gospel choir (Reverend Billy and the Stop Shopping Choir) uses a politics of interruption and embarrassment to preach an end to consumerism and an "Earth Revolution." Most shops seem to cater to hippies and stoners. There are a large number of tattoo parlors and vintage clothing stores. Handmade signs on noticeboards advertise herbology classes, foraging workshops, doula training, and a lot of yoga classes. This feels like crunchy, radical America at its finest. People downtown are drinking coffee, skateboarding, smoking cigarettes and pot, and loitering.

Olympia is in the coastal rainforest. The city is misty, rainy, surrounded by large cedar and Douglas-fir trees, and the Pacific Ocean. Although the downtown doesn't feel centered on these natural assets, the people we spoke with described the natural environment reverentially. It seems like a place where people are less focused on spending time in natural settings (local parks and trails were seemingly under-utilized) and more focused on ways to engage in conscientious consumption. An upcoming event, Procession of the Species, is Olympia's answer to the Earth Day parade, an event that celebrates biodiversity.

PULLMAN, THE STATE UNIVERSITY TOWN

Pullman is where college football happens. This is a place where people go to university, work for the university, or work in sectors that make life easy and fun for university students, faculty, and staff. The college mascot, the Cougars, features prominently here: the streets are painted with Cougars insignia, Cougars flags hang from the lampposts, and the Cougars football stadium seats more people than there are residents of the town. As people will tell you, Pullman is a wonderful place to raise a family and a terrible place to be single, if you're not a student. People are drawn to the benefits of a small town, from safety to minimal sprawl and urbanization, to free parking. But residents appreciate the cultural amenities that come with having an R1 university in town: frequent events from concerts to documentary screenings and talks. People stay for the friendly community and the ease of life, and they leave when they graduate, when they or their partner can't find employment, or when they find another university job.

Being in Pullman is relaxed. There is no one speeding, there are few traffic lights, no one honks, and there is little traffic to speak of. People run into acquaintances in local shops and, while the local businesses are fairly frequently patronized, there are seldom line-ups for service. No one feels busy, and chitchat between vendors and customers is friendly and often quite extensive.

There is a pronounced lack of political signage. Other than some "shop local" messaging and a barbershop featuring an assault rifle portrayed in a Lite Brite screen, we saw no other indications of political views downtown. As one of my students noted, "All the localness seems to emphasize commonalities while trying not to alienate anyone." In residential neighborhoods, quite a few houses displayed the sign, "No Matter Where You're From, We're Glad You're Our Neighbor," and this is as political as things got in Pullman.

The culture of Pullman feels very mainstream and middle-of-the-road. In contrast to Olympia, with its evidence of counter-cultural bookstores, news stories, signs, and overheard talk, Pullman does not at all appear counter-cultural. The downtown shops seem to cater largely to moms who might be visiting their children at university, with several gift stores, flower shops, and cafes. People in public spaces are typically working on laptops or meeting up with others to talk. Aside from the odd person wearing camo-print clothes, most people wear something with a WSU Cougars insignia and jeans or sweatpants. There are very few high-end cars, or other ostentatious displays of wealth. There are a lot of Christian churches in town, but few resemble churches; instead they are located in office buildings or old movie theaters.

Pullman sits in the Palouse, so named because early French settlers thought the landscape looked like lawn (*palus*). The gently rolling hills are a prominent feature of the town. The town itself is built around them: the university is on one hill (aptly named "College Hill"), and the majority of the housing stock is on the three other hills (named Pioneer, Sunnyside, and Military Hills). The businesses are centered on Main Street, which cuts between Sunnyside, Pioneer, and College Hill, and Grand Avenue, which circles around the town, meeting the base of each hill. Beyond these suburbanized hills is a cultivated landscape of monoculture agriculture: wheat and lentils. Within town, natural assets are understated. Several creeks run through town but often alongside a busy roadway. There are bike paths and urban parks that are relatively well used for exercise, play, and commuting.

PACIFICA, PICTURESQUE SEASIDE COMMUNITY

Pacifica is a place where people wave and say hello, even to strangers. People are drawn to the laid-back, island pace of life, but feel a tension around the financial clout that's needed to make it in this expensive community, given the lack of affordable housing and well-paying jobs. Despite stories of bucolic island living, there is a lot of hustle here, with lower-income people working several jobs and well-educated people working in retail and manual labor.

The stories that are told about Pacifica call into focus life on the island, while the wider world fades into the background. There is an active community calendar, and stories about cuts to social services in the local weekly paper. The letters written to the paper are almost all about local environmental issues, and most take a pro-environmental protection stance. Informal conversations center on complaints about the number of people in town (hard to find parking) and about economic vulnerability (people struggling to find housing and work). The town seems to invest heavily in telling a nostalgic story about itself: the buildings are preserved historical sites, and new buildings emulate this architectural style. The whole place feels like a museum. Retail spaces boast being the "oldest [tavern, inn, etc.] in town," the pharmacy has a picture of the men who started it in 1920, and there is a large mural of a Native American man on a beach with canoes, while a white settler looks on from a ship in the harbor. As one man I spoke with outside the hardware store described Pacifica, "it's like Mayberry, from the Andy Griffith's Show."

To be in Pacifica is to amble, meander, window-shop, and linger. The downtown seems almost entirely oriented toward well-to-do tourists: kitschy stores selling expensive candles, baby clothes, and local handicrafts; bookstores; ice-cream parlors; coffee shops; real-estate offices; and places to arrange whale watching, or bike and kayak rentals. There are numerous benches on each street, and they are mostly occupied. A look at the menu in a deli on Main Street reveals foodie-fare: a sandwich costs $19 and comes with hand-cut, house-made chips. The sidewalks are bustling from mid-morning to early evening.

This is not an ostensibly political town. We saw the odd bumper sticker for Bernie Sanders and a sign reading "Local food/Less oil" on a community noticeboard. But most posters promote wellness. For instance, an advertisement for a yoga teacher reads, "Feeling overwhelmed? Are you stuck in survival mode? Ready to SIMPLIFY and THRIVE?" Other than that, there were some calls to sign a "Save the Orca" petition. Most people in Pacifica seem to be white, relatively high-status, and thin.

The cultural practices of the town cater to consumers with aesthetically sophisticated and ethically aware tastes. Shops sell goods with a high-end folksy feel. There are a lot of Toyota Priuses on the road. The Subaru seems like the most common car, though there are quite a few pick-up trucks as well. We saw a couple of Christian churches here, but these are not as prominent as they are in Pullman. A film festival that is coming up advertises environmental documentaries. The community arts building looks new and beautiful. The grocery store has a large organic and natural section and a lot of local and organic produce for sale.

The environment in Pacifica is seemingly pristine and is what drew most participants to the island. People have kayaks on their porches and the roads are often more heavily populated with cyclists than drivers. It is the natural environment that brings in tourists (for whale watching, hiking, cycling, kayaking, etc.) and seasonal workers who support the tourist industry and benefit from living in this place. The natural environment is the focal point of the island.

WHITMAN, AFFORDABLE AGRICULTURAL COMMUNITY

Whitman is a place where people can enjoy an affordable, relaxed quality of life among easygoing people. It's close enough to a major urban center that residents who work in the city can get there easily, but far enough away to avoid the noise and pollution and high costs of city living. People here enjoy small talk and they know everyone's business. As my research assistant, Darcy Hauslik wrote, "If Pacifica is Mayberry, this is the bar from Cheers. Not only does everyone know your name and every other thing about you, but this place also seems much more real than the tourist town of Pacifica. You can see Whitman, warts and all, any afternoon."

The stories that are told about this place are centered around the residents of the town, past and present. There are posters announcing the commemoration of a battle that took place at a local butte, where the Indigenous Nez Perce successfully fended off attacks from white settlers, led by General Steptoe (after whom the butte is now named). The event doesn't honor the

Native Americans, but valorizes the heroism of the settlers. The event is officially called "Battle Days," but owing to the prodigious alcohol consumption that takes place each year, locals use the moniker "Bottle Days" instead. The residents of Whitman celebrate Battle Days in grand yet contradictory fashion, with car shows, pin-up contests, a rodeo, and a beer garden. Present-day stories could be described as gossip—our research team is the subject of much discussion. Groups of people lingering on the streets, in the bar, in the coffee shop, and in the town's restaurant are mainly discussing the three of us, or speculating as to who will be the most inebriated at the upcoming Battle Days event.

Being in Whitman, and not from Whitman, makes us feel highly visible and scrutinized. This does not seem to be a place that is often visited by strangers. People describe leaving their door unlocked and the owner of the café left us unattended while she walked home to get something. While we looked around the local scrapbooking store, an employee from the bar stopped by with lunch for the owner. The people we spoke with all know their neighbors, the mayor, the school principal, and the owners of the town's few businesses. It also feels like a place in decline. There are many commercial spaces that are either closed for good, or open very intermittently—the dentist is open Wednesday, by appointment. The billboards only advertise the opportunity to advertise, and people describe the town as being livelier and even "hopping" 20 years ago, before the highway was rerouted away from Whitman. The town's decor celebrates Americana, with flags and bunting on the streetlights, antique cars in shop windows, and shop names like "Granny's Thrift Store."

The politics here are conservative. There are many American flags and several Veterans' memorials. There is a notable absence of any symbolic markers of progressive political themes (e.g., pride, Black Lives Matter). The town's upcoming event, though, with a car show and a pin-up contest where women are evaluated on their sex appeal, speaks to a traditionally masculine culture. At the same time, all of the leaders in the community appear to be women (the mayor, the business owners, the school principal). Although only 500 people live in Whitman, there are four churches, and people report that church attendance is high.

Whitman is a blue-jeans-and-pick-up-truck kind of town. It also seems to be entirely white—we didn't see any people of color in the town. There are quite a few overweight people. It's hard to find fresh vegetables for sale, and the only advertisement in town was for a pesticide company. The only things we saw people buy at the grocery store were coffee (in Styrofoam cups) and milk. There are no organic products for sale, or local produce. Most of the vehicles are American-made.

The natural environment forms the backdrop of life in Whitman, rather than the heart of the town. There's a small creek that runs along the train tracks, and there are trees planted alongside the streets. Many houses have gardens with some flower beds and a lot of lawn. But the town is noticeably surrounded by large, monoculture farms, and people spoke of the fertile soils as an asset of the place.

Appendix D: Survey Methodology

After analyzing the qualitative data, I used excerpts from the transcripts to construct survey questions measuring affinity, severity, morality, efficacy, and relationality. I hired an undergraduate research assistant, Chi-pan Wong, to work with me to identify the practices that participants identified as pro-environmental, and included 19 of the most commonly mentioned practices. I hired another undergraduate student, Liam Larson, to help me compile the questions needed to estimate a household carbon footprint. I tested the clarity, reliability, and parsimony of the measures for eco-social relationships, practices, and carbon footprint on three convenience samples recruited through the survey research firm, Prolific. This allowed me to refine the survey instrument to its final state, which is included below.

I hired the survey research firm, Qualtrics, to administer the survey to a sample of their online panel. I selected quotas on income, education, and political ideology. The survey was put into the field on December 12, 2019, and data were collected by January 13, 2020. The sample included 2,619 US residents, aged 18 or older, from all 50 states. The final sample overrepresented female respondents, so I weighted all analyses on gender (see tables A.4 and A.5 in appendix E for sample details).

The first step in the quantitative analysis was to delineate the eco-types. To do so, I entered the 12 eco-social relationship items (see questions 7 through 10 in the survey instrument below) into a k-means cluster analysis, estimating 2, 3, 4, 5, 6, and 7-cluster solutions. The 5-cluster solution was the best solution, based on a replication of the analysis after randomly splitting the file into two groups. I then conducted descriptive statistics to estimate average scores for each cluster on affinity, severity, morality, and efficacy and used the mean values to label the clusters and create nominal variables for each eco-type. I also created variables for eco-friendly practices based on principal components factor analysis with varimax rotation, resulting in three variables: eco-consumption, reduced consumption, and sufficiency consumption.

The remaining analyses included additional descriptive statistics and regression analyses. I calculated descriptive statistics for each eco-social relationship category on environmental concerns, engagement in eco-friendly practices, and carbon footprint. Using Analyses of Variance (ANOVA) with Sheffé's post hoc tests, I identified significant differences in these outcomes across the five eco-social relationships. Finally, I used binary logistic regression techniques to determine the sociodemographic correlates of the five eco-types. Ordinary Least Squares regression analyses were used to understand variation in carbon footprint and the four bases of eco-social relationships. I conducted all statistical analyses in SPSS (Statistical Package for the Social Sciences) for Mac, Version 25.

THE SURVEY INSTRUMENT

Before we get started, we are asking a few demographic questions.

1. What year were you born? (YYYY)

2. What is the highest level of school you have completed?
   Less than high school
   High school graduate
   Some college
   Associate's degree
   Bachelor's degree
   Master's
   Doctorate or Professional degree (e.g., M.D., J.D.)

3. Information about income is very important for us to understand. Please indicate the answer that includes your total HOUSEHOLD income last year before taxes.
   Less than $15,000
   $15,000—$29,999
   $30,000—$44,999
   $45,000—$59,999
   $60,000—$74,999
   $75,000—$99,999
   $100,000—$149,999
   $150,000 or more

4. How would you describe your political views in general?
   Far Left   Very liberal
   Liberal
   Slightly liberal
   Moderate
   Slightly conservative
   Conservative
   Far Right   Very conservative
   Uninterested

5. How would you describe your political opinions on SOCIAL issues (e.g., Global warming, women's rights, gay marriage)?
   Far Left   Very liberal
   Liberal
   Slightly liberal
   Moderate
   Slightly conservative
   Conservative
   Far Right   Very conservative
   Uninterested

6. How would you describe your political opinions on ECONOMIC issues (e.g., Universal health care, foreign aid, taxes and other government programs)?
   Far Left   Very liberal
   Liberal
   Slightly liberal
   Moderate
   Slightly conservative
   Conservative
   Far Right   Very conservative
   Uninterested

This is a survey about environmental issues, and we would first like to know how interested you are in this subject.

7. How much do you disagree or agree with the following statements? [1 = SD (Strongly disagree), 5 = SA (Strongly agree)]
   I am very interested in issues relating to the natural environment.
   The natural environment is very important to me.
   I often think about environmental topics.

Now we'd like to learn more about your views on how serious these issues are.

8. How much do you disagree or agree with the following statements? [1 = SD, 5 = SA]
   Environmental problems are much more serious now than they used to be.
   Humans are using up the earth's resources.
   Protecting the environment should be among our country's top priorities.

9. Next, please answer a few questions about how responsible you feel for protecting the environment. [1 = SD, 5 = SA]
   I have a moral responsibility to reduce my impact on the environment.
   I worry about my impact on the natural environment.
   I try to reduce the amount I consume in order to protect the environment.

10. And now, please answer a few questions about how capable you feel of responding to environmental problems.
    [1 = SD, 5 = SA]
    I always do what I can to reduce my impact on the environment.
    I have oriented my life around my desire to reduce my impact on the environment.
    I am able to do what it takes to reduce my impact on the environment.

11. If you had to pick one description of your views on environmental issues, which of the following options is the best fit?
    I care about the environment, but it's not a major focus in my life.
    I care about the environment, but I think people exaggerate the seriousness of environmental problems.
    I think environmental problems are serious, but I don't think there's much I can do to help.
    I think environmental problems are serious and I wish I could do more to help.
    I think environmental problems are serious and I mostly do what I can to help.
    I don't care about environmental issues at all.

12. Next, we'd like to know about the people you spend time with. How much do you disagree or agree with the following statements? [1 = SD, 5 = SA]

    Most of the people I'm close to are very worried about the environment.

    Most of the people I'm close to try to reduce their impact on the environment.

    I prefer to spend time with people who care about the environment.

13. Now, we'd like to learn a little more about your normal household routines. In a typical month, how often do you (Never, Once in a while, Sometimes, Most of the time, All the time, Not available near me):

    Buy organic foods and/or products?

    Buy local food (when in season) and/or products?

    Buy eco-friendly products?

14. And in a typical month, how often do you (Never, Once in a while, Sometimes, Most of the time, All the time, Not available near me):

    Use cloth bags for shopping?

    Try not to buy too much stuff?

    Buy recycled products (e.g., paper towels)?

15. In a typical week, how often do you (Never, Once in a while, Sometimes, Most of the time, All the time):

    Try to reduce how much waste you produce?

    Try to reduce how much water you use?

    Try to reduce how much electricity you use?

16. And generally, how often do you (Never, Once in a while, Sometimes, Most of the time, All the time):

    Carry a reusable mug and/or water bottle?

    Pick up litter in your community?

    Hang laundry to dry?

17. Next, please indicate how often you (Never, Once in a while, Sometimes, Often, Always):

    Eat food that you or someone you know hunted or fished?

    Eat food that you or someone you know grew in a garden?

    Eat food that you or someone you know canned (preserved)?

18. And how often do you (Never, Once in a while, Sometimes, Often, Always):

    Spend time in nature (e.g., fishing, hunting, hiking)?

    Watch TV shows or documentaries about nature?

    Read books or magazines about nature?

19. How often do you try to improve the natural environment in your area (e.g., by planting trees, restoring natural areas)? (Never, Once in a while, Sometimes, Often, Always.)

20. Please answer a couple questions about environmentally friendly products.

    Ideally, I would only buy eco-friendly products.

    I have no interest in buying eco-friendly products.

    I've never noticed eco-friendly products for sale.

21. If you had all the money and time you needed, what would be your ideal choice of vehicle?

    No vehicle at all.

    A Tesla, or something like it.

    A Ford Taurus, or something like it.

    A Porsche 911, or something like it.

22. If you had all the money and time you needed, what would be your ideal choice of cleaning product?

    Something homemade, e.g., vinegar-based solution.

    An eco-friendly brand, e.g., Seventh Generation.

    A high-end brand, e.g., Williams Sonoma.

    A strong cleaner, e.g., Ajax.

23. Next, please select the statement about YOUR household's environmental impact relative to others' that best captures your opinion:

    My household creates LESS damage to the environment than the average US household.

    My household creates the SAME level of damage to the environment as the average US household.

    My household creates MORE damage to the environment than the average US household.

The next few questions ask about your household's energy consumption, transportation, food consumption, and recycling behaviors. You may not always know the exact answer, but please use your best guess.

24. Please estimate the size of your home (in square feet).
    Less than 1,000 sq. ft
    1,000–1,499 sq. ft
    1,500–1,999 sq. ft
    2,000–2,499 sq. ft
    2,500–2,999 sq. ft
    3,000 sq. ft or more

25. Based on your best estimate, please fill in the amount of your most recent monthly electricity bill (*either in dollars OR kilowatt hours (kWh)*):
    kWhs _____
    Dollars _____

26. If you own solar panels, please estimate what percentage of your typical monthly electricity comes from solar power?
    I don't have solar panels.
    I have solar panels but I don't know.
    My best estimate (% electricity from solar): _____

    _____

27. Next, we're going to ask a couple questions about transportation. First, please tell us about the vehicle you own and drive most often:
    I don't own a vehicle.
    I own and drive a hybrid vehicle.
    I own and drive an electric vehicle.
    I own and drive a normal gasoline or diesel vehicle.

28. Now, please estimate how far you (or someone in your household) drives each vehicle *you own and insure*, on a typical weekday or weekend day.
    Vehicle (1–5): distance traveled (miles) on a typical weekday.
    Vehicle (1–5): distance traveled (miles) on a typical weekend day.

29. On a normal day, how far do you travel (in miles):
    On a bus: distance traveled (miles) on a typical weekday.
    On a bus: distance traveled (miles) on a typical weekend day.
    On a train, subway, or streetcar: distance traveled (miles) on a typical weekday.
    On a train, subway, or streetcar: distance traveled (miles) on a typical weekend day.

Commuting by bicycle: distance traveled (miles) on a typical weekday.

Commuting by bicycle: distance traveled (miles) on a typical weekend day.

Commuting on foot: distance traveled (miles) on a typical weekday.

Commuting on foot: distance traveled (miles) on a typical weekend day.

Using a carshare: distance traveled (miles) on a typical weekday.

Using a carshare: distance traveled (miles) on a typical weekend day.

And now, just a few more questions about your flights in 2019, your recycling behaviors, and your diet.

30. For flights, please include any *upcoming flights as well as ones you've already taken* this year. How many roundtrip flights did you take this year (2019)?

    Short (under 300 miles, e.g., Boston to Philadelphia): Number of roundtrip flights in 2019

    Medium (300–2,299 miles, e.g., Chicago to Los Angeles): Number of roundtrip flights in 2019

    Long (over 2,300 miles, e.g., New York to Seattle): Number of roundtrip flights in 2019

31. Do you recycle (Yes, No, Not possible in my community):

    Aluminum and steel cans?

    Plastic?

    Glass?

    Newspaper?

    Magazines?

32. Which of the following terms best describes your diet?

    Omnivore (I eat meat most days)

    Flexitarian (I try to limit my meat consumption)

    Pescatarian (I don't eat meat but I do eat fish)

    Vegetarian (I don't eat meat or fish, but I do eat eggs and/or dairy)

    Vegan (I don't eat meat, fish, eggs, or dairy)

    Now we'd like to know what you think about who should take responsibility for protecting the environment.

33. For each actor, please indicate if you think they should be not at all or very responsible for protecting the environment [1 = Not at all RESPONSIBLE, 5 = Very RESPONSIBLE].
Individuals should be . . .
Businesses should be . . .
Government should be . . .
Local communities should be . . .
Nonprofit organizations should be . . .

34. Now, please indicate how much you TRUST each of these actors to act in a way that is positive for environmental protection [1 = Not at all, 5 = Very much].
Individuals
Businesses
Governments
Local communities
Nonprofit organizations

35. Generally speaking, on a scale of 1 to 5, where 1 means you are not at all concerned and 5 means you are very concerned, how concerned are you about environmental issues?

36. Now, looking at specific issues and using the same scale, how concerned are you about the following environmental issues [1 = Not at all concerned, 5 = Very concerned]:
Climate change
Plastic pollution
Extinction of plants and animals
Air pollution
Water pollution
Health risks from toxic chemicals

37. What is your gender?
Male
Female
Other _____

38. What race best describes you? (check all that apply):
Hispanic or Latino (of any race)
White
Black or African American
American Indian or Alaska Native

Asian
Arab/Middle Eastern
Native Hawaiian or Pacific Islander
Mixed race
Other _____

39. What type of business or industry are you currently working in
(or were you last working in, if you're not currently employed)?
(for example: hospital, bank, newspaper publishing) _____
_____

40. What is your current occupation, or most recent if not currently
working (for example: management consultant, accountant,
personnel manager)?
_____

41. What state do you live in?
Alabama . . . Wyoming

42. Which of the following best describes the area where you now
live?
A large city
A suburb near a large city
A small city or town
A rural area

43. [For rural only:] Which of the following descriptions best fits the
community you live in? (Select all that apply)
A resource-dependent community (i.e., people could earn a living
from farming, forestry, oil & gas, fishing, etc.).
An amenity-rich community (i.e., tourists like to visit this town).
A community in decline (i.e., more people seem to leave town
than move to town).

44. How many people live in your household, including yourself?

45. Do you own or rent the place where you live?

We'd like to ask a few questions about your upbringing.

46. Growing up, how active were your parents or guardians in each
of the following [1 = NOT AT ALL active, 5 = VERY active,
Don't Know]:
Trying to reduce their environmental impact
Spending time in nature (e.g., camping, fishing)

Discussing environmental issues
Buying eco-friendly products
Recycling waste
Growing their own food

47. What is the highest level of school your mother completed?
Less than high school
High school graduate
Some college
Associate's degree
Bachelor's degree
Master's
Doctorate or Professional degree (e.g., M.D., J.D.)

48. What is the highest level of school your father completed?
Less than high school
High school graduate
Some college
Associate's degree
Bachelor's degree
Master's
Doctorate or Professional degree (e.g., M.D., J.D.)

49. During your childhood, how frequently did your parents or
guardians engage you with the arts (e.g., music, theatre)?
Not at all
Very rarely
Somewhat rarely
Sometimes
Somewhat frequently
Very frequently
All the time

50. And what about now? How would you rate yourself on
engagement with the arts (e.g., music, theatre)?
Very low
Low
Somewhat low
Medium
Somewhat high
High
Very high

51. Lastly, what is your religion?
    No religion
    Christian (all denominations)
    Buddhist
    Hindu
    Jewish
    Muslim
    Sikh
    Any other religion, write in: _____

Appendix E: Survey Sample

In Table A.2, I include information on the survey sample as a whole, compared to estimates from the US Census. Table A.2 shows that my weighted sample is equivalent or roughly equivalent to the US adult population in terms of gender and age. There are more racial minorities in the survey sample than in the national adult population. My sample has a smaller share of low-income households than the national average, and a larger share of high-income households. The respondents in my sample have comparable levels of education to the national average and are roughly representative in terms of political ideology, though my sample slightly overrepresents liberals and underrepresents political moderates.

Table A.3 provides sociodemographic information on the same measures broken down by eco-type. Here, you can see that the Self-Effacing eco-type has the largest proportion of females, while the Indifferent has the largest proportion of males. The Fatalists are the youngest group and the Indifferent are the oldest, and most likely to be white. The Eco-Engaged are the most racially diverse category. In terms of income, there are more Eco-Engaged earning a high than a low income, and this pattern is inverted for the Self-Effacing, the Fatalists, and the Optimists. The Indifferent have a bimodal distribution, with extremes at the low and high ends of the income scale. The Fatalists have the lowest level of educational attainment, while the Eco-Engaged have the highest levels. Finally, patterns by political ideology are interesting. The categories that align with the ideal environmentalist (Eco-Engaged and Self-Effacing) are far more balanced in terms of political representation compared to the other categories, although political liberals make up the largest share of Eco-Engaged. In contrast, the groups opposed to or disinterested in the ideal environmentalist (Fatalists, Optimists, Indifferent) include a far greater proportion of conservatives than liberals.

TABLE A.2. Comparison of Survey Sample with US Adult Population

	Survey Sample n (%)	US Population (estimates from US Census Bureau unless otherwise noted)
Female [1]	50.8%	50.8%
Age (median) [2]	39.0 years	37.9 years
Race [1]		
Non-white	31.9%	27.3%
White	68.1%	72.7%
Income [3]		
Less than $15,000	12.9%	23.0%
$15,000–$29,999	15.6%	21.5%
$30,000–$44,999	13.0%	17.0%
$45,000–$59,999	11.6%	11.8%
$60,000–$74,999	9.6%	8.1%
$75,000–$99,999	11.3%	7.6%
$100,000 and over	26.0%	11.1%
Education [4,5]		
Less than high school	11.9%	12.4%
High school graduate	26.6%	27.1%
Some college	21.2%	20.6%
Associate's degree	7.7%	8.4%
Bachelor's degree	20.8%	19.4%
Graduate or Professional degree (e.g., M.D., J.D.)	11.8%	12.1%
Political ideology [6]		
Liberal	30.9%	26.0%
Moderate	29.0%	35.0%
Conservative	40.1%	39.0%

Notes:

[1] U.S. Census Bureau. 2019. "Table DP05: 2018: ACS 5-Year Estimates Data Profiles." https://www.census.gov/programs-surveys/acs

[2] U.S. Census Bureau. 2019. "Table S0101: 2018: ACS 5-Year Estimates Subject Tables." https://www.census.gov/programs-surveys/acs

[3] U.S. Census Bureau. 2019. "Current Population Survey, 2019 Annual Social and Economic Supplement". https://www.census.gov/programs-surveys/cps.html

[4] U.S. Census Bureau. 2019. "Table S1501: 2018: 5-Year Estimates Subject Tables." https://www.census.gov/programs-surveys/acs

[5] Population 25 and older

[6] Saad, Lydia. 2020. "The U.S. Remained Center-Right, Ideologically, in 2019." https://news.gallup.com/poll/275792/remained-center-right-ideologically-2019.aspx

TABLE A.3. Key Sociodemographic Attributes of Eco-Types

	Eco-Engaged	Self-Effacing	Optimists	Fatalists	Indifferent
Female	49.8%	55.2%	47.4%	53.2%	43.7%
Age (median)	37 years	40 years	41 years	36 years	48 years
Race					
Non-white	36.0%	28.3%	32.8%	31.7%	25.0%
White	64.0%	71.7%	67.2%	68.3%	75.0%
Income					
Less than $15,000	11.5%	11.1%	14.1%	14.7%	19.0%
$15,000–$29,999	14.0%	17.6%	16.3%	18.3%	8.9%
$30,000–$44,999	11.1%	14.8%	14.5%	11.8%	13.0%
$45,000–$59,999	11.3%	12.1%	11.9%	12.8%	8.0%
$60,000–$74,999	12.1%	8.1%	10.3%	6.4%	7.0%
$75,000–$99,999	12.7%	11.7%	8.7%	10.6%	11.9%
$100,000–$149,999	14.5%	13.5%	13.0%	13.3%	15.5%
$150,000 or more	12.7%	11.0%	11.1%	12.1%	16.5%
Education					
Less than high school	10.1%	12.4%	11.1%	16.2%	12.7%
High school graduate	25.2%	28.2%	27.7%	26.7%	23.3%
Some college	18.0%	23.7%	24.0%	21.5%	18.2%
Associate's degree	8.8%	8.0%	7.2%	6.4%	5.6%
Bachelor's degree	21.8%	18.6%	20.3%	20.1%	27.3%
Master's	13.7%	6.5%	8.1%	6.9%	9.4%
Doctorate or Professional degree (e.g., M.D., J.D.)	2.4%	2.6%	1.6%	2.1%	3.6%
Political ideology					
Liberal	41.5%	31.2%	21.2%	24.8%	17.7%
Moderate	26.4%	32.1%	31.6%	23.9%	15.1%
Conservative	32.1%	36.7%	47.2%	51.3%	67.2%

Appendix F: Regression Results

In the chapters on the eco-social relationships, I presented sociodemographic data about the sort of person most likely to embody that eco-type. When describing what an eco-social relationship looks like, I presented descriptive data in the text and discussed results of multivariate analyses.

Later, when examining variation within each of the elements of the model of eco-social relationships, I present results of multivariate analyses in the text. Here, I include all of these tables. Note that the analyses are weighted to reflect the gender distribution in the population.

SOCIODEMOGRAPHIC CORRELATES OF THE ECO-TYPES

In order to examine the relationships between gender, age, race, political ideology, socioeconomic status (income and education), residence, and cultural capital (eco-upbringing, parents' education, engagement in high culture), I ran a series of binary logistic regressions in SPSS (Version 25). For gender, male and nonbinary are the reference categories and a dummy variable for "female" is entered into the model. Age is measured in years. The measure for race uses a dummy variable where those who described their race as "white" are coded as "1" and all other responses are coded as "0." The scale for political ideology ranges from 1 through 7. I recoded those selecting numbers 1 through 3 as leaning conservative and use this variable as the reference category. Moderates selected "4," the middle of the scale, and I created a dummy variable and entered it into the model. Likewise, those who selected 5 through 7, I coded as leaning liberal and entered this dummy variable into the model. I recoded income and education into terciles and use the low tercile as the reference category in both cases. I use "rural" as the reference category for residence by adding town, suburb, and urban as dummy variables into the analysis. Eco-upbringing is a composite score of respondents' level of engagement in environmentally relevant activities in their family of origin and is treated as a continuous variable. The final four variables measure cultural capital. Mothers' and fathers' education level are the first two measures. I use dummy variables where 1 = parent has a Bachelor's degree or higher level of educational attainment. The variable "child-arts" is a dummy variable where 1 represents those whose parents somewhat frequently or very frequently engaged them in the arts. "Current-arts" indicates those who characterize their current level of engagement in the arts as somewhat high, high, or very high. These results are displayed in Table A.4.

The results in Table A.4 show that political ideology and eco-upbringing explain a lot of variation in people's membership in the different eco-types. The Eco-Engaged are over twice as likely to lean liberal than conservative. They, more than any other eco-social relationship, reveal high cultural capital: they are 88% more likely to have been raised in environmentally active

TABLE A.4. Binary Logistic Regression of Eco-Social Relationships

	Eco-Engaged (n=729)	Self-Effacing (n=528)	Optimists (n=411)	Fatalists (n=261)	Indifferent (n=150)
Female	1.148 (.103)	1.155 (.105)	.887 (.114)	.878 (.141)	.696 (.187)
Age	.385 (.003)	1.001 (.003)	1.003 (.004)	.978*** (.005)	1.012* (.006)
White	.975 (.116)	1.373** (.122)	.906 (.132)	.787 (.163)	.782 (.231)
Lean liberal	2.284*** (.128)	1.497** (.132)	.507*** (.157)	.607 *** (.191)	.375*** (.323)
Moderate	1.376* (.130)	.872 (.130)	1.091 (.135)	.872 (.170)	1.181 (.259)
Mod Income	1.322 (.279)	.810 (.158)	.926 (.170)	1.087 (.215)	.732 (.290)
High Income	1.108 (.103)	.912 (.155)	.907 (.170)	1.203 (.203)	.846 (.264)
Mod Educ	.854 (.148)	1.123 (.146)	1.171 (.158)	.852 (.199)	.929 (.267)
High Educ	1.322 (.151)	1.109 (.153)	.920 (.246)	.755 (.203)	1.034 (.261)
Town	.787 (.177)	1.950*** (.190)	.762 (.187)	.760 (.213)	1.138 (.129)
Suburban	.776 (.160)	2.188*** (.176)	.889 (.166)	.582** (.199)	.943 (.282)
Urban	.995 (.169)	1.889** (.189)	.760 (.183)	.443*** (.227)	1.387 (.298)
Eco-upbringing	1.876*** (.048)	.887** (.046)	1.012 (.050)	.551*** (.067)	.417*** (.100)
Mother-degree	1.209 (.144)	.833 (.151)	.829 (.167)	1.398 (.190)	.745 (.267)
Father-degree	1.019 (.143)	.846 (.147)	.996 (.163)	1.010 (.191)	1.441 (.249)
Child-arts	.801 (.124)	1.081 (.128)	.997 (.142)	1.234 (.172)	1.032 (.248)
Current-arts	1.389** (.119)	1.054 (.123)	.813 (.140)	.743 (.175)	.697 (.247)

Notes: ***, $p < .001$; **, $p < .010$; *, $p < .050$.

households and nearly 40% more likely to participate in high cultural capital aesthetic consumption. The Self-Effacing, who strive to be like the Eco-Engaged, are no more or less likely to be conservative or liberal, but they are 12% less likely to have grown up in an environmentally active household. They are, however, much more likely to live in a community that is not rural—they are roughly twice as likely to live in a town, suburb near a big city, or urban area than a rural community. They are also more likely to be white than in a racially diverse category—and this is the only eco-social relationship for which race is significant, net of other sociodemographic variables. The only sociodemographic measure that significantly predicts an Optimist eco-social relationship is the measure of leaning liberal—Optimists are 50% less likely to report having a liberal political ideology than a conservative one. Fatalists are younger, on average, and roughly 40% less likely to lean liberal than conservative. They are also less likely to live in a town, suburban community, or urban area compared with a rural community. They are unlikely to have grown up in an eco-engaged household. Finally, the Indifferent are older, and are over 60% less likely to lean liberal than conservative. Like the Fatalists and the Self-Effacing, they are unlikely to have been raised in an eco-engaged household.

VARIATION WITHIN ECO-TYPES

In Tables A.5–A.9, I present results for how these same sociodemographic measures can account for variation in the elements of eco-social relationships. I display these results for each of the five eco-types separately, beginning with the Eco-Engaged.

Among the Eco-Engaged, race and father's education are significantly related to variation in affinity. White Eco-Engaged whose fathers have a university degree have higher self-reported scores on affinity for the environment. Severity scores among the Eco-Engaged tend to be high, but among conservatives and those with an eco-upbringing, these scores are on the lower end of the range. While severity is a quality of the environment, morality and efficacy are qualities people perceive about themselves, in relationship with the environment. Perhaps because moral responsibility scores are consistently high among the Eco-Engaged, there are no sociodemographic correlates that can account for variation. The final quality that shapes eco-social relationships is efficacy. Among the Eco-Engaged, only eco-upbringing is associated with efficacy—those who were raised in households that practiced environmentally relevant behaviors evaluate their own actions more positively. The measure of relationality captures the extent

TABLE A.5. Binary Logistic Regression of Eco-Social Relationships for the Eco-Engaged

	Affinity	Severity	Morality	Efficacy	Relationality
Female	.003	−.006	.042	−.024	.019
	(.095)	(.090)	(.081)	(.113)	(.174)
Age	.058	.061	.034	.066	.093*
	(.003)	(.003)	(.003)	(.004)	(.006)
White	.127**	−.012	−.037	−.063	.051
	(.100)	(.095)	(.086)	(.120)	(.183)
Political ideology	−.073	−.136***	−.069	.010	−.061
(high = cons)	(.024)	(.023)	(.020)	(.028)	(.043)
Income	−.055	−.097	−.070	−.030	.058
	(.024)	(.022)	(.021)	(.029)	(.044)
Education	.004	.020	.052	.027	.095*
	(.036)	(.034)	(.031)	(.043)	(.066)
Town	.001	.023	.014	−.005	−.028
	(.165)	(.156)	(.142)	(.197)	(.303)
Suburban	−.006	.059	−.013	−.048	.057
	(.147)	(.139)	(.126)	(.176)	(.270)
Urban	.028	−.022	−.057	.046	.121*
	(.154)	(.145)	(.132)	(.184)	(.282)
Eco-upbringing	.019	−.100*	.046	.285***	.373***
	(.041)	(.038)	(.035)	(.049)	(.074)
Mother-degree	−.055	.074	−.018	.001	−.013
	(.155)	(.128)	(.116)	(.161)	(.248)
Father-degree	.112*	.020	.032	−.041	.043
	(.133)	(.126)	(.114)	(.159)	(.245)
Child-arts	.038	.019	−.027	−.079	−.008
	(.109)	(.103)	(.094)	(.131)	(.200)
Current-arts	−.009	−.035	−.028	−.009	−.019
	(.102)	(.087)	(.088)	(.122)	(.188)

Notes: ***, p < .001; **, p < .010; *, p < .050.

to which survey respondents use cues about a person's relationship with the environment to evaluate their moral worth. The model in Table A.5 shows that this is most common among older, educated Eco-Engaged who live in urban areas and grew up in environmentally active families.

There is little variation in affinity among the Self-Effacing (Table A.6). This limited variation can be partially accounted for by attending to age, as older Self-Effacing express slightly weaker affinity than younger Self-Effacing. But when we look at severity, politics and eco-upbringing matter:

TABLE A.6. Binary Logistic Regression of Eco-Social Relationships for the Self-Effacing

	Affinity	Severity	Morality	Efficacy	Relationality
Female	−.026	.083	.094*	.006	−.037
	(.157)	(.109)	(.125)	(.145)	(.187)
Age	−.096*	−.013	.004	.183***	.198***
	(.005)	(.004)	(.004)	(.005)	(.006)
White	.078	−.065	.088	−.199**	−.021
	(.186)	(.129)	(.148)	(.172)	(.221)
Political ideology	−.043	−.201***	−.014	.106**	−.145***
(cons = high)	(.048)	(.034)	(.039)	(.045)	(.058)
Income	.031	−.033	.159**	−.072	.109*
	(.038)	(.026)	(.030)	(.035)	(.145)
Education	.099	−.024	−.012	.059	.016
	(.057)	(.040)	(.046)	(.053)	(.068)
Town	.024	−.020	.095	.053	.037
	(.292)	(.204)	(.233)	(.271)	(.348)
Suburban	−.079	−.019	.126	.151*	.082
	(.273)	(.190)	(.235)	(.253)	(.326)
Urban	−.060	.006	.123	.001	.050
	(.249)	(.205)	(.235)	(.273)	(.350)
Eco-upbringing	.050	−.157**	.060	.362***	.392***
	(.075)	(.052)	(.060)	(.070)	(.090)
Mother-degree	−.008	.007	.007	−.052	.007
	(.221)	(.154)	(.177)	(.205)	(.264)
Father-degree	.030	.037	−.024	.001	.068
	(.213)	(.148)	(.170)	(.197)	(.254)
Child-arts	.050	.048	.023	−.068	.018
	(.187)	(.130)	(.149)	(.173)	(.222)
Current-arts	.052	−.051	−.021	−.069	−.013
	(.179)	(.125)	(.143)	(.166)	(.213)

Notes: ***, $p < .001$; **, $p < .010$; *, $p < .050$.

Self-Effacing who lean conservative and who were raised in eco-engaged households perceive ecological decline to be less severe. Income and gender are related to morality among the Self-Effacing, with women who earn a high income more likely to report higher scores on the morality measures (Table A.6). There are several correlates of efficacy scores among the Self-Effacing. Older and conservative Self-Effacing who live in suburban areas and were raised in eco-engaged households score higher than their counterparts. White Self-Effacing score lower than minority respondents.

TABLE A.7. Binary Logistic Regression of Eco-Social Relationships for the Optimists

	Affinity	Severity	Morality	Efficacy	Relationality
Female	−.139**	−.028	.141**	.011	.023
	(.160)	(.152)	(.142)	(.150)	(.186)
Age	−.018	.033	.055	.087	.055
	(.006)	(.006)	(.005)	(.006)	(.007)
White	−.044	−.003	.035	.045	.026
	(.202)	(.192)	(.180)	(.190)	(.236)
Political ideology	.140**	−.165**	−.047	−.113*	−.019***
(cons=high)	(.054)	(.051)	(.048)	(.051)	(.063)
Income	.010	−.043	.182**	−.004	.019
	(.043)	(.041)	(.038)	(.040)	(.050)
Education	.051	−.041	.015	−.025	−.075
	(.064)	(.061)	(.057)	(.060)	(.075)
Town	.154**	.103	−.060	−.043	.015
	(.265)	(.252)	(.236)	(.250)	(.310)
Suburban	.184**	.134	−.154	−.038	.005
	(.230)	(.219)	(.232)	(.217)	(.269)
Urban	.134*	.078	−.054	.042	.054
	(.260)	(.247)	(.233)	(.245)	(.304)
Eco-upbringing	.075	.014	.207***	.310***	.391***
	(.087)	(.082)	(.077)	(.082)	(.101)
Mother-degree	−.005	−.084	−.002	−.018	−.018
	(.260)	(.247)	(.231)	(.245)	(.303)
Father-degree	.066	−.015	−.064	−.004	−.033
	(.245)	(.233)	(.218)	(.231)	(.286)
Child-arts	.065	.072	−.134*	.042	.062
	(.211)	(.201)	(.188)	(.199)	(.247)
Current-arts	.049	−.040	.022	.069	.048
	(.210)	(.199)	(.187)	(.197)	(.245)

Notes: ***, $p < .001$; **, $p < .010$; *, $p < .050$.

The final model in Table A.6 shows that older, wealthier, politically liberal Self-Effacing who grew up in eco-engaged households are most likely to use cues about a person's relationship with the environment to evaluate how ethical and appealing they are.

The range of Optimists' affinity is related to gender, political ideology, and residence (Table A.7). Female Optimists have lower affinity scores than male Optimists. And conservative Optimists have higher affinity scores than liberal Optimists. Optimists living in towns, suburbs, and urban areas all have higher scores than those in rural areas. Scores on perceived severity—the quality of the environment that I argue most strongly shapes affinity—are lower for conservative Optimists than liberal Optimists. A sense of moral responsibility to take individual actions to protect the environment is stronger among female Optimists, those who earn more money, and those who were raised in environmentally active households. Optimists who were engaged in the arts as children reported lower morality scores. Variation in self-reported efficacy among Optimists is related to political ideology and eco-upbringing: conservative Optimists are likely to report lower scores and those raised in eco-engaged households report higher scores for efficacy. Optimists who will use cues about a person's eco-social relationship to evaluate their interest and approval of that person (relationality) are politically liberal and grew up in eco-engaged households.

Only eco-upbringing is associated to affinity among the Fatalists, as those with an eco-upbringing report higher affinity scores than others (Table A.8). Severity scores for the Fatalists are influenced by political ideology, education, and eco-upbringing. Having a conservative ideology, more education, and an eco-upbringing are associated with reporting lower severity scores. Fatalists' scores on morality vary by gender, residence, and eco-habitus. Female Fatalists in urban areas, who were raised by mothers with university degrees and were engaged in environmental behaviors report a stronger sense of moral responsibility to protect the environment than others. Older Fatalists and those who grew up in eco-engaged households score higher on the measures of self-efficacy than others. The model of relationality in Table A.8 shows that the only variable significantly related to evaluating a person based on their relationship with the environment is eco-upbringing.

For the Indifferent, only income is related to affinity scores, as those with high incomes are likely to score lower on affinity (Table A.9). And only eco-upbringing is related to severity—the Indifferent who were raised in eco-engaged households have lower scores on severity. There are no sociodemographic measures that are significantly related to the Indifferent respondents' sense of moral responsibility to protect the environment. As with the other eco-social relationships, variation in efficacy among the Indifferent is influenced by eco-upbringing. Those who grew up in eco-engaged households are more likely to positively evaluate their contributions to environmental protection. Eco-upbringing is also the only variable significantly associated with relationality—Indifferent respondents who grew up in eco-engaged households report higher scores when asked if they use evidence of a person's relationship with the environment when evaluating them.

TABLE A.8. Binary Logistic Regression of Eco-Social Relationships for the Fatalists

	Affinity	Severity	Morality	Efficacy	Relationality
Female	−.094	.048	.211**	.096	.110
	(.252)	(.263)	(.197)	(.202)	(.271)
Age	−.008	−.067	.079	.215**	−.070
	(.009)	(.009)	(.007)	(.007)	(.009)
White	.075	−.103	−.011	−.023	−.012
	(.295)	(.307)	(.231)	(.236)	(.317)
Political ideology	.097	−.146*	−.052	−.038	−.076
(cons = high)	(.083)	(.087)	(.065)	(.067)	(.089)
Income	−.036	.074	.039	.058	−.008
	(.061)	(.064)	(.048)	(.049)	(.066)
Education	−.015	−.169*	.009	−.038	.080
	(.097)	(.102)	(.087)	(.078)	(.105)
Town	−.094	−.117	.165	.110	.131
	(.378)	(.395)	(.296)	(.303)	(.407)
Suburban	−.030	−.045	.163	.127	.050
	(.374)	(.390)	(.293)	(.299)	(.402)
Urban	−.065	−.096	.155*	.147	.034
	(.412)	(.430)	(.323)	(.330)	(.443)
Eco-upbringing	.125*	−.263***	.141*	.151*	.176**
	(.131)	(.167)	(.103)	(.105)	(.141)
Mother-degree	−.020	.034	.188*	.008	.095
	(.352)	(.367)	(.276)	(.282)	(.379)
Father-degree	.012	−.006	−.040	−.042	−.088
	(.340)	(.355)	(.267)	(.273)	(.366)
Child-arts	−.026	.067	.039	.105	.076
	(.316)	(.330)	(.247)	(.253)	(.340)
Current-arts	.043	.119	−.009	−.017	.102
	(.325)	(.340)	(.255)	(.261)	(.350)

Notes: ***, $p < .001$; **, $p < .010$; *, $p < .050$.

ENGAGEMENT IN ENVIRONMENTAL PRACTICES ACROSS ECO-TYPES

In the survey, I asked questions aimed at capturing the environmentally relevant practices mentioned most frequently by participants in the Washington-based interviews. All of the items included were measured on a five-point scale of frequency, where 1 = never. After conducting a factor analysis that groups the items into three categories, I created scales for each category. The scales are averaged so that the range remains from 1 to 5. The

TABLE A.9. Binary Logistic Regression of Eco-Social Relationships for the Indifferent

	Affinity	Severity	Morality	Efficacy	Relationality
Female	.103	.019	.127	.176	.046
	(.393)	(.304)	(.294)	(.337)	(.317)
Age	−.041	−.126	−.022	−.009	−.084
	(.011)	(.009)	(.008)	(.010)	(.009)
White	.078	−.106	−.008	−.188	−.042
	(.513)	(.397)	(.383)	(.439)	(.412)
Political ideology	.061	.002	.051	.042	−.040
(cons = high)	(.128)	(.099)	(.096)	(.110)	(.103)
Income	−.199*	.025	.054	.037	.050
	(.089)	(.069)	(.066)	(.076)	(.071)
Education	.089	.104	.034	.055	.049
	(.157)	(.121)	(.117)	(.134)	(.126)
Town	−.019	−.054	−.127	.104	.024
	(.615)	(.476)	(.460)	(.527)	(.495)
Suburban	−.090	−.111	−.070	.076	−.019
	(.592)	(.458)	(.442)	(.507)	(.476)
Urban	−.080	−.083	−.150	.060	−.014
	(.615)	(.476)	(.460)	(.527)	(.495)
Eco-upbringing	−.020	−.309**	.082	.546**	.271***
	(.215)	(.166)	(.161)	(.184)	(.173)
Mother-degree	−.066	.111	−.026	−.082	−.017
	(.526)	(.428)	(.413)	(.474)	(.445)
Father-degree	.028	−.100	.026	−.068	−.016
	(.553)	(.407)	(.393)	(.451)	(.423)
Child-arts	.119	.033	.095	−.200	−.041
	(.523)	(.404)	(.403)	(.448)	(.420)
Current-arts	.014	.105	.080	.493	.097
	(.540)	(.418)	(.390)	(.463)	(.434)

Notes: ***, $p < .001$; **, $p < .010$; *, $p < .050$.

three environmental practices are eco-friendly consumption (e.g., buying organic foods, using a cloth bag to shop), reducing consumption (e.g., using less water, energy), and self-sufficiency practices (e.g., hunting, gardening).

Table A.10 displays results for the models of frequency of engagement in eco-friendly consumption practices for each eco-type. Interestingly, while political ideology is most relevant for shaping people's eco-types, within these clusters, indicators of eco-habitus are most significant for accounting for variation in engagement. Across all models, people who grew up in

TABLE A.10. Ordinary Least Squares Regression of Frequency of Engagement in Eco-Friendly Consumption

	Eco-Engaged	Self-Effacing	Optimists	Fatalists	Indifferent
Female	.031	.069	.070	−.005	.129
	(.049)	(.054)	(.066)	(.077)	(.131)
Age	.012	.202***	.080	.009	.014
	(.002)	(.002)	(.002)	(.003)	(.004)
White	.059	−.002	.011	.031	.043
	(.012)	(.064)	(.084)	(.091)	(.169)
Political ideology	.029	−.156***	−.104	−.055	−.049
(cons = high)	(.012)	(.017)	(.022)	(.026)	(.042)
Income	.089*	.062	.047	−.019	.136
	(.012)	(.014)	(.018)	(.019)	(.030)
Education	.088	.097*	.115	.095	−.001
	(.019)	(.020)	(.027)	(.031)	(.051)
Town	−.100*	.094	.023	.132	.228
	(.085)	(.100)	(.111)	(.114)	(.205)
Suburban	−.016	.145*	.100	.161	.113
	(.075)	(.093)	(.095)	(.115)	(.196)
Urban	.032	.063	−.017	.107	.095
	(.021)	(.091)	(.108)	(.125)	(.203)
Eco-upbringing	.258***	.334***	.201***	.364***	.316**
	(.069)	(.026)	(.037)	(.042)	(.070)
Mother-degree	−.080	.095	.037	.029	−.010
	(.069)	(.076)	(.107)	(.107)	(.182)
Father-degree	.085	−.009	−.040	−.004	−.042
	(.068)	(.072)	(.101)	(.103)	(.171)
Child-arts	−.046	.008	.116*	.213**	.134
	(.056)	(.064)	(.087)	(.101)	(.171)
Current-arts	.078*	.095*	.047	−.026	−.045
	(.053)	(.061)	(.087)	(.100)	(.170)

Notes: ***, $p < .001$; **, $p < .010$; *, $p < .050$.

environmentally active households report higher levels of engagement in eco-friendly consumption compared to those who did not. And arts engagement, which is a measure of a person's cultural capital, is also positively related to engagement in eco-friendly consumption. That is, holding all other variables constant, people who attended high culture performances as children or who currently do so as adults report more frequent eco-friendly consumption than others. There are some other significant relationships

TABLE A.11. Ordinary Least Squares Regression of Frequency of Engagement in Reducing Consumption

	Eco-Engaged	Self-Effacing	Optimists	Fatalists	Indifferent
Female	.029	.073	.084	−.011	−.058
	(.056)	(.063)	(.078)	(.111)	(.193)
Age	.199***	.309***	.274***	.179	.019
	(.002)	(.002)	(.003)	(.004)	(.006)
White	.034	−.060	−.125*	.084	.086
	(.059)	(.075)	(.098)	(.129)	(.252)
Political ideology	.026	.055	.036	.127	−.164
(cons = high)	(.014)	(.020)	(.026)	(.036)	(.063)
Income	.076	−.055	.075	−.025	−.095
	(.014)	(.015)	(.021)	(.027)	(.044)
Education	−.124*	.041	.025	−.030	.098
	(.032)	(.023)	(.031)	(.043)	(.077)
Town	.016	.006	−.066	.198*	−.093
	(.097)	(.118)	(.129)	(.166)	(.302)
Suburban	.004	−.040	−.076	.284**	−.207
	(.087)	(.110)	(.112)	(.164)	(.291)
Urban	−.018	−.059	−.133*	.125	−.297*
	(.091)	(.119)	(.127)	(.181)	(.302)
Eco-upbringing	.098*	.158**	.092	.173**	.209*
	(.024)	(.030)	(.042)	(.058)	(.106)
Mother-degree	.000	−.021	−.037	−.009	−.001
	(.080)	(.089)	(.126)	(.155)	(.272)
Father-degree	.067	.118*	.064	−.038	.127
	(.079)	(.086)	(.119)	(.150)	(.258)
Child-arts	−.051	.013	.038	.113	.073
	(.065)	(.075)	(.103)	(.139)	(.257)
Current-arts	.000	.061	.061	−.116	−.011
	(.06)	(.072)	(.102)	(.143)	(.265)

Notes: ***, p < .001; **, p < .010; *, p < .050.

within specific eco-types—for instance, older, well-educated, and politically liberal Self-Effacing report more frequent eco-friendly consumption than younger, less-educated, conservative people in this eco-social relationship. And wealthier Eco-Engaged engage in eco-friendly consumer practices more often than those with lower incomes.

Table A.11 displays the models of engagement in reducing consumption for the five eco-types. Again, eco-upbringing is significantly and positively related to engagement, but the relationship is not as strong as for eco-consumption and does not account for variation within the Optimists. Age seems to be the factor that accounts for most variation within the Eco-Engaged, Self-Effacing, and Optimists, with older respondents reporting higher levels of engagement in reducing consumption than younger respondents. For Fatalists and the Indifferent, place of residence matters. Among Fatalists, those in towns and suburbs reduce consumption more often than those in rural areas; among the Indifferent, those in urban areas reduce consumption less frequently than those in rural areas. There are other relationships that are isolated within one eco-social relationship—for instance, racialized Optimists report reducing consumption less frequently than white Optimists.

Table A.12 reports models of the last scale of environmentally relevant practices: self-sufficiency. Again, eco-upbringing is significantly related to engagement across all eco-types. In addition, younger Eco-Engaged and Optimists are engaging in self-sufficiency practices. Aside from these patterns, there are isolated relationships within each model. For instance, liberal Eco-Engaged report more frequent engagement in sufficiency practices, suburban Eco-Engaged and urban Self-Effacing engage in sufficiency practices less often than their rural counterparts, and Self-Effacing and Optimists who attend artistic events also engage in self-sufficiency practices more often than others.

CARBON FOOTPRINT ANALYSES ACROSS ECO-TYPES

Table A.13 presents Ordinary Least Squares regression analyses of the measure of household carbon footprint. The independent variables are all identical to the models above, except that I have added a measure of home ownership (1 = owns home; 0 = rent or other). I include this measure because a person's ability to reduce home energy use will presumably be more limited if they do not own their home. A few interesting patterns emerge. First, political ideology is not associated with the carbon footprint of any of the eco-types. Second, income is positively related to carbon footprint, but only among Fatalists and the Indifferent. The only factor explaining variation in carbon footprint among the Eco-Engaged is home ownership—those who own their home have smaller footprints than those who do not. Among the Self-Effacing, respondents who live in towns have a smaller footprint than those who live in rural areas, and those who grew up in eco-engaged

TABLE A.12. Ordinary Least Squares Regression of Frequency of Engagement in Self-Sufficiency Practices

	Eco-Engaged	Self-Effacing	Optimists	Fatalists	Indifferent
Female	−.060	−.081	.003	−.020	−.083
	(.057)	(.054)	(.056)	(.077)	(.117)
Age	−.090**	−.008	−.118*	−.107	.065
	(.002)	(.002)	(.002)	(.003)	(.003)
White	.049	−.008	−.008	−.070	−.016
	(.060)	(.064)	(.070)	(.090)	(.152)
Political ideology	.138***	.067	−.048	.082	−.167
(cons = high)	(.014)	(.017)	(.019)	(.025)	(.038)
Income	.062	−.060	−.044	−.052	−.015
	(.014)	(.013)	(.015)	(.019)	(.026)
Education	.036	.084	.055	.078	−.049
	(.022)	(.020)	(.022)	(.030)	(.046)
Town	−.045	−.067	.008	−.073	.026
	(.099)	(.100)	(.092)	(.116)	(.182)
Suburban	−.100*	−.099	−.119	−.129	−.065
	(.088)	(.094)	(.080)	(.114)	(.175)
Urban	−.047	−.152*	−.099	−.111	−.167
	(.092)	(.101)	(.091)	(.126)	(.182)
Eco-upbringing	.423***	.482***	.415***	.495***	.439***
	(.024)	(.026)	(.030)	(.040)	(.064)
Mother-degree	−.085	.029	.077	−.056	−.035
	(.081)	(.076)	(.091)	(.108)	(.164)
Father-degree	.113**	−.010	−.056	−.040	.038
	(.080)	(.073)	(.085)	(.104)	(.156)
Child-arts	−.008	−.025	.031	−.020	−.005
	(.066)	(.064)	(.074)	(.097)	(.155)
Current-arts	.055	.090*	.112*	.046	.092
	(.061)	(.061)	(.073)	(.099)	(.160)

Notes: ***, p < .001; **, p < .010; *, p < .050.

households have smaller footprints, on average. Finally, female Optimists have smaller footprints than male Optimists.

I was curious about why these sociodemographic measures explain so little variation in carbon footprint. In order to try to understand this, I ran a regression for the sample as a whole, rather than split by eco-type. This analysis suggests that the eco-types account for a great deal of the variation across measures such as age, income, political ideology, and so on. In the

TABLE A.13. Ordinary Least Squares Regression of Household Carbon Footprint

	Eco-Engaged	Self-Effacing	Optimists	Fatalists	Indifferent
Female	−.042	−.012	−.110*	−.123	.005
	(6.131)	(6.808)	(8.784)	(10.814)	(15.648)
Age	−.027	.045	.016	.011	.039
	(.214)	(.228)	(.327)	(.381)	(.465)
White	.032	.055	.098	.038	.083
	(6.466)	(8.145)	(11.347)	(12.771)	(21.755)
Political ideology	.062	.085	.037	.049	.074
(cons = high)	(1.539)	(2.148)	(2.971)	(3.545)	(5.545)
Income	.034	.068	−.062	.196*	.251*
	(1.676)	(1.774)	(2.494)	(2.730)	(3.803)
Education	.042	.032	.109	.059	.069
	(2.311)	(2.507)	(3.534)	(4.187)	(6.607)
Town	−.018	−.193**	−.015	−.033	−.089
	(10.279)	(12.550)	(14.289)	(15.997)	(23.612)
Suburban	.016	−.182*	−.069	−.119	−.175
	(9.459)	(11.887)	(12.581)	(15.752)	(22.786)
Urban	−.045	−.130	−.138	.075	.000
	(10.049)	(12.823)	(14.290)	(17.829)	(24.265)
Eco-upbringing	−.044	−.130**	−.071	−.049	.002
	(2.613)	(3.295)	(4.892)	(5.788)	(8.448)
Mother-degree	−.045	−.062	−.009	.064	−.026
	(8.598)	(9.749)	(14.009)	(14.868)	(21.461)
Father-degree	−.099	.073	.104	−.131	−.022
	(8.554)	(9.299)	(13.258)	(14.701)	(20.161)
Child-arts	.024	.029	−.089	.090	−.034
	(7.075)	(8.196)	(11.776)	(13.262)	(20.990)
Current-arts	.057	.004	.026	−.107	−.016
	(6.615)	(7.719)	(11.547)	(13.964)	(21.994)
Owns home	−.139**	−.051	−.004	−.004	−.002
	(7.230)	(7.846)	(10.222)	(13.498)	(20.230)

Notes: ***, $p < .001$; **, $p < .010$; *, $p < .050$.

whole sample analysis of household carbon footprint, I found that older respondents had smaller footprints (B = −.115, s.e. = .301), wealthier respondents had larger footprints (B = .209, s.e. = 2.347)—in fact, income explains the greatest proportion of variation—conservatives had slightly larger footprints than liberals (B = .078, s.e. = 2.459), white survey respondents had larger footprints than racial minorities (B = .064, s.e. = 10.171), people in rural communities have larger footprints than those in urban areas (B = .095, s.e. = 14.702), those raised in environmentally active households have smaller footprints (B = −.096, s.e. = 3.881), and people who own their home have smaller footprints (B = −.091, s.e. = 10.429). These relationships are consistent with past literature on household carbon footprints. The discrepancy with the table above, where so few variables explain a significant proportion of variation, indicates the explanatory power of eco-social relationships.

NOTES

Preface

1. From Domestico, "An Interview with George Saunders."

Introduction

1. As Gorski points out in *American Covenant*, it is too simplistic to see this as only a two-sided argument—it is multi-sided. Further, stressing the various sides of the conflict acts to obscure the common ground that exists.

2. There are competing explanations for why political ideology might shape identities and lifestyle choices. Some argue that our political beliefs are tied in with the foundations of our moral compass and that liberals and conservatives place different emphases on moral values like care and fairness (which liberals typically value) and respect for authority, sanctity, and loyalty (which conservatives tend to value) (see Haidt, *The Righteous Mind*). Others argue that differences like this are basically random—that once we start to sense that people like us prefer one thing over another (e.g., shopping at Cabellas or shopping at Whole Foods Market), then we start to defend that preference as reflecting our identity (see DellaPosta, Shi, and Macy, "Why Do Liberals Drink Lattes?").

3. See, for instance, Hornsey et al., "Meta-Analyses," for politically polarized views on climate change. See Pearson et al., "Diverse Segments," for an example of misjudging other people's concern for the environment. See also Moore-Berg et al., "Exaggerated Meta-Perceptions," for an understanding of the impacts of inaccurate judgments across political ideology on social trust.

4. Catton and Dunlap, "Environmental Sociology." Note that alternative, and more recent, terms are the New *Ecological* Paradigm and the Human *Exemptionalist* Paradigm (Dunlap et al., "New Trends in Measuring Environmental Attitudes.")

5. See, for example, Dunlap and Van Liere, "The 'New Environmental Paradigm,'" p. 19.

6. Catton and Dunlap, "Environmental Sociology"; Dunlap and Van Liere, "The 'New Environmental Paradigm.'"

7. Later versions of the NEP scale include two additional facets—the extent to which people feel humans are exempt from the laws of nature, and people's perception of the likelihood of an imminent ecological crisis (cf. Dunlap, "The New Environmental Paradigm Scale").

8. Dunlap and Van Liere, "The New Environmental Paradigm."

9. Some of these studies are described in the following articles: Berenguer, Corraliza, and Martín, "Rural-Urban Differences"; Fransson and Gärling, "Environmental Concern"; Gifford and Nilsson, "Personal and Social Factors"; Hawcroft and Milfont, "The Use (and Abuse) of the New Environmental Paradigm Scale"; Jones and Dunlap, "The Social Bases of Environmental Concern"; and Laidley, "The Influence of Social Class."

10. Gifford and Nilsson note this in their meta-analysis of research on individual-level environmental outcome measures, "Personal and Social Factors."

11. Stern, Paul, and Thomas Dietz. "The Value Basis of Environmental Concern."

12. Jones and Dunlap, "The Social Bases of Environmental Concern"; Nawrotzki, "The Politics of Environmental Concern."

13. See Antonio and Brulle, "The Unbearable Lightness of Politics" for a focus on polarization in how elected representatives vote on climate action proposals, and Dunlap, McCright, and Yarosh, "The Political Divide on Climate Change" for politically polarized patterns among voters and elected representatives.

14. McCright and Dunlap, "Cool Dudes."

15. Aldy, Kotchen, and Leiserowitz, "Willingness to Pay"; McCright and Dunlap, "Cool Dudes"; McCright, Xiao, and Dunlap, "Political Polarization."

16. Ballew et al., "Climate Change in the American Mind."

17. McCright and Dunlap, "Anti-Reflexivity."

18. McCright, "Anti-Reflexivity and Climate Change Skepticism."

19. Oreskes, "My Facts Are Better than Your Facts."

20. Yoder, "Big Oil."

21. Farrell, "Corporate Funding."

22. Antonio and Brulle, "The Unbearable Lightness of Politics."

23. For instance, see Brulle, "Institutionalizing Delay"; Farrell, "Corporate Funding"; and Dunlap and Brulle, *Climate Change and Society*, particularly chapter 10, by Dunlap and McCright, "Challenging Climate Change." Brulle, "Institutionalizing Delay" analyzed data from the Internal Revenue Service (IRS) to document investments from fossil-fuel corporations (via philanthropic foundations) into organizations that exist to cast doubt about climate science and extoll the virtues of economic growth.

24. Coley and Hess, "Green Energy Laws," p.576 (emphasis mine).

25. See Dunlap, "The New Environmental Paradigm Scale," for a historical overview of the emergence of environmental sociology; see also Catton and Dunlap, "Environmental Sociology," for a thorough discussion of the aims of this relatively recent field of sociology.

26. Steg, "Values, Norms, and Intrinsic Motivation," p. 279.

27. The argument that environmental values influence environmental behaviors is derived from the theory of planned behavior. See Ajzen, "The Theory of Planned Behavior."

28. Schwartz, "Universals in the Content and Structure of Values."

29. For example, see Bouman and Steg, "Motivating Society-Wide Pro-Environmental Change."

30. See, for example, Jansson, Marell, and Nordlund, "Exploring Consumer Adoption"; Nordlund and Garvill, "Value Structures." Note that Stern's "New Environmental Theories" distinguishes between intention versus impact. He observes that often, people believe they are doing the right thing for the environment, when in fact they are not.

31. Mills, "Situated Actions and Vocabularies of Motive."

32. Two excellent sources for a much richer discussion of these dynamics are Martin and Lembo, "On the Other Side of Values," and Strand and Lizardo, "Beyond World Images." See also a rebuttal from Vaisey, "Welcome to the Real World."

33. See Bernstein, "(Dis)Agreement over What?"; Ford and Norgaard, "Whose Everyday Climate Cultures?"; and Miles and Upenieks, "An Expanded Model of the Moral Self."

34. Kempton, Boster, and Hartley. *Environmental Values in American Culture*, p. 10.

35. A complementary approach to the one I take in this book is Alison Ford and Kari Norgaard's work on "environmental subjectivities," which they define as "the lived experience of relating to the environment in a social context that recognizes the effects of power and culture on individual practice," (see "Whose Everyday Climate Cultures?" p.47). By contrasting interviews

with members of the Karuk Tribe to interviews with urban homesteaders, Ford and Norgaard argue that studying relationships to the environment should not involve an analysis of values so much as a focus on environmental subjectivities.

36. Greider, "Claims-Making as Social Science," notes some idiosyncrasies in the survey methods of Kempton et al., arguing that the sampling strategy the authors used, "does not permit any type of generalization beyond the respondents themselves," p. 32. For this book, I hired a survey research firm to administer the questionnaire to a sample of respondents who filled quotas for income, education, and political ideology. Ultimately, this means that the survey sample I report on has roughly the same composition in these categories as the US adult population.

37. See Martin and Lembo, "On the Other Side of Values."

38. Martin devotes a great deal of chapters 6 and 9 of *The Explanation of Social Action* to the idea that the qualities of objects are important for determining interests.

39. Other scholars use the term "threat perception." There is a strong tradition of focusing on perceived ecological risks in environmental psychology. For instance, Séguin, Pelletier, and Hunsley, "Toward a Model of Environmental Activism," found that people who perceived risks to be more severe were more likely to participate in environmental activism.

40. Resilience is also a quality of the environment that fossil-fuel companies in particular have spent great sums of money trying to influence. The way in which we evaluate the severity of ecological decline does not typically emerge from our own carefully conducted research, but rather is influenced by the people we talk to, the news we rely on, and leaders we trust.

41. Note that recent research examines political differences in threat perception, based on survey evidence indicating liberals are more likely than conservatives to sense that ecological decline is urgent and severe (Schwaller et al., "From Abstract Futures to Concrete Experiences").

42. Environmental psychologists have a similar concept that they call "personal norm," which refers to a moral obligation to do something to protect the environment, see Steg, "Values, Norms, and Intrinsic Motivation."

43. Environmental psychologists identified this characteristic of human-environment relationships over two decades ago—noting the same two facets I observed: a sense of self-efficacy to have the power to choose what one sees as the "right" actions and a belief that those actions are powerful and meaningful. For instance, Xu, Wei, and Chen, "Determinants and Mechanisms," use this Value-Identity-Personal Norm model to understand environmentally responsible behavior among tourists in China. Recent research employing similar models points to a third facet of efficacy—our sense of what others do. For instance, Bouman and Steg, "Motivating Society-Wide Pro-Environmental Change," summarize research that shows that people are more likely to act in an eco-friendly way when they believe that others will do so as well. In later chapters, I bring in survey data measuring the extent to which people trust that various actors and institutions in society will uphold their responsibility to protect the environment.

44. In what way might efficacy seem to be tangential to human-environment relationships? Well, many frameworks for measuring human-environment relationships, from Dunlap and Van Liere's NEP Scale (see "The 'New Environmental Paradigm'") to measures of biospheric values exclude any measures of efficacy.

45. For previous research demonstrating the significance of place of residence in shaping human-environment relationships, see Armstrong and Stedman, "Understanding Local Environmental Concern." For research indicating the significance of political ideology and education, see Gifford and Nilsson, "Personal and Social Factors." The maximum variation sampling approach is described by Suri, "Purposeful Sampling."

46. By focusing on the everyday routines and beliefs of people who I did not recruit for their committed environmental activism, this research reflects many of the "mundane methods" described in Holmes and Hall, *Mundane Methods*.

47. In the first phase of this study, I only interviewed people in Washington State. Although past research does not suggest that there is geographic variation within the US that is significant for understanding abstract outcomes like environmental concern or environmental worldviews, there are of course regional variations in what sorts of issues people care about and what sorts of environmental solutions people see as attractive and feasible.

48. Because the rural communities have such small populations, I use pseudonyms for the towns and for all participants.

49. In appendix C, I describe each of the four communities in more detail.

50. For more details, see Washington Secretary of State, "Elections & Voting: November 8, 2016 General Election Results."

51. See Box A.3 in appendix A in this volume for a full list of codes.

52. For those who are more interested in methodology, there are a number of appendixes of relevance in this volume. Appendix A contains the interview guide and qualitative analytic framework and appendix B provides an overview of the sociodemographic characteristics of the interview sample. Appendix C contains detailed descriptions of the communities where I conducted interviews. Appendix D includes the survey questions and a summary of the quantitative analyses. Appendix E includes a table summarizing survey sample characteristics. Finally, appendix F includes full results for the statistical analyses I discuss in chapters 2–6.

53. For those unfamiliar with the term circular economy, the concept grew out of the industrial ecology literature as a critique of the prodigious generation of waste and inefficient use of resources characteristic of a linear economy. In a linear economy, natural resources enter the economy as inputs to production and they are either wasted in the production of a good or wasted at the end of a product's life. In contrast, in a circular economy, the aspiration is to cycle more resources from their end-of-life back into the economy as inputs to production. Other approaches to making the economy more "circular" include increased product durability and greater engagement in sharing and lending of goods and services among households and industrial and commercial actors. Those interested in learning more about the definition of the circular economy might read Kirchherr, Reike, and Hekkert, "Conceptualizing the Circular Economy." Those interested in a critical perspective on the circular economy would do well to read Hobson's articles on the topic, including: "The Limits of the Loops."

54. Kennedy, Krahn, and Krogman, "Are We Counting What Counts" and Kennedy et al., "Egregious Emitters"; see also Gore, *Extreme Carbon Inequality*.

55. Leiserowitz et al., "Politics and Global Warming," and Leiserowitz at al., "Global Warming's Six Americas in 2020."

Chapter 1

1. Weng, *The Good Place*.

2. Acker, "Hierarchies, Jobs, Bodies"; Williams, Blair-Loy, and Berdahl, "Cultural Schemas."

3. Brumley, "It's More Appropriate for Men."

4. In the geographer Laura Pulido's words, the ideal environmentalist has "ecological legitimacy," see Pulido, "Ecological Legitimacy."

5. Josée Johnston, Shyon Baumann, and Merin Oleschuk offer a compelling argument that people use prototypes to categorize and evaluate the social world, in a way that can reinforce but also make transparent how social categories like gender, race, and class are implicated in social judgments. See Johnston, Baumann, and Oleschuk "Capturing Inequality."

6. I identified these themes through the process of analyzing the interview data (see appendix A in this volume for more details).

7. Horton, "Green Distinctions."

8. This approach of focusing on consumption in domains of daily life is particularly common among practice theorists. For example, see Spaargaren, "Theories of Practices."

9. Environmental social scientists have worked to identify the sorts of behaviors that have the most impact on mitigating climate change. Some of these are found in my participants' characterizations of the environmentalist—like solar panels and electric vehicles, but many are not. See Dietz et al., "Household Actions," for more on identifying high-impact, high-plasticity behaviors.

10. In this context, I use the term "high-status" to refer to my participants' sense of someone who is at the top of our social hierarchy.

11. Something that cultural sociologists since Pierre Bourdieu have noted is that income alone isn't enough to garner social status. See Bourdieu, "The Forms of Capital." For example, a rich pig farmer would not be seen as high-status in our social hierarchy because of the relatively low prestige of their job. A high-status person has both economic capital (wealth) and cultural capital, which refers to prestige, highly regarded titles and degrees, knowledge and manners, as well as preferences for goods and services that are aesthetically valued. See Lamont and Lareau, "Cultural Capital." For example, a professor of agriculture would likely be seen as having more status than the pig farmer, even if the professor earned less income.

12. Kennedy and Horne, "Accidental Environmentalist or Ethical Elite?"

13. Anderson, "The White Space"; see also Anderson, *Black in White Space*.

14. For example, Parker and McDonough, "Environmentalism of African Americans"; Taylor, "American Environmentalism"; and Hegvedt et al., "Framing and Feeling Fuel." See also Pearson et al., "Diverse Segments," for evidence of these patterns in a nationally representative survey of US households.

15. Pearson et al., "Diverse Segments."

16. Sturgeon, *Environmentalism in Popular Culture*.

17. See Bacon, "Settler Colonialism," for a more thorough treatment of this topic. And see Leddy, "Intersections of Indigenous and Environmental History," especially pages 83–85 for a discussion of the critique of the "ecological Indian" and the way environmental historians balance such critiques with some Indigenous people's land-based cultural identities.

18. At the county level, Washington is generally Democrat-leaning in the state's west side, and Republican-leaning in the state's central and eastern counties. However, federally, Washington has supported Democrat candidates for every election since the late 1980s. This east/west contrast is often evoked by conservatives on the eastern side of the state, who express a sense that their views are not reflected in the state's leadership. This is an example of where the tensions that my Washington State participants raised may not reflect patterns in other parts of the US.

19. This cycle that Hannah observes begs the question, what might these dynamics look like in a state that does not have a Democrat as Governor? This is a limitation of conducting interviews in one state and an example of why replicating this study in other jurisdictions would help unpack the relationship between political representation and people's experiences of ecological decline.

20. See table A.3 in appendix E, and A.4 in appendix F in this volume.

21. Three articles that are foundational for defining the ecological habitus, or eco-habitus, are Haluza-Delay's, "A Theory of Practice for Social Movements," Kasper's "Ecological Habitus," and Carfagna et al.'s, "An Emerging Eco-Habitus."

22. One more spoiler from Weng, *The Good Place*—in the show, even buying the right tomato dooms us to the Bad Place because of the myriad invisible impacts of our consumption choices.

23. See, for example, Ziltener and Künzler, "Impacts of Colonialism."

24. See, for example, Bacon, "Settler Colonialism," and Whyte, "Way beyond the Lifeboat." Robin Wall Kimmerer also makes this point beautifully in her book, *Braiding Sweetgrass*.

25. See Bessire, *Running Out*, for a personal and anthropological analysis of the impacts of settler colonialism on the Ogallala Aquifer. See geographer Andrew Curley's work (e.g., Curley,

"Unsettling Indian Water Settlements,") for an explanation of how these patterns shape access to water and water quality.

26. Ford and Norgaard, "Whose Everyday Climate Cultures?"

27. Foster and York are only two of many scholars in this tradition, but those readers interested in a more fulsome discussion of the ecological effects of capitalism would do well to begin with Foster, Clark, and York, *The Ecological Rift*.

28. Raj Patel has written many books and articles on this topic, see for instance Patel, *Stuffed and Starved*.

29. See, for example, Micheletti, Føllesdal, and Stolle, *Politics, Products, and Markets*.

30. Extended producer responsibility (EPR) refers to policies that shift the work of managing the environmental impacts of a good from the consumer (and governments) to the producer. For example, many electronics companies now have programs where the consumer mails back empty toner cartridges rather than disposing of them in municipal landfills.

31. Jaeger, "Forging Hegemony."

32. Rome, *The Genius of Earth Day*.

33. Dietz, "Earth Day."

34. Kennedy, "Sustainable Consumption."

35. For example, see Miller, *Building Nature's Market*. See Haenfler, Johnson, and Jones, "Lifestyle Movements," for a description of lifestyle movements with additional examples.

36. Dietz, "Earth Day"; Rome, *The Genius of Earth Day*.

37. Newman and Bartels, "Politics at the Checkout Line."

38. Bennett et al., "Disavowing Politics."

39. In addition to hearing from product marketing that eco-friendly consumption is rewarding, many people also experience this mode of engagement in environmental protection as pleasurable. Kate Soper terms this phenomenon "alternative hedonism" in her book, *Post-Growth Living*, p.35.

40. See Gabriel and Lang, *The Unmanageable Consumer*.

41. See Lizardo, "Improving Cultural Analysis," p.91.

42. Warde, "Consumption and Theories of Practice."

43. Schelly, in *Dwelling in Resistance*, has studied ecologically oriented intentional communities—these are physical spaces that people construct with the objective of leaving a light footprint on the earth. Voluntary simplicity was popularized by Elgin, "Voluntary Simplicity," and refers to efforts that individuals can make to cultivate less materially intensive well-being via working less and having more leisure time. See also Grigsby, *Buying Time and Getting By*; Reisch et al., "Frontiers in Sustainable Consumption Research."

Chapter 2

1. A note is required to talk about the term "upper-class." There are many debates in sociology about how to measure the social hierarchy. We might be able to easily ascertain that the Queen is in a higher class than someone who is houseless, but class is more complex than income. In *Distinction*, Bourdieu valuably drew our attention to how cultural capital, in addition to economic capital, affects a person's place in the social hierarchy. Cultural capital includes a person's titles (degrees, job title) as well as their tastes for consumer goods and services, and their knowledge and manners (Bourdieu, "The Forms of Capital"; Lamont and Lareau, "Cultural Capital"). For this book, I organize interview participants into thirds based on their economic capital (income and home-ownership) and cultural capital (education, occupational prestige). There is more detail about this process in Kennedy and Givens, "Eco-Habitus or Eco-Powerlessness?".

2. See Oleschuk, "Gender, Cultural Schemas, and Learning to Cook," and Bowen, Brenton, and Elliott, *Pressure Cooker*, for more on these dynamics.

3. In appendix F in this volume, interested readers can look at results of the binary logistic regression analyses on which these comments are based.

4. Attending artistic performances is a commonly used measure of cultural capital. See DiMaggio, "Cultural Capital and School Success."

5. While I use pseudonyms for participants' names, I use them only for the rural communities. Because the rural areas have such small populations, this step is necessary to ensure confidentiality for the people I interviewed.

6. See Bourdieu, "The Forms of Capital." Regarding the data reported here, these results are based on an Ordinary Least Squares regression analysis. With affinity as the outcome variable, I estimated the relationships between affinity and several sociodemographic measures. The measures I discuss are those that were significantly related to affinity. In other words, some of the variation in affinity is related to variation in these measures. See appendix F in this volume for full results.

7. Carfagna et al., "An Emerging Eco-Habitus."

8. Precautionary consumption is when consumers seek to reduce the chemical residues in their bodies by purchasing products that promise to be cleaner and greener (see, MacKendrick, *Better Safe than Sorry*). This is an example of the response to environmental issues that Szasz in *Shopping Our Way to Safety* calls "inverted quarantine."

9. See McCright, "Political Orientation."

10. I designed the survey to reflect the interviews. So, while some people I interviewed talked about public-sphere actions like protesting or talking to people about environmental issues, this was not nearly as common as the private-sphere behaviors I included.

11. Kennedy et al., "Why We Don't 'Walk the Talk.'"

12. Bourdieu, *Distinction*, and "Social Space."

13. Lamont and Molnár, "The Study of Boundaries."

14. Lamont, *Money, Morals, and Manners.*

15. The carbon footprint is only an estimate of environmental impact. There are concerns, first of all, about how accurately a person can respond to questions about things many people may not be conscious of—how many miles they drive, how many flights they take in a year, how much energy they use in a month. Second, the footprint measure focuses on behaviors that people may have little control over. Perhaps you fly for work, or perhaps you rent your home and have no control over whether it has solar panels or how insulated it is. However, despite these weaknesses, the measure is helpful here as a big-picture snapshot of impact compared to perception of impact (see, Dietz, Shwom, and Whitley, "Climate Change and Society").

16. See Kaufman, "The Carbon Footprint Sham."

17. CO_2e stands for "carbon dioxide equivalent." It is a unit of analysis that converts the environmental impacts of a range of carbon emissions into a single unit based on carbon dioxide. It is difficult to compare carbon footprint estimates across studies because of the variation in how these estimates are calculated. As a result, I simply compare people within my sample to the sample average.

18. A couple of examples of sociological literature that takes aim at consumer-based solutions to environmental problems include Szasz, *Shopping Our Way to Safety*, and Johnston, "The Citizen-Consumer Hybrid."

19. See, for instance, Latané, "The Psychology of Social Impact."

20. Maniates, "Individualization."

21. See Micheletti, Føllesdal, and Stolle, *Politics, Products, and Markets.*

Chapter 3

1. This question, how concerned are you about the environment, from "not at all concerned" on the low end to "extremely concerned" on the high end, is used on the General Social Survey, and employed on many other scholarly surveys of environmentalism.

2. See appendix F in this volume for full results of the multivariate analysis.

3. Tom is referring here to the idea that distinguishing "humans" from "nature" is problematic. Commonly discussed in environmental studies and environmental ethics, the argument is basically that the category "natural" is merely conceptual, and is a legacy of colonialism. The corollary is that humans are just as much a part of the natural world as any other species. Among the varied stated dangers in separating humans and the nonhuman world is that this distinction falsely casts "wilderness" as a place without humans, obscuring Indigenous people's existence, and that this distinction creates a hierarchy in which humans feel entitled to exploit other species (e.g., Dussault, "Ecological Nature").

4. Although climate change was the leading concern among Self-Effacing interviewees, in the survey data, the average scores of Self-Effacing respondents for the five issues I asked about are actually lowest for climate change (though still high, at 4.22 out of 5). Digging into that a little deeper, I noted sharp political contrasts. Among Self-Effacing liberals, three-quarters rank their concern for climate change a 5 out of 5. But only 45% of moderates and conservatives rank their concern at the same level.

5. See Cruz, "The Relationships of Political Ideology."

6. Norgaard, *Living in Denial.*

7. There are at least two complementary reasons why age may be inversely related to self-efficacy. First, it may be that competition over the cultural capital tied to the ideal environmentalist is more intense among people who have yet to establish secure economic capital (since people generally reach peak-earning years later in life). Second, this could be a generational pattern, where older respondents associate with an environmentalism less tied to conscious consumerism and thus are not holding themselves to the same standards as younger Self-Effacing.

8. Environmental studies scholar Manisha Anantharaman makes this point in the paper "Critical Sustainable Consumption."

9. Carfagna et al., "An Emerging Eco-Habitus"; Laidley, "The Influence of Social Class."

Chapter 4

1. Religion was not a focus of my interviews and, with the exception of four Optimists, the people I interviewed did not make references to their religious beliefs as influencing their relationship with the environment. Still, it is noteworthy that the people who did call attention to the significance of their religion were all Optimists. Readers interested in a more nuanced look at the relationships between religion, morality, and environmental protection might read Justin Farrell's *Battle for Yellowstone.*

2. The way in which Optimists stressed the importance of economic security for their neighbors reminds me very much of Colin Jerolmack's ethnography of a Pennsylvania town whose residents supported fracking (*Up to Heaven and Down to Hell*). Jerolmack rejects arguments that townspeople's support for fracking is a simple matter of economic interests, because some of the people who backed the fracking industry did not benefit economically at all. Instead, Jerolmack attributed their support of fracking to a hope that doing so would help their neighbors become more economically secure.

3. See appendix F in this volume for the logistic regression results.

4. Michael S. Carolan in "Do You See What I See?" uses the term "epistemic distance" to make sense of the ways that many farmers ignore problematic aspects of food production that cannot be seen. For instance, while research might indicate that use of a particular pesticide compromises soil health, if this is inconsistent with the tangible evidence they see, farmers can dismiss this sort of claim out of hand. Similarly, I suggest that because the Optimists relate to the environment immediately around them, they are skeptical of claims of a global deterioration in ecological integrity, as this simply doesn't align with what they see with their own eyes.

5. For example, see McCright and Dunlap, "Cool Dudes."

6. For example, see Dunlap and McCright, "Challenging Climate Change."

7. McCright and Dunlap, "Cool Dudes."

8. See table A.7 in appendix F of this volume for full results.

9. This point about experiencing an environment that is tangible and present is consistent with sociologist Michael Carolan's concept of "epistemic distance." See Carolan, "Do You See What I See?"

10. The political differences I observed in the ways that wildfires affected perceptions of climate change are reflected in quantitative research on this topic. For example, Mildenberger et al., in "The Effect of Public Safety Power Shutoffs," found that wildfire frequency did affect survey respondents' engagement in household-level climate adaptation, but that liberals were more likely than conservatives to report feeling more concerned about climate change after the fires.

11. See, for instance, Farrell's "Corporate Funding" and Supran and Oreskes, "Assessing ExxonMobil's Climate Change Communications."

Chapter 5

1. Bobo, "Racism in Trump's America."

2. Lieberson, "Unhyphenated Whites," p. 167.

3. Sapinski, "Constructing Climate Capitalism."

4. In some ways, Ted's arguments here are reminiscent of the Jevons' paradox. The Jevons' paradox is named after William Stanley Jevons, a British economist who first documented this paradox in a book published in 1865. His book was an analysis of the coal industry in Britain, and he noticed something curious: after the steam engine was produced—an engine that used coal far more efficiently than its predecessor—coal consumption actually increased. Because the new engine was so efficient, industrialists could increase production for the same input costs, leading to an expansion in coal consumption.

5. York, in "Why Petroleum Did Not Save the Whales," offers a compelling illustration of the tendency for new innovations to add to, rather than displace, older technology.

6. Elizabeth Shove has written a highly readable and sharp diagnosis of how the normal routines of everyday life can culminate in extraordinary environmental impacts (Shove, *Comfort, Cleanliness and Convenience*). Noting how water and energy consumption per person has increased over time, Shove points to how evolving social norms around comfort, cleanliness, and convenience are implicated in an upward creep of material consumption.

7. See appendix F in this volume for the full logistic regression results.

8. See Newman and Fernandes, "A Re-Assessment of Factors."

9. Hungerford and Volk, "Changing Learner Behavior."

10. Kennedy and Muzzerall, "Morality, Emotions, and the Ideal Environmentalist."

11. Schnaiberg, *The Environment*.

12. See, for example, Gould, Pellow, and Schnaiberg's accessible overview of Treadmill theory, which discusses corporate efforts to promote the social value of industrialization: Gould, Pellow, and Schnaiberg "Interrogating the Treadmill of Production."

13. It's worth noting that both the claim of overpopulation and overconsumption are gendered. Even though Ted doesn't implicate women as being more responsible for ecological decline, charging population as ecologically destructive typically castigates women's reproduction choices (Gaard, *Ecofeminism*), and the image of hysterical and excessive shoppers is a highly feminized one. Kennedy and Dzialo in "Locating Gender in Environmental Sociology," summarized much of this research on gendered responsibilities for environmental issues and protection.

Chapter 6

1. Jasper and Poulsen, "Recruiting Strangers and Friends."

2. Spaargaren, "Sustainable Consumption."

3. In fact, increasing frequency and intensity of wildfires in this region are consistent with predictions from climate modeling and thus linked to rising concentrations of greenhouse gasses in the atmosphere (Macias Fauria and Johnson, "Climate and Wildfires."

4. See appendix F in this volume for full results.

5. Park and Pellow offer a more extensive definition, in their book, *The Slums of Aspen*. On page 4 they define environmental privilege as resulting "from the exercise of economic, political and cultural power that some groups enjoy," noting that this "enables them exclusive access to coveted environmental amenities such as forests, parks, mountains, rivers, coastal property, open lands and elite neighborhoods." Overall, they argue, "Environmental privilege is embodied in the fact that some groups can access spaces and resources which are protected from the kinds of ecological harm that other groups are forced to contend with everyday."

6. Sennett and Cobb, *The Hidden Injuries of Class*.

7. The Indifferent engage in some of the strategies that Norgaard's Norwegian participants described in *Living in Denial*. For instance, they rationalized their own low levels of concern for the environment by contrasting the state of the environment in their community, or the United States as a whole, with places where they perceive environmental issues to be more severe (primarily the Global South).

Chapter 7

1. See, for instance, Fisher, Waggle, and Leifeld, "Where does political polarization come from?" They argue that there is a growing consensus among US representatives across political lines on climate science. The source of polarization, they show, is on the economic costs of climate action and on choosing the right policies to tackle climate change. McCright, Xiao, and Dunlap, in "Political Polarization," trace polarization among the electorate back to 1992, when politically polarized views on environmental policy first emerged.

2. Arlie Hochschild's account of libertarians' opposition to environmental protection policies in Louisiana is a compelling example of these patterns (see Hochschild, *Strangers in Their Own Land*).

3. See De Keere, "Finding the Moral Space" for a detailed empirical study of how cultural and economic capital are related to a sense of personal moral responsibility across social class. See Prieur and Savage, "Emerging Forms of Cultural Capital" for a more general discussion of so-called "new cultural capital."

4. As I said, my focus in this chapter is on how political ideology shapes people's commonplace, instinctual judgments of one another's eco-social relationships. However, cultural capital is an important factor here. I wrote about this in greater detail with Jennifer Givens ("Eco-Habitus or Eco-Powerlessness?"). For readers interested in interactions between political ideology and cultural capital, recall that the Eco-Engaged and the Optimists are most likely to have grown

up in environmentally active households. This upbringing affords these two orientations to the environment a confidence and relative effortlessness that those who did not grow up in eco-conscious households lack.

5. Cultural sociologists use the terms "symbolic boundaries" and "social boundaries" to describe the practice of establishing in- and out-groups based on moral, cultural, and economic criteria. See, for example, Lamont, *Money, Morals, and Manners.*

6. In other contexts, this pattern is called ethnocentrism. It refers to the practice of judging someone else's beliefs and practices on the basis of one's own culture. It is typically applied in very different settings; for example, when a white, Christian American labels another person's eating practices (eating, for example, dogs or horses) as disgusting or inhumane, while happily consuming the meat of pigs and cows.

7. See Jaeger, "Forging Hegemony."

8. Ridgeway and Nakagawa, "Is Deference the Price of Being Seen as Reasonable?"

9. Feinberg and Willer, "The Moral Roots of Environmental Attitudes."

10. As an example of school curricula, note that the state of New Jersey has been applauded by environmental organizations for being the first state to integrate evidence of the climate crisis into K-12 education (Davidson, "New Jersey Becomes First State"); and, for an example of a novel, see author Kiley Reid's review of the book *A Good Neighborhood* (Reid, "When You Hate Your Neighbor"). In her review, Reid notes that, "Good characters love trees . . . They compost their leftovers and forego foie gras." In contrast, the "villain" of the story "is defined by his gaudy home, his six televisions, the celebratory Maserati window sticker that he tacks on his bulletin board and the déclassé pride he takes in his HVAC company's local commercials."

11. Kobe De Keere's research illustrates this point clearly. Through a correspondence analysis of the distribution of moral opinions across social class, he found that people who have the most cultural and economic capital hold egalitarian views on climate change. Egalitarian views capture the impulses of the ideal environmentalist, described in De Keere's research with the following vignette: "The climate problem can best be solved by changing our way of living and all of us together start living a more balanced life" (De Keere, "Finding the Moral Space," p.7).

12. Pasek et al., "Biased and Inaccurate Meta-Perceptions."

Chapter 8

1. This is an example of what Jasper and Poulsen, "Recruiting Strangers and Friends," call a "moral shock."

2. Carfagna et al., "An Emerging Eco-Habitus."

3. Kennedy, Baumann, and Johnston, "Eating for Taste."

4. Gaard, "Toward a Queer Ecofeminism"; Plumwood, "Ecofeminism: An Overview."

5. Pearson et al., "Diverse Segments."

6. My point about conservative eco-types having less cultural power than liberals' may strike some readers as failing to recognize significant ways that conservatives exert authority and control over environmental issues. Counterarguments to my claim may point out that Republican politicians regularly block Democrats' efforts to pass climate legislation, or draw attention to conservative billionaires who spend money on manipulating public views on climate change and back Republican representatives who promise to oppose climate action. As I've discussed elsewhere in this book, these points are all well-evidenced. Still, that doesn't negate the cultural power of progressive voices to establish a moral monopoly on orientations to the environment. I saw this argument reflected in David Brooks' column, "Democrats Need to Confront Their Privilege," in the *New York Times.* Brooks argues that Democrats, "dominate the cultural commanding heights," pointing to the majority of progressives that make up "the elite universities, the elite media, the

entertainment industry, the big tech companies, the thriving elite places like Manhattan, San Francisco and Los Angeles." Brooks suggestion to Democrats is strikingly similar to my suggestion to readers: that we need a "positive moral vision" and leaders who distance themselves from polarized divides and seek to bridge those divides. Whenever a person finds themselves engaging in us/them thinking, that should be a cue that there is space to cultivate curiosity in the biography and contextual parameters that make a view diametrically opposed to one's own nonetheless feel right for someone else.

7. I made the point that the Optimists and Fatalists are something of a cultural underdog given their representation within my survey sample, contrasted to the Eco-Engaged and Self-Effacing. This point should not take away from overwhelming evidence that well-funded organizations linked to fossil-fuel companies spend profligately to lobby elected representatives and shape public opinion to oppose climate action. In the US, coverage of these patterns is documented in Supran and Oreskes' "Assessing ExxonMobil's Climate Change Communications." In Canada, the Corporate Mapping Project has published accounts of similar dynamics (cf., Carroll, *Regime of Obstruction*).

8. For instance, see Clive Hamilton's research "What History Can Teach Us About Climate Change Denial" on corporate interference in voters' beliefs about climate change; and Hoffman's analysis of how people across the political spectrum interpret climate science in Hoffman, *How Culture Shapes the Climate Change Debate*.

9. Ridgeway and Nakagawa, "Is Deference the Price of Being Seen as Reasonable?"

10. Taylor, "American Environmentalism" and "Race, Class, Gender, and American Environmentalism."

11. Bacon, "Settler Colonialism."

12. It is worth noting a potential limitation in this argument, which is that carbon footprint measurements are not a perfect tool. A more robust approach to capture a household's environmental impact would be a life cycle analysis.

13. Mills, *The Sociological Imagination*.

14. For recent examples of literature that deploys a sociological imagination to study environmental justice, see Pellow, *What Is Critical Environmental Justice?*

15. Maniates, "Individualization."

16. Willis and Schor, "Does Changing a Light Bulb Lead to Changing the World?"

17. The idea of having a stronger capacity to imagine addressing socioecological problems is called a "democratic imagination" in Perrin, *Citizen Speak*.

18. Schnaiberg, *The Environment*; Foster and Clark, *The Robbery of Nature*.

19. This point echoes a similar argument that Pulido makes in "Ecological Legitimacy."

20. In Strand and Lizardo's framework, we could describe many Fatalists as existing in a state of "radical doubt." See Strand and Lizardo, "Beyond World Images."

21. Another take on this idea that individuals' concern for climate change captures too much scholarly and public attention is Joane Nagel's argument in "Climate Change, Public Opinion, and the Military Security Complex." Nagel argued that while social scientists and others wring their hands about the lack of public acceptance of climate change, large and powerful institutions such as the military and the insurance industry have quietly begun adopting quite drastic climate adaptation measures. This is very different from my argument, but ultimately serves the same argument that we overstate the significance of individuals' perceptions of ecological decline.

22. Bessire, *Running Out*.

23. Some readers might think, wait—how to protect the environment is precisely what conservatives and liberals tend to disagree over. Yes, that's true. But I suggest that we are more likely to achieve bipartisan support for policies that will have environmental benefits (such as fuel emissions standards and rebates for reducing energy loss from buildings) in a context where we minimize the likelihood of reactive effects.

24. In 2017, the Carbon Disclosure Project (CDP) published a high-impact report demonstrating that 100 fossil-fuel producers are responsible for 53% of the greenhouse gasses emitted since the global economy began to industrialize in 1751. See Griffin, "The Carbon Majors Database." Reports focused on individuals call attention to the disproportionate impact that the wealthiest households in the world have. For instance, a collaboration between Oxfam and the Stockholm Environment Institute reports that 52% of emissions released between 1990 and 2015 can be traced to the wealthiest 10% of the world's population. See Gore, "Confronting Carbon Inequality." Looking at 2018 emissions data, Johannes Friedrich, Mengpin Ge, and Andrew Pickens report for the World Resources Institute that the top three emitters of greenhouse gasses are China, the European Union, and the United States. These governments make up 41.5% of emissions. See Friedrich, Ge, and Pickens, "Changes in the World's Top 10 Emitters."

25. For recent data on Americans' trust in government, see the 2021 Pew Research Center, *Public Trust in Government: 1958–2021*. The data show low and declining levels of trust in government over time.

Conclusion

1. Guterres' statement was published on the United Nations' website in response to the report of the IPCC Working Group 1, 2021.

2. Anantharaman, "Critical Sustainable Consumption."

3. See Kennedy and Horne, "Accidental Environmentalist or Ethical Elite?"

4. Horton, "Green Distinctions."

5. Hess and Brown, "Green Tea"; Hess, Quan, and Brown, "Red States, Green Laws"; Horne and Kennedy, "Explaining Support for Renewable Energy." See also the recent report on politics and global warming from the Yale Program on Climate Communication (Leiserowitz et al., "Global Warming's Six Americas in 2020"), which shows that while support for global warming is politically polarized, there is much stronger consensus on support for climate friendly policies.

6. See John L. Martin's discussion of this tendency for social scientists to assume an authority relationship over their research subjects in his book, *The Explanation of Social Action*.

7. There are important limitations in basing this research in only one state. Readers from other areas may identify stereotypically west coast sentiments among my interview participants. It may be that eco-types look and feel different in other contexts. It is an open question—that I hope other researchers will endeavor to ask—how regional differences influence eco-social relationships.

8. See Dietz et al., "Household Actions."

9. Maki et al., "Meta-Analysis"; Rivera-Camino, "Corporate Environmental Market Responsiveness."

10. Pasek et al., "Biased and Inaccurate Meta-Perceptions."

11. Simard, *Finding the Mother Tree*.

Appendices

1. Dunlap, "The New Environmental Paradigm Scale."

2. Kennedy and Givens, "Eco-Habitus or Eco-Powerlessness?"

3. Paulsen, "Making Character Concrete."

BIBLIOGRAPHY

Acker, Joan. "Hierarchies, Jobs, Bodies: A Theory of Gendered Organizations." *Gender & Society* 4, no. 2 (1990): 139–58. https://doi.org/10.1177/089124390004002002

Ajzen, Icek. "The Theory of Planned Behavior." *Organizational Behavior and Human Decision Processes* 50, no. 2 (1991): 179–211. https://doi.org/10.1016/0749-5978(91)90020-T.

Aldy, Joseph E., Matthew J. Kotchen, and Anthony A. Leiserowitz. "Willingness to Pay and Political Support for a US National Clean Energy Standard." *Nature Climate Change* 2, no. 8 (2012): 596–99. https://doi.org/10.1038/nclimate1527.

Anantharaman, Manisha. "Critical Sustainable Consumption: A Research Agenda." *Journal of Environmental Studies and Sciences* 8, no. 4 (2018): 553–61. https://doi.org/10.1007/s13412-018-0487-4.

Anderson, Elijah. *Black in White Space: The Enduring Impact of Color in Everyday Life.* Chicago: University of Chicago Press, 2021.

———. "The White Space." *Sociology of Race and Ethnicity* 1, no. 1 (2015): 10–21. https://doi.org/10.1177/2332649214561306.

Antonio, Robert J., and Robert J. Brulle. "The Unbearable Lightness of Politics: Climate Change Denial and Political Polarization." *The Sociological Quarterly* 52, no. 2 (May 2011): 195–202. https://doi.org/10.1111/j.1533-8525.2011.01199.x.

Armstrong, Andrea, and Richard C. Stedman. "Understanding Local Environmental Concern: The Importance of Place: Local Environmental Concern and Place." *Rural Sociology* 84, no. 1 (March 2019): 93–122. https://doi.org/10.1111/ruso.12215.

Bacon, Jules M. "Settler Colonialism as Eco-Social Structure and the Production of Colonial Ecological Violence." *Environmental Sociology* 5, no. 1 (2019): 59–69. https://doi.org/10.1080/23251042.2018.1474725.

Ballew, Matthew T., Anthony Leiserowitz, Connie Roser-Renouf, Seth A. Rosenthal, John E. Kotcher, Jennifer R. Marlon, Erik Lyon, Matthew H. Goldberg, and Edward W. Maibach. "Climate Change in the American Mind: Data, Tools, and Trends." *Environment: Science and Policy for Sustainable Development* 61, no. 3 (2019): 4–18. https://doi.org/10.1080/00139157.2019.1589300.

Bennett, Elizabeth A., Alissa Cordner, Peter Taylor Klein, Stephanie Savell, and Gianpaolo Baiocchi. "Disavowing Politics: Civic Engagement in an Era of Political Skepticism." *The American Journal of Sociology* 119, no. 2 (2013): 518–48. https://doi.org/10.1086/674006.

Berenguer, Jaime, José A. Corraliza, and Rocío Martín. "Rural-Urban Differences in Environmental Concern, Attitudes, and Actions." *European Journal of Psychological Assessment* 21, no. 2 (2005): 128–38. https://doi.org/10.1027/1015-5759.21.2.128.

Bernstein, Jennifer. "(Dis)Agreement over What? The Challenge of Quantifying Environmental Worldviews." *Journal of Environmental Studies and Sciences* 10, no. 2 (2020): 169–77. https://doi.org/10.1007/s13412-020-00593-x.

Bessire, Lucas. *Running Out: In Search of Water on the High Plains*. Princeton: Princeton University Press, 2021.

Bobo, Lawrence D. "Racism in Trump's America: Reflections on Culture, Sociology, and the 2016 US Presidential Election." *The British Journal of Sociology* 68 (2017): S85–104. https://onlinelibrary.wiley.com/doi/full/10.1111/1468-4446.12324.

Bouman, Thijs, and Linda Steg. "Motivating Society-Wide Pro-Environmental Change." *One Earth* 1, no. 1 (September 2019): 27–30. https://doi.org/10.1016/j.oneear.2019.08.002.

Bourdieu, Pierre. *Distinction: A Social Critique of the Judgement of Taste*. Cambridge, MA: Harvard University Press, 1984.

———. "Social Space and Symbolic Power." *Sociological Theory* 7, no. 1 (1989): 14–25. https://doi.org/10.2307/202060.

———. "The Forms of Capital." In *The Sociology of Economic Life*, edited by M. Granovetter, 78–92. New York: Routledge, 1986.

Bowen, Sarah, Joslyn Brenton, and Sinikka Elliott. *Pressure Cooker: Why Home Cooking Won't Solve Our Problems and What We Can Do about It*. New York: Oxford University Press, 2019.

Brooks, David. "Democrats Need to Confront Their Privilege." *New York Times*, November 4, 2021. https://www.nytimes.com/2021/11/04/opinion/democrats-culture-wars.html.

Brulle, Robert J. "Institutionalizing Delay: Foundation Funding and the Creation of U.S. Climate Change Counter-Movement Organizations." *Climatic Change* 122, no. 4 (February 2014): 681–94. https://doi.org/10.1007/s10584-013-1018-7.

Brumley, Krista M. " 'It's More Appropriate for Men': Management and Worker Perceptions of the Gendered Ideal Worker." *Sociological Spectrum* 38, no. 6 (2018): 406–21. https://doi.org/10.1080/02732173.2018.1564096.

Carfagna, Lindsey B., Emilie A. Dubois, Connor Fitzmaurice, Monique Y. Ouimette, Juliet B. Schor, Margaret Willis, and Thomas Laidley. "An Emerging Eco-Habitus: The Reconfiguration of High Cultural Capital Practices among Ethical Consumers." *Journal of Consumer Culture* 14, no. 2 (2014): 158–78. https://doi.org/10.1177/1469540514526227.

Carolan, Michael S. "Do You See What I See? Examining the Epistemic Barriers to Sustainable Agriculture." *Rural Sociology* 71, no. 2 (2006): 232–60. https://doi.org/10.1526/003601106777789756.

Carroll, William K., ed. *Regime of Obstruction: How Corporate Power Blocks Energy Democracy*. Athabasca University Press, 2021.

Catton, William R., and Riley E. Dunlap. "Environmental Sociology: A New Paradigm." *The American Sociologist* 13, no. 1 (1978): 41–49. http://www.jstor.org/stable/27702311.

Coley, Jonathan S., and David J. Hess. "Green Energy Laws and Republican Legislators in the United States." *Energy Policy* 48, (2012): 576–83. https://doi.org/10.1016/j.enpol.2012.05.062.

Cruz, Shannon M. "The Relationships of Political Ideology and Party Affiliation with Environmental Concern: A Meta-Analysis." *Journal of Environmental Psychology* 53 (2017): 81–91. https://doi.org/10.1016/j.jenvp.2017.06.010.

Curley, Andrew. "Unsettling Indian Water Settlements: The Little Colorado River, the San Juan River, and Colonial Enclosures." *Antipode* 53, no. 3 (2021): 705–23. https://doi.org/10.1111/anti.12535.

Davidson, Jordan. "New Jersey Becomes First State to Put the Climate Crisis in Its K-12 Curriculum." *EcoWatch*, June 4, 2020. https://www.ecowatch.com/new-jersey-schools-climate-science-curriculum-2646152515.html.

De Keere, Kobe. "Finding the Moral Space: Rethinking Morality, Social Class and Worldviews." *Poetics* 79 (April 2020): 101415. https://doi.org/10.1016/j.poetic.2019.101415.

DellaPosta, Daniel, Yongren Shi, and Michael Macy. "Why Do Liberals Drink Lattes?" *The American Journal of Sociology* 120, no. 5 (2015): 1473–1511. https://doi.org/10.1086/681254.

Dietz, Thomas. "Earth Day: 50 Years of Continuity and Change in Environmentalism." *One Earth* 2, no. 4 (April 2020): 306–8. https://doi.org/10.1016/j.oneear.2020.04.003.

Dietz, Thomas, Gerald T. Gardner, Jonathan Gilligan, Paul C. Stern, and Michael P. Vandenbergh. "Household Actions Can Provide a Behavioral Wedge to Rapidly Reduce US Carbon Emissions." *Proceedings of the National Academy of Sciences—PNAS* 106, no. 44 (2009): 18452–56. https://doi.org/10.1073/pnas.0908738106.

Dietz, Thomas, Rachael L. Shwom, and Cameron T. Whitley. "Climate Change and Society." *Annual Review of Sociology* 46 (2020): 135–58. https://doi.org/10.1146/annurev-soc-121919 -054614.

DiMaggio, Paul. "Cultural Capital and School Success: The Impact of Status Culture Participation on the Grades of US High School Students." *American Sociological Review* 47, no. 2 (1982): 189–201. https://doi.org/10.2307/2094962.

Domestico, Anthony. "An Interview with George Saunders: A Kindly Presence of Mind." *Commonweal Magazine*, June 10, 2017. https://www.commonwealmagazine.org/interview-george -saunders.

Dunlap, Riley E. "The New Environmental Paradigm Scale: From Marginality to Worldwide Use." *The Journal of Environmental Education* 40, no. 1 (2008): 3–18. https://doi.org/10.3200/JOEE .40.1.3-18.

Dunlap, Riley E., and Robert J. Brulle, eds. *Climate Change and Society: Sociological Perspectives*. Oxford: Oxford University Press, 2015. https://doi.org/10.1093/acprof:oso/9780199356102 .001.0001.

Dunlap, Riley E., and Aaron M. McCright. "Challenging Climate Change." In *Climate Change and Society: Sociological Perspectives*, edited by Riley E. Dunlap and Robert J. Brulle. Oxford: Oxford University Press, 2015. https://doi.org/10.1093/acprof:oso/9780199356102.001.0001.

Dunlap, Riley E., Aaron M. McCright, and Jerrod H. Yarosh. "The Political Divide on Climate Change: Partisan Polarization Widens in the US." *Environment: Science and Policy for Sustainable Development* 58, no. 5 (2016): 4–23. https://doi.org/10.1080/00139157.2016.1208995.

Dunlap, Riley E., and Kent D. Van Liere. "The 'New Environmental Paradigm.'" *The Journal of Environmental Education* 40, no. 1 (1978): 19–28. https://doi.org/10.3200/JOEE.40.1.19-28.

Dunlap, Riley E., Kent D. Van Liere, Angela G. Mertig, and Robert Emmet Jones. "New Trends in Measuring Environmental Attitudes: Measuring Endorsement of the New Ecological Paradigm: A Revised NEP Scale." *Journal of Social Issues* 56, no. 3 (2000): 425–42. https://doi .org/10.1111/0022-4537.00176.

Dussault, Antoine C. "Ecological Nature: A Non-Dualistic Concept for Rethinking Humankind's Place in the World." *Ethics and the Environment* 21, no. 1 (2016): 1–37. https://doi.org/10 .2979/ethicsenviro.21.1.01.

Elgin, Duane. "Voluntary Simplicity and the New Global Challenge." In *The Environment in Anthropology: A Reader in Ecology, Culture, and Sustainable Living*, edited by N. Haenn and R. Wilk, 458–68. New York: New York University Press, 2005.

Farrell, Justin. *Battle for Yellowstone: Morality and the Sacred Roots of Environmental Conflict*. Princeton: Princeton University Press, 2015.

———. "Corporate Funding and Ideological Polarization about Climate Change." *Proceedings of the National Academy of Sciences—PNAS* 113, no. 1 (2016): 92–97. https://doi.org/10.1073 /pnas.1509433112.

Feinberg, Matthew, and Robb Willer. "The Moral Roots of Environmental Attitudes." *Psychological Science* 24, no. 1 (January 2013): 56–62. https://doi.org/10.1177/0956797612449177.

Fisher, Dana R., Joseph Waggle, and Philip Leifeld. "Where Does Political Polarization Come From? Locating Polarization Within the US Climate Change Debate." *American Behavioral Scientist* 57, no. 1 (2013): 70–92. https://doi.org/10.1177/0002764212463360.

Ford, Allison, and Kari Marie Norgaard. "Whose Everyday Climate Cultures? Environmental Subjectivities and Invisibility in Climate Change Discourse." *Climatic Change* 163, no. 1 (November 2020): 43–62. https://doi.org/10.1007/s10584-019-02632-1.

Foster, John Bellamy, and Brett Clark. *The Robbery of Nature: Capitalism and the Ecological Rift.* New York: New York University Press, 2020.

Foster, John Bellamy, Brett Clark, and Richard York. *The Ecological Rift: Capitalism's War on the Earth.* New York: New York University Press, 2011.

Fransson, N., and T. Gärling. "Environmental Concern: Conceptual Definitions, Measurement Methods, and Research Findings." *Journal of Environmental Psychology* 19, no. 4 (1999): 369–82. https://doi.org/10.1006/jevp.1999.0141.

Friedrich, Johannes, Mengpin Ge, and Andrew Pickens. "This Interactive Chart Shows Changes in the World's Top 10 Emitters." World Resources Institute, 2020. https://www.wri.org/insights/interactive-chart-shows-changes-worlds-top-10-emitters.

Gaard, Greta. "Toward a Queer Ecofeminism." *Hypatia* 12, no. 1 (1997): 114–37. https://doi.org/10.1111/j.1527-2001.1997.tb00174.x.

———. *Ecofeminism: Women, Animals, Nature.* Philadelphia: Temple University Press, 1993.

Gabriel, Yiannis, and Tim Lang. *The Unmanageable Consumer.* London: SAGE, 2015.

Gifford, Robert, and Andreas Nilsson. "Personal and Social Factors That Influence Pro-Environmental Concern and Behaviour: A Review." *International Journal of Psychology* 49, no. 3 (2014): 141–57. https://doi.org/10.1002/ijop.12034.

Gore, Timothy. "Extreme Carbon Inequality: Why the Paris Climate Deal Must Put the Poorest, Lowest Emitting and Most Vulnerable People First." Oxfam International, 2015. https://policy-practice.oxfam.org/resources/extreme-carbon-inequality-why-the-paris-climate-deal-must-put-the-poorest-lowes-582545/.

———. "Confronting Carbon Inequality: Putting Climate Justice at the Heart of the COVID-19 Recovery." Oxfam International, 2020. https://policy-practice.oxfam.org/resources/confronting-carbon-inequality-putting-climate-justice-at-the-heart-of-the-covid-621052/.

Gorski, Philip S. *American Covenant: A History of Civil Religion from the Puritans to the Present.* Princeton: Princeton University Press, 2019.

Gould, Kenneth A., David N. Pellow, and Allan Schnaiberg. "Interrogating the Treadmill of Production: Everything You Wanted to Know About the Treadmill but Were Afraid to Ask." *Organization & Environment* 17, no. 3, 2004: 296–316. https://doi.org/10.1177/1086026604268747.

Greider, Thomas. "Claims-Making as Social Science: A Review of Environmental Values in American Culture, by Willett Kempton, James S. Boster, and Jennifer A. Hartley; Cambridge, MA: MIT Press, 1995." *Journal of Political Ecology* 2, no. 1 (1995): 30–36. https://doi.org/10.2458/v2i1.20162.

Griffin, Paul. "The Carbon Majors Database: CDP Carbon Majors Report 2017." London: Carbon Disclosure Project (CDP) UK, 2017. https://studylib.es/doc/8820778/carbon-majors-report-2017.

Grigsby, Mary. *Buying Time and Getting By: The Voluntary Simplicity Movement.* Albany: State University of New York Press, 2004.

Guterres, António. "Secretary-General Calls Latest IPCC Climate Report 'Code Red for Humanity', Stressing 'Irrefutable' Evidence of Human Influence". https://www.un.org/press/en/2021/sgsm20847.doc.htm.

Haenfler, Ross, Brett Johnson, and Ellis Jones. "Lifestyle Movements: Exploring the Intersection of Lifestyle and Social Movements." *Social Movement Studies* 11, no. 1 (2012): 1–20. https://doi.org/10.1080/14742837.2012.640535.

Haidt, Jonathan. *The Righteous Mind: Why Good People Are Divided by Politics and Religion.* New York: Vintage Books, 2012.

Haluza-DeLay, Randolph. "A Theory of Practice for Social Movements: Environmentalism and Ecological Habitus." *Mobilization* 13, no. 2 (2008): 205–18. https://doi.org/10.17813/maiq.13.2.k5015r82j2q35148.

Hamilton, Clive. "What History Can Teach Us About Climate Change Denial." In *Engaging with Climate Change: Psychoanalytic and Interdisciplinary Perspectives*, edited by S. Weintrobe, 16–32. New York: Routledge, 2013. https://doi.org/10.4324/9780203094402.

Hawcroft, Lucy J., and Taciano L. Milfont. "The Use (and Abuse) of the New Environmental Paradigm Scale over the Last 30 Years: A Meta-Analysis." *Journal of Environmental Psychology* 30, no. 2 (2010): 143–58. https://doi.org/10.1016/j.jenvp.2009.10.003.

Hegtvedt, Karen A., Christie L. Parris, and Cathryn Johnson. "Framing and Feeling Fuel Environmentally Responsible Behaviors of Black Residents in the United States." *Sociological Perspectives* 62, no. 5 (2019): 603–26. https://doi.org/10.1177/0731121419852946.

Hess, David J., and Kate Pride Brown. "Green Tea: Clean-Energy Conservatism as a Countermovement." *Environmental Sociology* 3, no. 1 (2017): 64–75. https://doi.org/10.1080/23251042.2016.1227417.

Hess, David J., Quan D. Mai, and Kate Pride Brown. "Red States, Green Laws: Ideology and Renewable Energy Legislation in the United States." *Energy Research & Social Science* 11 (2016): 19–28. https://doi.org/10.1016/j.erss.2015.08.007.

Hobson, Kersty. "The Limits of the Loops: Critical Environmental Politics and the Circular Economy." *Environmental Politics* 30, no. 1–2 (2021): 161–79. https://doi.org/10.1080/09644016.2020.1816052.

Hochschild, Arlie Russell. *Strangers in Their Own Land: Anger and Mourning on the American Right*. New York: The New Press, 2016.

———. "The Ecstatic Edge of Politics: Sociology and Donald Trump." *Contemporary Sociology: A Journal of Reviews* 45, no. 6 (November 2016): 683–89. https://doi.org/10.1177/0094306116671947.

Hoffman, Andrew J. *How Culture Shapes the Climate Change Debate*. Stanford: Stanford University Press, 2015.

Holmes, Helen, and Sarah Marie Hall, eds. *Mundane Methods: Innovative Ways to Research the Everyday*. Manchester: Manchester University Press, 2020.

Horne, Christine, and Emily Huddart Kennedy. "Explaining Support for Renewable Energy: Commitments to Self-Sufficiency and Communion." *Environmental Politics* 28, no. 5 (July 29, 2019): 929–49. https://doi.org/10.1080/09644016.2018.1517917.

Hornsey, Matthew J., Emily A. Harris, Paul G. Bain, and Kelly S. Fielding. "Meta-Analyses of the Determinants and Outcomes of Belief in Climate Change." *Nature Climate Change* 6, no. 6 (June 2016): 622–26. https://doi.org/10.1038/nclimate2943.

Horton, Dave. "Green Distinctions: The Performance of Identity among Environmental Activists." *The Sociological Review* 51, no. 2 (2003): 63–77. https://doi.org/10.1111/j.1467-954X.2004.00451.x.

Hungerford, Harold R., and Trudi L. Volk. "Changing Learner Behavior through Environmental Education." *The Journal of Environmental Education* 21, no. 3 (1990): 8–21. https://doi.org/10.1080/00958964.1990.10753743.

Hunter, James Davison. *Culture Wars: The Struggle to Define America*. New York: Basic Books, 1991.

Intergovernmental Panel on Climate Change. "Climate Change 2021: The Physical Science Basis," 2021.

———. "Global Warming of 1.5 °C," 2018.

Jaeger, Andrew Boardman. "Forging Hegemony: How Recycling Became a Popular but Inadequate Response to Accumulating Waste." *Social Problems* 65, no. 3 (2018): 395–415. https://doi.org/10.1093/socpro/spx001.

Jansson, Johan, Agneta Marell, and Annika Nordlund. "Exploring Consumer Adoption of a High Involvement Eco-Innovation Using Value-Belief-Norm Theory." *Journal of Consumer Behaviour* 10, no. 1 (2011): 51–60. https://doi.org/10.1002/cb.346.

Jasper, James M., and Jane D. Poulsen. "Recruiting Strangers and Friends: Moral Shocks and Social Networks in Animal Rights and Anti-Nuclear Protests." *Social Problems* 42, no. 4 (1995): 493–512. https://doi.org/10.2307/3097043.

Jerolmack, Colin. *Up to Heaven and Down to Hell: Fracking, Freedom, and Community in an American Town*. Princeton: Princeton University Press, 2021.

Johnston, Josée. "The Citizen-Consumer Hybrid: Ideological Tensions and the Case of Whole Foods Market." *Theory and Society* 37, no. 3 (2008): 229–70. https://doi.org/10.1007/s11186 -007-9058-5.

Johnston, Josée, Shyon Baumann, and Merin Oleschuk. "Capturing Inequality and Action in Prototypes: The Case of Meat-Eating and Vegetarianism." *Poetics* 87 (2021): 101530. https:// doi.org/10.1016/j.poetic.2021.101530.

Jones, Robert Emmet, and Riley E. Dunlap. "The Social Bases of Environmental Concern: Have They Changed Over Time?" *Rural Sociology* 57, no. 1 (1992): 28–47. https://doi.org/10.1111 /j.1549-0831.1992.tb00455.x.

Kasper, Debbie V. S. "Ecological Habitus: Toward a Better Understanding of Socioecological Relations." *Organization & Environment* 22, no. 3 (September 2009): 311–26. https://doi.org /10.1177/1086026609343098.

Kaufman, Mark. "The Carbon Footprint Sham: A 'Successful, Deceptive' PR Campaign." *Mashable*. Accessed October 19, 2021. https://mashable.com/feature/carbon-footprint-pr -campaign-sham.

Kempton, Willett, James S. Boster, and Jennifer A. Hartley. *Environmental Values in American Culture*. Cambridge, MA: MIT Press, 1995.

Kennedy, Emily Huddart. "Sustainable Consumption." In *The Cambridge Handbook of Environmental Sociology*. Vol. 2, edited by Katharine Legun, Julie C. Keller, Michael Carolan, and Michael M. Bell, 221–35. Cambridge: Cambridge University Press, 2020.

Kennedy, Emily H. and Parker Muzzerall. "Morality, Emotions, and the Ideal Environmentalist: Toward A Conceptual Framework for Understanding Political Polarization." *American Behavioral Scientist* (2021). https://doi.org/10.1177%2F00027642211056258.

Kennedy, Emily Huddart, Shyon Baumann, and Josée Johnston. "Eating for Taste and Eating for Change: Ethical Consumption as a High-Status Practice." *Social Forces* 98, no. 1 (2019): 381–402. https://doi.org/10.1093/sf/soy113.

Kennedy, Emily Huddart, Thomas M. Beckley, Bonita L. McFarlane, and Solange Nadeau. "Why We Don't 'Walk the Talk': Understanding the Environmental Values/Behaviour Gap in Canada." *Human Ecology Review* 16, no. 2 (2009): 151–60.

Kennedy, Emily Huddart, and Liz Dzialo. "Locating Gender in Environmental Sociology." *Sociology Compass* 9, no. 10 (2015): 920–29. https://doi.org/10.1111/soc4.12303.

Kennedy, Emily Huddart, and Jennifer E. Givens. "Eco-Habitus or Eco-Powerlessness? Examining Environmental Concern across Social Class." *Sociological Perspectives* 62, no. 5 (October 2019): 646–67. https://doi.org/10.1177/0731121419836966.

Kennedy, Emily Huddart, and Christine Horne. "Accidental Environmentalist or Ethical Elite? The Moral Dimensions of Environmental Impact." *Poetics* 82 (October 2020): 101448. https://doi .org/10.1016/j.poetic.2020.101448.

Kennedy, Emily Huddart, Harvey Krahn, and Naomi T. Krogman. "Are We Counting What Counts? A Closer Look at Environmental Concern, Pro-Environmental Behaviour, and Carbon Footprint." *Local Environment* 20, no. 2 (2015): 220–36. https://doi.org/10.1080 /13549839.2013.837039.

———. "Egregious Emitters: Disproportionality in Household Carbon Footprints." *Environment and Behavior* 46, no. 5 (2014): 535–55. https://doi.org/10.1177/0013916512474986.

Kimmerer, Robin Wall. *Braiding Sweetgrass: Indigenous Wisdom, Scientific Knowledge and the Teachings of Plants*. Minneapolis: Milkweed Editions, 2013.

Kinder, Colleen. "How Sailing Across the Pacific Changed My Thinking About Plastic." *Bloomberg Businessweek*, June 26, 2020.

Kirchherr, Julian, Denise Reike, and Marko Hekkert. "Conceptualizing the Circular Economy: An Analysis of 114 Definitions." *Resources, Conservation and Recycling* 127, (2017): 221–32. https://doi.org/10.1016/j.resconrec.2017.09.005.

Laidley, Thomas M. "The Influence of Social Class and Cultural Variables on Environmental Behaviors: Municipal-Level Evidence from Massachusetts." *Environment and Behavior* 45, no. 2 (2013): 170–97. https://doi.org/10.1177/0013916511416647.

Lamont, Michèle. *Money, Morals, and Manners: The Culture of the French and American Upper-Middle Class*. Chicago: University of Chicago Press, 1992.

Lamont, Michele, and Annette Lareau. "Cultural Capital: Allusions, Gaps and Glissandos in Recent Theoretical Developments." *Sociological Theory* 6, no. 2 (1988): 153–68. https://doi.org/10.2307/202113.

Lamont, Michèle, and Virág Molnár. "The Study of Boundaries in the Social Sciences." *Annual Review of Sociology* 28, no. 1 (August 2002): 167–95. https://doi.org/10.1146/annurev.soc.28.110601.141107.

Latané, Bibb. "The Psychology of Social Impact." *The American Psychologist* 36, no. 4 (1981): 343–56. https://doi.org/10.1037/0003-066X.36.4.343.

Leddy, Lianne C. "Intersections of Indigenous and Environmental History in Canada." *Canadian Historical Review* 98, no. 1 (2017): 83–95. https://doi.org/10.3138/chr.98.1.Leddy.

Leiserowitz, Anthony A., Edward W. Maibach, Seth A. Rosenthal, John E. Kotcher, Jennifer Carman, Xinran Wang, Matthew H. Goldberg, Karine Lacroix, and Jennifer Marlon. "Politics and Global Warming, December 2020." Yale Program on Climate Change Communication, 2021.

Leiserowitz, Anthony A., Jennifer Marlon, Xinran Wang, Parrish Bergquist, Matthew H. Goldberg, John E. Kotcher, Edward W. Maibach, and Seth A. Rosenthal. "Global Warming's Six Americas in 2020." Yale Program on Climate Change Communication, 2020.

Lieberson, Stanley. "Unhyphenated Whites in the United States." *Ethnic and Racial Studies* 8, no. 1 (January 1, 1985): 159–80. https://doi.org/10.1080/01419870.1985.9993479.

Limbaugh, Rush. "Rush Limbaugh on Whether Trump is Justified Taking Executive Action to Secure Funding for His Border Wall." Fox News, February 17, 2019. Video, 13:34. https://video.foxnews.com/v/6003164394001#sp=show-clips.

Lizardo, Omar. "Improving Cultural Analysis: Considering Personal Culture in its Declarative and Nondeclarative Modes." *American Sociological Review* 82, no. 1 (February 2017): 88–115. https://doi.org/10.1177/0003122416675175.

Macias Fauria, Marc, and E. A. Johnson. "Climate and Wildfires in the North American Boreal Forest." *Philosophical Transactions of the Royal Society B: Biological Sciences* 363, no. 1501 (2008): 2315–27. https://doi.org/10.1098/rstb.2007.2202.

MacKendrick, Norah. *Better Safe than Sorry: How Consumers Navigate Exposure to Everyday Toxics*. Oakland: University of California Press, 2018.

Maki, Alexander, Amanda R. Carrico, Kaitlin T. Raimi, Heather Barnes Truelove, Brandon Araujo, and Kam Leung Yeung. "Meta-Analysis of Pro-Environmental Behaviour Spillover." *Nature Sustainability* 2, no. 4 (2019): 307–15. https://doi.org/10.1038/s41893-019-0263-9.

Maniates, Michael F. "Individualization: Plant a Tree, Buy a Bike, Save the World?" *Global Environmental Politics* 1, no. 3 (2001): 31–52. https://doi.org/10.1162/152638001316881395.

Martin, John Levi. *The Explanation of Social Action*. New York: Oxford University Press, 2011. https://doi.org/10.1093/acprof:oso/9780199773312.001.0001.

Martin, John Levi, and Alessandra Lembo. "On the Other Side of Values." *American Journal of Sociology* 126, no. 1 (July 1, 2020): 52–98. https://doi.org/10.1086/709778.

McCright, Aaron M. "Anti-Reflexivity and Climate Change Skepticism in the US General Public." *Human Ecology Review* 22, no. 2 (2016): 77–108. https://doi.org/10.22459/HER.22.02.2016.04.

———. "Political Orientation Moderates Americans' Beliefs and Concern about Climate Change." *Climatic Change* 104, no. 2 (2011): 243–53. https://doi.org/10.1007/s10584-010-9946-y.

McCright, Aaron M., and Riley E. Dunlap. "Anti-Reflexivity." *Theory, Culture & Society* 27, no. 2–3 (March, 2010): 100–133. https://doi.org/10.1177/0263276409356001.

———. "Cool Dudes: The Denial of Climate Change among Conservative White Males in the United States." *Global Environmental Change* 21, no. 4 (October 2011): 1163–72. https://doi.org/10.1016/j.gloenvcha.2011.06.003.

McCright, Aaron M., Chenyang Xiao, and Riley E. Dunlap. "Political Polarization on Support for Government Spending on Environmental Protection in the USA, 1974–2012." *Social Science Research* 48, (2014): 251–60. https://doi.org/10.1016/j.ssresearch.2014.06.008.

Micheletti, Michele, Andreas Føllesdal, and Dietlind Stolle. *Politics, Products, and Markets: Exploring Political Consumerism Past and Present.* New Brunswick: Transaction Publishers, 2004.

Mildenberger, Matto, Samuel Trachtman, Peter Howe, Leah Stokes, and Mark Lubell. "The Effect of Public Safety Power Shutoffs on Climate Attitudes and Behavioral Intentions." *Nature Energy* (2022, forthcoming).

Miles, Andrew, and Laura Upenieks. "An Expanded Model of the Moral Self: Beyond Care and Justice." *Social Science Research* 72, (2018): 1–19. https://doi.org/10.1016/j.ssresearch.2018.02.004.

Miller, Laura J. *Building Nature's Market: The Business and Politics of Natural Foods.* Chicago: University of Chicago Press, 2017.

Mills, C. Wright. "Situated Actions and Vocabularies of Motive." *American Sociological Review* 5, no. 6 (1940): 904–13. https://doi.org/10.2307/2084524.

———. *The Sociological Imagination.* New York; Oxford University Press, 2000.

Moore-Berg, Samantha L., Lee-Or Ankori-Karlinsky, Boaz Hameiri, and Emile Bruneau. "Exaggerated Meta-Perceptions Predict Intergroup Hostility between American Political Partisans." *Proceedings of the National Academy of Sciences—PNAS* 117, no. 26 (2020): 14864–72. https://doi.org/10.1073/pnas.2001263117.

Nagel, Joane. "Climate Change, Public Opinion, and the Military Security Complex." *Sociological Quarterly* 52, no. 2 (2011): 203–10. https://doi.org/10.1111/j.1533-8525.2011.01200.x.

Nawrotzki, Raphael J. "The Politics of Environmental Concern: A Cross-National Analysis." *Organization & Environment* 25, no. 3 (2012): 286–307. https://doi.org/10.1177/1086026612456535.

Newman, Benjamin J., and Brandon L. Bartels. "Politics at the Checkout Line: Explaining Political Consumerism in the United States." *Political Research Quarterly* 64, no. 4 (2011): 803–17. https://doi.org/10.1177/1065912910379232.

Newman, Todd P., and Ronald Fernandes. "A Re-Assessment of Factors Associated with Environmental Concern and Behavior Using the 2010 General Social Survey." *Environmental Education Research* 22, no. 2 (2016): 153–75. https://doi.org/10.1080/13504622.2014.999227.

Nordlund, Annika M., and Jörgen Garvill. "Value Structures behind Pro-Environmental Behavior." *Environment and Behavior* 34, no. 6 (2002): 740–56. https://doi.org/10.1177/001391602237244.

Norgaard, Kari Marie. *Living in Denial: Climate Change, Emotions, and Everyday Life.* Cambridge, MA: MIT Press, 2011.

Oleschuk, Merin. "Gender, Cultural Schemas, and Learning to Cook." *Gender & Society* 33, no. 4 (2019): 607–28. https://doi.org/10.1177/0891243219839669.

Oreskes, Naomi. "My Facts Are Better Than Your Facts: Spreading Good News about Global Warming." In *How Well Do Facts Travel?* 136–66. New York: Cambridge University Press, 2010. https://doi.org/10.1017/CBO9780511762154.008.

Park, Lisa Sun-Hee, and David Pellow. *The Slums of Aspen: Immigrants Versus the Environment in America's Eden.* New York: New York University Press, 2011.

Parker, Julia Dawn, and Maureen H. McDonough. "Environmentalism of African Americans: An Analysis of the Subculture and Barriers Theories." *Environment and Behavior* 31, no. 2 (1999): 155–77. https://doi.org/10.1177/00139169921972047.

Pasek, Michael H., Lee-Or Ankori-Karlinsky, Alex Levy-Vene, and Samantha L. Moore-Berg. "Biased and Inaccurate Meta-Perceptions About Out-Partisans' Support for Democratic Principles May Erode Democratic Norms." *PsyArXiv*, 2021. https://doi.org/doi:10.31234/osf.io/qjy6t.

Patel, Raj. *Stuffed and Starved: Markets, Power and the Hidden Battle for the World Food System.* Melbourne: Black Inc, 2007.

Patterson, Orlando. "Making Sense of Culture." *Annual Review of Sociology* 40, no. 1 (July 30, 2014): 1–30. https://doi.org/10.1146/annurev-soc-071913-043123.

Paulsen, Krista E. "Making Character Concrete: Empirical Strategies for Studying Place Distinction." *City & Community* 3, no. 3 (2004): 243–62. https://doi.org/10.1111/j.1535-6841.2004.00080.x.

Pearson, Adam R., Jonathon P. Schuldt, Rainer Romero-Canyas, Matthew T. Ballew, and Dylan Larson-Konar. "Diverse Segments of the US Public Underestimate the Environmental Concerns of Minority and Low-Income Americans." *Proceedings of the National Academy of Sciences—PNAS* 115, no. 49 (2018): 12429–34. https://doi.org/10.1073/pnas.1804698115.

Pellow, David N. *What Is Critical Environmental Justice?* Cambridge; Polity Press, 2018.

Perrin, Andrew J. *Citizen Speak: The Democratic Imagination in American Life.* Chicago: University of Chicago Press, 2006.

Pew Research Center. "Public Trust in Government: 1958–2021," 2021. http://www.pewresearch.org/politics/2021/05/17/public-trust-in-government-1958-2021/.

Plumwood, Val. "Ecofeminism: An Overview and Discussion of Positions and Arguments." *Australasian Journal of Philosophy* 64, (1986): S120–38. https://doi.org/10.1080/00048402.1986.9755430.

Prieur, Annick, and Mike Savage. "Emerging Forms of Cultural Capital." *European Societies* 15, no. 2 (2013): 246–67. https://doi.org/10.1080/14616696.2012.748930.

Pulido, Laura. "Ecological Legitimacy and Cultural Essentialism: Hispano Grazing in the Southwest." *Capitalism Nature Socialism* 7, no. 4 (December, 1996): 37–58. https://doi.org/10.1080/10455759609358707.

Reid, Kiley. "When You Hate Your Neighbor, and Then Your Kids Start Dating." *New York Times*, March 10, 2020. https://www.nytimes.com/2020/03/10/books/review/a-good-neighborhood-therese-anne-fowler.html

Reisch, Lucia A., Maurie J. Cohen, John B. Thøgersen, and Arnold Tukker. "Frontiers in Sustainable Consumption Research." *Gaia* 25, no. 4 (2016): 234–40. https://doi.org/10.14512/gaia.25.4.4.

Ridgeway, Cecilia L., and Sandra Nakagawa. "Is Deference the Price of Being Seen as Reasonable? How Status Hierarchies Incentivize Acceptance of Low Status." *Social Psychology Quarterly* 80, no. 2 (June 2017): 132–52. https://doi.org/10.1177/0190272517695213.

Rivera-Camino, Jaime. "Corporate Environmental Market Responsiveness: A Model of Individual and Organizational Drivers." *Journal of Business Research* 65, no. 3 (2012): 402–11. https://doi.org/10.1016/j.jbusres.2011.07.002.

Rome, Adam. *The Genius of Earth Day: How a 1970 Teach-in Unexpectedly Made the First Green Generation.* New York: Hill and Wang, 2013.

Sapinski, Jean Philippe. "Constructing Climate Capitalism: Corporate Power and the Global Climate Policy-Planning Network." *Global Networks* 16, no. 1 (2016): 89–111. https://doi.org/10.1111/glob.12099.

Schelly, Chelsea. *Dwelling in Resistance: Living with Alternative Technologies in America*. New Brunswick: Rutgers University Press, 2017.

———. "Residential Solar Electricity Adoption: What Motivates, and What Matters? A Case Study of Early Adopters." *Energy Research & Social Science* 2, (2014): 183–91. https://doi.org/10.1016/j.erss.2014.01.001.

Schnaiberg, Allan. *The Environment, from Surplus to Scarcity*. New York: Oxford University Press, 1980.

Schwaller, Nora Louise, Sophie Kelmenson, Todd K. BenDor, and Danielle Spurlock. "From Abstract Futures to Concrete Experiences: How Does Political Ideology Interact with Threat Perception to Affect Climate Adaptation Decisions?" *Environmental Science & Policy* 112, (2020): 440–52. https://doi.org/10.1016/j.envsci.2020.07.001.

Schwartz, Shalom H. "Universals in the Content and Structure of Values: Theoretical Advances and Empirical Tests in 20 Countries." In *Advances in Experimental Social Psychology*, 25: 1–65. New York: Elsevier Science & Technology, 1992. https://doi.org/10.1016/S0065-2601(08)60281-6.

Séguin, Chantal, Luc G. Pelletier, and John Hunsley. "Toward a Model of Environmental Activism." *Environment and Behavior* 30, no. 5 (1998): 628–52. https://doi.org/10.1177/001391659803000503.

Sennett, Richard, and Jonathan Cobb. *The Hidden Injuries of Class*. New York: Alfred A. Knopf, 1972.

Shove, E. A. *Comfort, Cleanliness and Convenience: The Social Organization of Normality*. Oxford: Berg, 2003.

Simard, S. *Finding the Mother Tree: Discovering the Wisdom of the Forest*. New York: Alfred A. Knopf, 2021.

Soper, Kate. *Post-Growth Living: For an Alternative Hedonism*. London: Verso Books, 2020.

Spaargaren, Gert. "Sustainable Consumption: A Theoretical and Environmental Policy Perspective." *Society & Natural Resources* 16, no. 8 (2003): 687–701. https://doi.org/10.1080/08941920309192.

———. "Theories of Practices: Agency, Technology, and Culture: Exploring the Relevance of Practice Theories for the Governance of Sustainable Consumption Practices in the New World-Order." *Global Environmental Change* 21, no. 3 (2011): 813–22. https://doi.org/10.1016/j.gloenvcha.2011.03.010.

Steg, Linda. "Values, Norms, and Intrinsic Motivation to Act Proenvironmentally." *Annual Review of Environment and Resources* 41, no. 1 (2016): 277–92. https://doi.org/10.1146/annurev-environ-110615-085947.

Stern, Paul C. "New Environmental Theories: Toward a Coherent Theory of Environmentally Significant Behavior." *Journal of Social Issues* 56, no. 3 (2000): 407–24. https://doi.org/10.1111/0022-4537.00175.

Stern, Paul, and Thomas Dietz. "The Value Basis of Environmental Concern." *Journal of Social Issues* 50 (April 14, 2010): 65–84. https://doi.org/10.1111/j.1540-4560.1994.tb02420.x.

Strand, Michael, and Omar Lizardo. "Beyond World Images: Belief as Embodied Action in the World." *Sociological Theory* 33, no. 1 (March 2015): 44–70. https://doi.org/10.1177/0735275115572397.

Sturgeon, Noël. *Environmentalism in Popular Culture: Gender, Race, Sexuality, and the Politics of the Natural*. Tucson: University of Arizona Press, 2009.

Supran, Geoffrey, and Naomi Oreskes. "Assessing ExxonMobil's Climate Change Communications (1977–2014)." *Environmental Research Letters* 12, no. 8 (2017): 84019. https://doi.org/10.1088/1748-9326/aa815f.

Suri, Harsh. "Purposeful Sampling in Qualitative Research Synthesis." *Qualitative Research Journal* 11, no. 2 (2011): 63–75. https://doi.org/10.3316/QRJ1102063.

Szasz, Andrew. *Shopping Our Way to Safety: How We Changed from Protecting the Environment to Protecting Ourselves.* Minneapolis: University of Minnesota Press, 2007.

Taylor, Dorceta. "American Environmentalism: The Role of Race, Class and Gender in Shaping Activism 1820–1995." *Race, Gender & Class* 5, no. 1 (1997): 16–62. https://www.jstor.org/stable/41674848.

———. "Race, Class, Gender, and American Environmentalism." US Department of Agriculture, Forest Service, Pacific Northwest Research Station, 2002.

Vaisey, Stephen. "Welcome to the Real World: Escaping the Sociology of Culture and Cognition." *Sociological Forum* 36, S1 (2021). https://doi.org/10.1111/socf.12770.

Vandenbergh, Michael P., and Jonathan M. Gilligan. *Beyond Politics.* Cambridge: Cambridge University Press, 2017.

Warde, Alan. "Consumption and Theories of Practice." *Journal of Consumer Culture* 5, no. 2 (2005): 131–53. https://doi.org/10.1177/1469540505053090.

Washington Secretary of State. "Elections & Voting: November 8, 2016 General Election Results," 2016. https://results.vote.wa.gov/results/20161108/.

Weng, Jude. "Chidi Sees the Time-Knife." *The Good Place.* Netflix Canada, 2019. Accessed August 22, 2020.

Whyte, Kyle. "Way beyond the Lifeboat: An Indigenous Allegory of Climate Justice." In *Climate Futures: Reimagining Global Climate Justice,* edited by Debashish Munshi, Kum-Kum Bhavnani, John Foran, and Priya Kurian. London: Zed Books, 2019.

Williams, Joan C., Mary Blair-Loy, and Jennifer L. Berdahl. "Cultural Schemas, Social Class, and the Flexibility Stigma: Cultural Schemas and Social Class." *Journal of Social Issues* 69, no. 2 (2013): 209–34. https://doi.org/10.1111/josi.12012.

Willis, Margaret M., and Juliet B. Schor. "Does Changing a Light Bulb Lead to Changing the World? Political Action and the Conscious Consumer." *The Annals of the American Academy of Political and Social Science* 644, no. 1 (2012): 160–90. https://doi.org/10.1177/0002716212454831.

Xu, Yongxun, Xuechao Wei, and Shih-Chih Chen. "Determinants and Mechanisms of Tourists' Environmentally Responsible Behavior: Applying and Extending the Value-Identity-Personal Norm Model in China." *Sustainability* 11, no. 13 (2019): 3711. https://doi.org/10.3390/su11133711.

Yoder, Kate. "Big Oil spent $10 million on Facebook ads last year—to sell what, exactly?" Salon.com, 2021. https://www.salon.com/2021/08/10/big-oil-spent-10-million-on-facebook-ads-last-year--to-sell-what-exactly_partner/.

York, Richard. "Why Petroleum Did Not Save the Whales." *Socius: Sociological Research for a Dynamic World* 3, (2017). https://doi.org/10.1177/2378023117739217.

Ziltener, Patrick, and Daniel Künzler. "Impacts of Colonialism–A Research Survey." *Journal of World-Systems Research* 19, no. 2 (2013): 290–311. https://doi.org/10.5195/jwsr.2013.507.

INDEX

Page numbers in *italics* refer to figures and tables.

A NOTE ON THE TYPE

This book has been composed in Adobe Text and Gotham.
Adobe Text, designed by Robert Slimbach for Adobe,
bridges the gap between fifteenth- and sixteenth-century
calligraphic and eighteenth-century Modern styles.
Gotham, inspired by New York street signs, was designed
by Tobias Frere-Jones for Hoefler & Co.